An American Journey

Roger K. Baer PhD

"I disapprove of what you say, but I will defend to the death your right to say it."

A quote from Evelyn Beatrice Hall under the pseudonym of S.G. Tallentyre

An American Journey was registered with the Library of Congress,

Copyright Office dated 2/13/15.

ID number is 7014 2120 0000 5432 6391.

CONTENTS

PROLOGUE

It's been a few years since I started to write this account of my life and related historical events in America and other parts of the world. Growing older, I felt a need to stimulate my mind; and writing seemed to be the best antidote. Also, I lamented over my disappointments as a teacher having witnessed the demise in the quality of education in America. And I became distressed over the course of social and political circumstances gripping this nation. Periodically I grumbled and expressed my dissatisfaction to my lovely wife who responded: "Why don't you stop complaining, and write about it!"

It took some time before I heeded her advice and began to write reaching back into a past filled with joys and sorrows. It was like a catharsis: a relief of repressed emotions. As I wrote, I felt overcome with feelings of being transported back to earlier times and distant places. Retracing my life experiences in tandem with other events was a lengthy journey. I did decide to relate it all through a fictitious character named Jack Rubin. This was done simply because I preferred telling my story in the third rather than the first person in order to avoid the repetition of "I" and "me". Pseudonyms identify characters in the narrative except for sociology faculty members of the Catholic University of America and the University of Chicago. They were outstanding teachers and scholars who I believe greatly influenced my life especially my career in sociology. I hold them all in high esteem even those with whom I had disagreeable and unfriendly relationships. The actual names of my Shotokan karate teachers are also disclosed. Training in karate contributed importantly to my physical and mental or spiritual development. Above all, it taught me to cultivate courage, tenacity, and respect for others.

Except for Jack Rubin's long sleep and flashbacks, all depicted events are factual. Questions might be raised concerning the accuracy of some historical materials largely gleaned from internet encyclopedia sources. The journey spans a time period of about eight decades beginning in the years of the Great Depression of the 1930's and in Boston, the birthplace of the author. These were tumultuous years when America existed in some kind of "splendid isolation" despite growing threats to world peace. Exposed to newsreels shown in Boston theaters, Jack Rubin was well aware of rising global conflict. At the same time, he grew up in a city torn by racial, religious, and ethnic prejudices and bigotry which he abhorred.

Although much of his early education was in Brookline, a suburb of Boston, Jack completed high school at a military academy nestled in the Shenandoah Valley of Virginia. Following the end of World War Two, he attended college first in upper New York State and later at American University in the nation's capital. It was the 1940's and a time when Washington, D.C. was a Jim Crow city and the campus of American University was a bastion of bigotry: Blacks were denied admittance to the university and Jewish students were barred from university fraternities and sororities. These were circumstances repugnant to Jack, but they could not be altered. Subsequently he left the university campus, moved to a rooming house, and completed his studies at the downtown campus of American University. There he majored in journalism, and after taking some sociology courses he chose sociology as an additional major. The subject, representing a new way of thinking, fascinated him. During his college years the civil rights movement had begun to gain momentum, and he joined a demonstration in front of the White House which was part of a national protest against the unjust execution of a black man, Willie McGee.

It was June, 1951 and the United Nations acted to repulse the North Korean invasion of the Republic of South Korea. America was at war again. Jack was drafted into the armed forces and underwent months of intense infantry basic training supervised by a cadre of Korean War veterans. His company was a racially integrated unit: white and black soldiers who trained together, ate together, and shared common living quarters. With the end of basic training, the troops received their future assignments. All white soldiers were ordered to serve in the American Army of Occupation in West Germany; and all black soldiers, with one exception, were ordered to Korea. There was a traumatic reaction among the men especially the black soldiers. All the men felt some shame and betrayal. It was if lightening had struck the barracks. Clearly the decision to break up the company appeared racially motivated.

After a brief furlough, Jack and other members of his company sailed on a troop ship to the port of Bremerhaven, Germany where they disembarked and boarded a train taking them to a replacement depot in the Bavarian Alps in southern Germany. For almost two years he served as a medical records specialist in an artillery battalion. These were the years of the Cold War when tensions were running high between Allied and Communist forces. Faced with uncertainties Jack lived from one day to the next without thoughts or plans for the future, He did have some interesting and enlightening experiences. And his sojourn there conjured up memories of the Holocaust and a father he never knew who had served in the American Expeditionary Force in World War One.

In the fall of 1953, Jack returned home and was separated from the U.S. Army. At this point, he felt he had to choose between a career in journalism or pursuing a graduate degree in sociology. For almost a year he worked as a copy boy on a major newspaper in Washington, D.C. where he obtained some experience in news reporting but then decided to take advantage of the educational benefits offered to Korean War veterans and enrolled in the graduate program of the Sociology Department of the Catholic University of America. As he worked toward the completion of a Masters degree in sociology, his enthusiasm for sociology grew;and completing requirements for the degree, he moved on to pursue a PhD in sociology at the University of Chicago. These were perhaps the most challenging and enriching years of his life in terms of academic experiences and relationships with other students. They were difficult times, too; and readers are given an inside look at the tensions and conflicts that occurred between faculty and graduate students.

While in Chicago Jack met his future wife, a wonderful woman ;and shortly after they married they moved to the nation's capital where Jack worked at the Population Division of the U.S. Bureau of the Census and engaged in research related to the War on Poverty. In 1968, amid the assassination of Martin Luther King and racial riots in major U.S. cities, he and his family: a wife and two children returned to Chicago so he could complete the doctoral dissertation and earn his PhD in sociology. For about a decade the nation had spent much treasure and blood in a futile war in Vietnam. The cost had been great. Also, it had ushered in growing national discord and signaled the beginning of the end of many Great Society programs.

As a graduate student in Chicago Jack had taught at a number of universities and on one occasion encountered some anti-Semitism when pressured and refusing to pass a failing student. Now he embarked upon a full time teaching career in Chicago at the Business School of Roosevelt University. During these few years he saw recurrent declines in the quality and integrity of higher education and became embroiled in conflict with older faculty resistant to academic reforms.

Most of his remaining teaching career was spent at Saint Cloud State University where he attempted to maintain a semblance of academic integrity. But it was an uphill struggle against the onslaught of Political Correctness and a dumbing down of academic standards. On one occasion, he clashed with certain university faculty and administrators and filed a grievance against Saint Cloud State University These were not unique circumstances for similar situations arose in other universities. But in the aftermath of the dispute, he became even more alienated from academia and finally retired from fulltime teaching.

Now he and Hilda headed farther west to Las Vegas, where they began living temporarily before building a retirement home in Prescott, Arizona. During their stint in Vegas, Hilda participated in a Swedish American group, and Jack became more involved in Shotokan karate. His testing for higher belts became more frequent than had been the case back in Minnesota; and before moving on to Prescott, he earned his black belt despite a continuing struggle with congestive heart failure.

As the 21st century began, America suffered a terrorist attack when hijacked airliners crashed into the twin towers of the World Trade Center in New York City causing the deaths of thousands. Another airliner struck the Pentagon, and courageous passengers sacrificed their lives by thwarting a third plane attack. As the years progressed, the War on Terror escalated with Islamic extremists dedicated to inflicting death and destruction upon all "infidels" or "nonbelievers". At first America was in the forefront forcefully leading an offensive against the attacks and other rising threats of terrorism. But later, under a new president and administration, the nation faltered incrementally abdicating its leadership role in the war against world terrorism. At home, the welfare of the republic was endangered, as many of our political leaders had become self indulgent disregarding the needs of the electorate. Promises of transparency in government were broken, and obfuscation, mendacity, and stonewalling became widespread.

Jack and Hilda experienced a dose of culture shock living in Prescott. They found it difficult to develop close interpersonal relationships. Human contact seemed very superficial. Of course neither of them was especially gregarious, and they were more accustomed to the cosmopolitan ambience of larger urban areas. However, there were certain advantages living in Prescott. High quality medical care was readily available, the sun radiated brightly nearly every day with all the seasons very mild, the air was fresh free of pollutants, and the surrounding mountains and verdant forests provided inspiring and extraordinary sights. It was a very quiet place, and it was here that Jack began to write about his past and events in the larger world.

The details of this story unfold in the following pages, and readers are invited to take a lengthy journey back in space and time. Beginning in the years of the Great Depression, it spans almost eight decades and travels from Boston to the nation's capital, to post World War Two Germany, to the wonders of ancient Greece and Crete, to the châteaux of southern France, westward in America to Chicago and Minnesota, and finally across the Great Divide to the glitter of

Las Vegas and the cowboy country of Arizona. But, most importantly, I believe it is a story conveying some meaningful and significant messages.

CHAPTER ONE:
THE HOME OF THE BEAN
AND THE COD

Jack Rubin relaxed in a soft chair in the shaded patio of his Arizona home. He gazed up at nearby rolling hills engulfed by a dense canopy of verdant trees and shrubs. More distant was an elongated range of mountains. His gaze followed the steep terrains leading down to valleys far below. The sun was slipping beyond the far horizon Twilight was fast approaching. Breathing deeply and slowly closing his eyes, he started to reminisce. He drifted back through time and space, back over his past experiences and events of many years. An American journey began.

It was the early 1930's when America was in the throes of the Great Depression, and   Jack Rubin was growing up in Brookline. Although a separate municipality, Brookline merged almost imperceptibly into the city of Boston: the hub of New England. It was a unique city, a blending of the Old and the New World. In the downtown area traffic languidly flowed along narrow, winding, cobblestone streets. Historical sites such as churches and even cemeteries from the colonial era dotted some of the streets. Lying below the dome of the state house and Beacon Hill were the Boston Common and Public Garden, a spacious park filled with pedestrians and pigeons. In its center swan boats, filled with children and adults, glided across the waters of a large pond. At one time, attempts were made to transform the Common into a car parking area since parking in downtown Boston was nearly impossible. But such efforts were fiercely resisted by Boston residents and tradition prevailed. The Common, the oldest city park in the United States dating back to 1634, had been used as cow pasture and for public hangings as well as for the quartering of British troops during the American Revolution. Moving east from Park Street Station, bordering on The Common, were the theater district and Chinatown. Extending to the north was Paul Revere House and Breeds Hill, site of the Battle of Bunker Hill; and, if you listened intently enough, you might hear the famous order: "Don't fire until you see the whites of their eyes." Suffering heavy losses, the British won the battle. But the colonists went on to win the war.

Life began for Jack Rubin in 1928, shortly before the difficult years of the Great Depression. He never knew his father who passed away just after his birth. But he remembered his sister, Marjorie. She suffered from leukemia and died at the age of twelve when Jack was only six. Sometimes he awoke from nightmares screaming: "Marjorie! Marjorie!" As he grew older, he delivered newspapers and went from door to door soliciting magazine subscriptions. During summers he set up a lemonade stand and sold lemonade for pennies a cup. His mother tirelessly plodded the streets selling life insurance policies, which in those days was more of a man's vocation.

In the late 1930's, life became easier. Jack's mother remarried; and the family dwelt along Beacon Street, a major thoroughfare, in the heart of Brookline. Nearby streetcar tracks stretched along Beacon to the Boston city line and disappeared into the darkness of a subway. The streetcar was Jack's major connection to distant parts of Brookline, downtown Boston, the beaches of Revere, and the Boston waterfront. Crossing Beacon he would often ride the trolley cars to Park Street or Boylston Street Station whenever he chose to explore the downtown area. With the arrival of spring came the beginning of the baseball season. Almost every Sunday he would head out to Fenway Park, the home of the Boston Red Sox and the "green monster": that green wall that loomed high beyond the left field. It was only a few miles from his home, so he could walk; otherwise he rode the streetcar. On Sundays, when there were double headers and the New York Yankees were in town, the ball park was filled to capacity. Admittance was less than a dollar, and vendors dressed in white coats and caps ran up and down the stairs shouting: "Popcorn, peanuts!" All stood for the national anthem followed by the cry: "Play ball!" The Sox took to the field amid loud cheers from their fans, and the Yankees came up to bat. The first was Babe Ruth, the "Bambino"; and the Red Sox fans vigorously booed perhaps recalling the "Bambino Curse" which they believed had haunted their team for many years and brought it misfortune from the time that Babe Ruth left the Sox to join the Yankees. On the first pitch, Ruth hit the ball hard. The third baseman fumbled it but quickly threw it to first base. It was still a close play, as stocky Ruth was not the fastest runner. The umpire called him safe, and there was an uproar of protest from the fans. In left field Ted Williams angrily threw his glove to the ground and stomped on it. But after a brief interruption, the game continued.

In warmer weather Jack would travel with a fishing pole and tackle box to Boston Harbor. He would cast a line from the docks and catch flounder, mackerel, and ocean perch, or he might sail out on a fishing boat in search of cod and haddock. Other times he would travel to Revere Beach usually with companions. Once he took a blanket along and slept all night on the beach. Waking early in the morning, he found himself spitting sand out of his mouth. He never tried that again.

Something unexpected happened soon after Jack's mother remarried. It was summer, and Jack began to suffer extreme headaches which became intolerable. A doctor was called to their vacation house and made a quick and tentative diagnosis.

"This boy must go to the hospital immediately. I think he has polio. Time is critical."

Wrapped in a blanket he was carried by his stepfather to a waiting car and rushed to the hospital. He had no idea about the seriousness of his condition. He was treated quickly and spent the rest of the summer in bed at the hospital. Returning home, he continued to be bedridden. Fortunately he suffered no paralysis which was a common effect of polio. At that time there was no Salk vaccine to combat the disease. He recovered slowly and was forced to miss a year of school.

Occasionally Jack and his friends engaged in mischievous acts. One they did after dark when Jack and another boy stood on opposite sides of a street, and each leaned forward pretending to pull an object such as a rope or chain. As an approaching car slowed, the two boys quickly disappeared into the night. Another prank involved randomly selecting a name and phone number from the telephone directory. The boys would then dial the number and might ask:

"Is John there?"

Of course they always asked for someone with a name differing from the one in the directory. And the response was often:

"There's no John living here."

They would repeat the call a few times, and when making a last call either Jack or his companion would say:

"Hi there! This is John. Have I had any calls?"

What about the people of Boston: their composition and disposition? Spread throughout the city was a medley of racial, ethnic and religious groups comprised of Asians, Blacks, Irish, Italians, Catholics, Protestants, and Jews. Prejudice and discrimination persisted among these as well as other groups. Divisions were sharpened and hardened by Old World animosities. The population could be described as a "stew pot" rather than a "melting pot". Jack was growing up in a household with a stepfather who was a devout orthodox Jew. This engendered some conflict. Jack's mother had been his sole parent until he was about nine years old and had not strongly imbued him with any particular religion only emphasizing the importance of being tolerant of all creeds. But Jack was well aware of his Jewish identity. He attended religious school at a reform synagogue where he was confirmed; and most of his friends were Jewish. At an early age, he spent a summer at a Cub Scout camp. He may have been the only Jewish boy in the camp, and there was one boy who continually antagonized him.

"You damn Jew! Christ killer!" the youth would shout at Jack.

Then he began shoving Jack and cursing him. The campers gathered around to witness a fight. Jack swung back at the boy, and they exchanged blows. On and on they went. No one really tried to stop them. Some of the other campers shouted similar epithets. But there was one boy who stood up for Jack shouting, "I'm in your corner Jack! Smack him good!" The boy was not Jewish, and his support gave Jack some consolation.

Similar incidents occurred where Jack was not directly involved. On St Patrick's Day there were sometimes reports of Jewish students being harassed by the "Southies": young men from South Boston known for their religious and racial bigotry. Jack learned, too that intolerance existed in the Jewish community as well, When he was in his early teens, he and a friend were planning to go out on a double date.

His friend, Roy asked, "Jack is your date Jewish?"

Jack replied: "No, what difference does it make?

"It won't work," Roy rejoined, "My date is Jewish, and she won't like it."

"To hell with her!" Jack snapped angrily. "Then you two can go alone!"

This isn't right, Jack thought, and the two boys never saw each other again. It was the end of their friendship.

Once Jack arranged a date between a Jewish girl and a Christian boy.

Later the girl's mother admonished him.

"Jack, don't you ever again fix my daughter up with a boy who's not Jewish."

These were just a few examples of the hostility and alienation between Jews and Christians.

Divisions and conflicts characterized other groups as well. Catholics and Protestants were at odds with one another as were various ethnic groups: Irish, Italians, Portuguese; and association between the different races was limited and sometimes antagonistic. Attempts were made by religious leaders and other entities to promote a better understanding among the different groups. It was even rumored that priests, ministers, and rabbis occasionally shared common pulpits trying to deliver messages of tolerance.

Beyond the confines of Boston and America, events were more foreboding. The fires of animosity and conflict had been spreading in Asia and Europe, and the threat of a global war was growing. Not long after Jack was born, the clouds of war had begun to gather. In 1931 Japan invaded Manchuria and continued to push farther into China. Despite censure by the League of Nations, Japan persisted in its aggression and in 1933 withdrew from the League. In 1935 the Italian dictator, Benito Mussolini ordered the invasion of Ethiopia. The poorly armed Ethiopians were helpless against modern military weapons and chemical weapons such as mustard gas. The League of Nations condemned Italy's aggression and imposed economic sanctions which proved ineffective. Finally the prelude to World War II in Europe occurred with the onset of the Spanish Civil War. At the start of the 1930's, elections in Spain gave broad support to the Republicans and Socialists which opened the door to the establishment of the Second Spanish Republic which persisted until the termination of the Spanish Civil War. A new and liberal constitution was drawn up, and there were great hopes for democratic reforms. However, right wing and conservative forces began to stir in opposition. They eventually identified themselves as Nationalists and were comprised of former monarchists, landowners, Catholic clergy and the fascist Falange. They labeled their adversaries as "red hordes" and "enemies of Christian civilization". In contrast, supporters of the Republic were made up of democratic liberals, Socialists, Communists, Marxist sympathizers, and were strongly anti- clerical They viewed the war as a conflict between tyranny and democracy. By 1936 General Francisco Franco led an army from Morocco seeking to overthrow the Republic. There was a good deal of foreign intervention particularly in support of the Nationalists or rebels. Both Nazi Germany and Fascist Italy provided much military aid to Franco's forces including aircraft, tanks, munitions and other modern weapons. Germany even provided training for Nationalist forces and submarine forays;and as many as 16,000 German citizens fought in the war. The Italian Navy helped to bombard Republican held ports in Spain and in Morocco and supplied the Nationalists with thousands of troops. The intervention of Germany and Italy was a rehearsal for their future aggressions. Surprisingly Great Britain favored a victory for Franco and considered him as a liberal as well as a bulwark against the spread of Communism. Also, they felt their Mediterranean ports would be more secure with Spain controlled by a Nationalist regime and supported a sea blockade against Spain which prevented the Republic from getting more help from abroad. Private parties in Great Britain, the United States, and other democracies sent considerable aid to Franco. There was much less support for the Republic. International volunteers or brigades came to help fight a war which many believed was a struggle of democracy against fascism. The most significant number, 10,000 came from France. Smaller units volunteered from a number of other countries. Military aid for the Republic came from the Soviet Union, Mexico, and from France; but it was not enough to stave off the final capitulation of the Republic in 1939 and the establishment of a fascist dictatorship under the leadership of Francisco Franco. The participation of Germany and Italy in this struggle was seen as the prelude to World War Two.

It was September 1939, and Germany had invaded Poland. Nazi troops, tanks, and cannon crossed the border under the pretext of a provocation. Subsequently, France and England declared war on

Germany. Both nations were committed to defending Poland. World War Two had begun. It was about this time that Jack frequented the movie theaters. There were two in Brookline; and he could board a nearby streetcar which would quickly transport him to either theatre. Sometimes he would venture farther into downtown Boston, hop off at Boylston or Park Street, and stroll his way to a theatre offering a double feature horror show. He had a special fascination for those monster movies. Often he would go alone. Admission was only a quarter, and he could munch on a chocolate bar or a box of popcorn for only five or ten cents. Typically, the theatres showed double features and in between there were newsreels like the "March of Time". They were informative and largely focused on current world events. It was something of an education experience for Jack. He would sit in the dark theatre intently watching as a report of the German invasion of Poland unfolded. Flashing across the theater screen were battle scenes of the massive devastation resulting from bombs dropped by screaming dive bombers and gunfire, people scurrying for cover, and the many broken and twisted bodies of the injured and dead. The defenders of Warsaw fought valiantly, but Poland capitulated in a matter of months and was occupied by both German and Russian military forces.

In November of the same year, Jack saw something else appear on theatre screens: the beginning of a terrible winter war with the onset of a Soviet Union invasion of Finland. The conflict lasted only four months, but the fighting was extremely fierce and casualties were very heavy. Although the League of Nations acted to expel the Soviet Union, it failed to deter the aggression. The Soviet Union demanded certain areas of Finland for reasons of security. Their major concerns were the future protection of Leningrad as well as continued access to the Baltic Sea and the Atlantic Ocean. The Soviet

Union insisted on the virtual cessation of the Karelian Isthmus. But Finland refused to comply with Soviet demands and the Winter War began. Jack viewed some vivid and memorable battle scenes against white frozen landscapes with temperatures falling as low as -45 degrees Fahrenheit. Accompanying commentaries were extensive and intense. Finnish forces, along with Swedish volunteers, fought off the Red Army hordes which outnumbered them as much as ten or twenty to one. Dressed in white ski suits with rifles slung over their shoulders, the defenders were very skilled in cross-country skiing and took advantage of the nature of weather conditions and the terrain. In the cold snow, long periods of darkness, and thick forests, they fought a guerrilla war and often ambushed the Red Army troops which advanced in columns and were especially vulnerable as at first they were dressed in khaki uniforms. Through the darkness, Jack could hear men screaming in anguish cut down by enemy fire; and, in brief spans of daylight, he could see Finnish soldiers and Swedish volunteers dressed in white snowsuits, firing their rifles or machine guns at the advancing Red Army troops, hurling Molotov cocktails (bottles of inflammable liquids), and creating log jams to stop the enemy tanks. Many of the defenders fell, their white snowsuits stained red with blood. They fought bravely, inflicted heavy casualties on the Red Army, but in the end they were overwhelmed. Again, the League of Nations had failed. The rest of the world stood passively by. England and France did offer to dispatch military aid to Norwegian ports and requested passage to Finland, but both Norway and Sweden were cowed by threats of Nazi retaliation and occupation. Much of the fighting occurred in the Karelian Isthmus where the Finnish defenders and Swedish volunteers were completely overwhelmed and forced to retreat. By March, 1940, the war ended with the entire Karelian Isthmus ceded to the Soviet Union and a signing of the Moscow Peace Treaty. Jack would come to understand the personal significance of these events in much later years.

Other times theater newsreels showed the waving swastikas, the goose stepping troops, columns of tanks and cannons rolling along the streets of Berlin and Nuremburg, and the on looking crowds shouting: "Sieg Heil! Sieg Heil!" Jack recalled how movie audiences responded with nonchalance and even laughter. Many years earlier in 1933 the Nazi Party had won a plurality in the Bundestag in the last democratic election in Germany, and a mad man Adolf Hitler had become the nation's new chancellor. By 1939 Hitler's armies had overan Austria and Czechoslovakia; and for a time many believed that peace would prevail in Europe and that the Nazi hordes would be a bulwark against the specter of Communism.

Here in America the Nazis began to spread their tentacles by organizing youth camps and rallies. At least one such rally occurred in Madison Square Garden in New York City where portraits of Adolf Hitler and George Washington were displayed, and the swastika and the stars and stripes hung side by side. As the Nazi war machine conquered countries throughout Europe, it was preceded by what was known as the "fifth column". It was an expression that originated during the Spanish Civil War when a Nationalist general led four columns of troops in an attack on Madrid and claimed that he had a fifth column inside the city. These were groups within a country who were working for the Nazi invaders. They employed a "divide and conquer" strategy in fermenting discontent and conflict among different religious, ethnic, and political groups making countries more vulnerable to conquest. The strategy was very effective in Germany where Social Democrats were turned against Communists, Protestants against Catholics, Christians against Jews. Later it worked effectively in other conquered countries. Then there were those who failed to take a stand or speak out. Martin Niemoller, a Lutheran minister who at first supported the Nazis but later opposed them and was imprisoned, expressed it well:

> *First they came for the socialists, and I did not speak out because I was not a socialist.*
>
> *Then they came for the trade unionists, and I did not speak out because I was not a trade unionist.*
>
> *Then they came for the Jews, and I did not speak out because I was not a Jew.*
>
> *Then they came for me and there was no one left to speak for me.*

Back in the relative serenity of Brookline, Jack was immersed in school work. The public school systems in Brookline and throughout Boston demanded high quality performance from teachers and students. Beginning in the fifth grade, drills in English grammar were common. In higher elementary grades the historical roots of America were highlighted: the original Thirteen Colonies, the American Revolution, the American Constitution, the War of 1812, the Civil War or "the War Between the States", followed by the rebirth of a nation. Memorable were the cries of early American patriots:

> *Give me liberty or give me death! I only regret that I have but one life to give to my country! I have not yet begun to fight!*

Students were expected to prepare written and oral reports about such historical events and related social issues. Jack struggled with these and other parts of the school curriculum. The importance of English composition was stressed even more at Brookline High School where Jack became inclined to write short stories especially about the supernatural.

By spring of 1940 the war in Europe had escalated considerably. In a blitzkrieg or lightning strike German forces swept through Belgium and Holland circumventing the Maginot defense line. Allied resistance was crumbling, and France was about to fall. The British Expeditionary Forces (BEF) retreated to the French port of Dunkirk trapped on the beaches with their backs to the sea. The Germans had seized the port of Boulogne and had surrounded Calais but had halted their advance on Dunkirk. Bad weather and marshes in proximity to Dunkirk impeded the use of motorized assault units and the effectiveness of the Luftwaffe. Also, the German military was concerned with the vulnerability of their flanks and their supply lines. The evacuation of British troops was miraculous. Soldiers on the beaches were being bombed and strafed continually, but squadrons of the Royal Air Force, ships of the Royal Navy, and many other vessels rescued the BEF.

It was the summer of 1940, and the Battle of Britain had begun. England was bombed almost constantly and was preparing for an anticipated invasion. At the time, Jack was living with his family in an apartment on Beacon Street. During evenings he visited some refugees from Czechoslovakia living in the same apartment building. Many evenings they would all hover about the radio listening intently to the nightly newscast and an emotional voice saying:

"Ah yes, there's good news tonight! Again the Luftwaffe suffered heavy losses. The Royal Air Force shot down numerous enemy bombers and fighter escorts. The skies over England are still controlled by the RAF!"

Jack and the others loudly cheered and clapped their hands.

Also, Jack was heartened by the speeches of the British Prime Minister, Winston Churchill. Stirring was Churchill's tribute to the valiant efforts of the pilots of the Royal Air Force:

Never in the field of human conflict was so much owed by so many to so few.

As England suffered from the relentless onslaughts of the Luftwaffe and the threat of an impending German invasion, Churchill spoke in the House of Commons:

I have nothing to offer but blood, toil, tears, and sweat.

And even though much of Europe had fallen under Nazi domination, he added:

We shall go on to the end. We shall fight in France, we shall fight on the seas and oceans, we shall fight with growing confidence and growing strength in the air, we shall defend our island whatever the cost may be. We shall fight on the beaches, we shall fight on the landing grounds, we shall fight in the fields and in the streets, we shall fight in the hills, we shall never surrender.

Britain held out and fought on alone. Although isolationism persisted in America, some help was provided by President Franklin Roosevelt. Without the approval of the Congress, the President secretly sent a flotilla of World War One destroyers to assist the British on the condition that the ships would be sunk if Great Britain fell. The war escalated even further in June of 1941 when Hitler, against the advice of his generals, ordered the invasion of the Soviet

Union. Initially the German invaders were very successful penetrating deep into Russia.

Then it happened! It was December 7, 1941 on a Sunday morning in Hawaii. It was a day earlier in Boston, and Jack was still in bed when he heard the shocking news come over the radio: an unexpected attack on Pearl Harbor by the Empire of Japan! The damage was devastating. Nearly the entire Pacific fleet was destroyed, and thousands lost their lives. Immediately America issued a declaration of war against the Empire of Japan; and Germany, in turn, declared war on the United States. Americans had lived in some kind of "splendid isolation" separated from the rest of the world by two great oceans. The war would rage on for four more years in Europe and Asia. Many of America's youth would die in the jungles of the South Pacific and on the blood soaked beaches of Tarawa and Normandy. A terrible price was paid for warnings gone unheeded in Ernest Hemingway's, *For Whom the Bells Toll*, and his quote from John Donne's 17th century poem, *No Man is an Island* which resonated throughout the world:

No man is an island entire of itself
Every man is a piece of the continent, a part of the main

If a clod be washed away by the sea,
Europe is the less, as a well as if a promontory were.

As well as if a manor of thy friends were

Any man's death diminished me, because I am involved
in mankind.

And therefore never send to know for whom the bell tolls
It tolls for thee.

The world was ablaze, and Jack was eager to join the fight. But he was still too young. And after spending two years at Brookline High, he wished to continue his high school education elsewhere. There was too much conflict at home involving his stepfather and other family members. Also, he felt stifled in Brookline. He had grown up in a community where all his friends and associates were Jewish. Certainly it was a healthy environment. The values of high aspirations, education, and hard work were extolled. But Jack yearned for adventure, to break out, and grow in the larger world. But where would he go? His mother had been born and had grown to adulthood in a small town in Georgia. There were things about Southern culture which attracted him. Notable was the fact that the South had contributed many of America's greatest writers: William Faulkner, Erskine Caldwell, Tennessee Williams, Mark Twain, and Margaret Mitchell. Not included, of course, was the caste system: the prejudice and discrimination practiced against blacks which he considered repugnant. Jack chose to attend a military academy nestled in the Shenandoah Valley of Virginia. Although he did not plan on any military career, he felt the experience would prepare him better to serve in the military in case the war raged on until he was old enough to enlist. It was a change that would carry him away from the confines of Brookline and into the larger world. Deep in a valley surrounded by the picturesque Blue Ridge Mountains, he continued his studies. During the few years he was there, he wrote short stories for the Bayonet, the school newspaper at the military academy. He was stimulated by the works of Edgar Allen Poe, Nathaniel Hawthorne, Jack London, John Steinbeck, Ernest Hemingway, and other American writers. He read the tragedies of William Shakespeare, the early writings of Geoffrey Chaucer, and the poems of John Milton, Rudyard Kipling, and John Donne. Also, Jack was influenced by some of the French writers: Francois Voltaire, Guy De Maupassant, Jean Paul Sartre, and Emile Zola. During these times students were required to read a list of fifty classical works. Academic achievement was the norm; and students who did excel proudly wore the honor roll band, a practice abandoned in later years when American education began to implement a leveling process.

There was something else he learned while at Augusta Military Academy. A preacher visited the school in search of converts; and the commandant ordered all cadets to attend his sermons. At first no objections were raised, and all attended. The preacher delivered his sermons suffused with much emotion, and Jack was really moved. This guy was good, he thought, almost another Billy Graham; and from time to time, the preacher would cry out entreating the cadets:

"Rise from your seats! Come forward and accept Jesus Christ as your Savior!"

Jack almost rose, but then was glued to his seat when the preacher added: "Remember, you cannot find happiness unless you accept Jesus Christ as your Savior!"

That just didn't sound right to Jack. Not long after that, a petition signed by cadets of different faiths: Catholic, Protestant, and Jewish was submitted to the commandant stating that the undersigned cadets would no longer attend the preacher's sermons. They felt it was an infringement on their religious freedom, and the commandant quickly rescinded his order. Jack, along with others, had signed the petition, and he was proud that they all had taken a stand.

If only the world had taken a stand earlier against Nazi aggression and tyranny, millions of lives could have been spared. As the years passed, the tides of war turned in favor of the Allied powers. At Stalingrad prolonged and intense fighting occurred street to street and house to house until the mighty Nazi war machine began its long retreat. There were the Allied victories in the deserts of Africa, the landings and assaults at Anzio and Normandy, and finally the liberation of Europe from Nazi tyranny. Japan capitulated after a terrible weapon: the atomic bomb was unleashed. It was either that or a loss of thousands or perhaps a million lives of American servicemen to bring an end to war in the Pacific. The world had entered the nuclear age, the United Nations emerged from global devastation, and America could no longer turn its back on the rest of the world.

CHAPTER TWO:
THE COLLEGE YEARS

It was June, 1946. Jack received his high school diploma at Augusta Military Academy and planned to move on to college. Some of the graduating cadets were going on to West Point and Annapolis. Other friends back in Brookline were expecting to attend prestigious Ivy League universities such as Harvard, Yale, and Columbia. Indeed Jack had applied to Columbia but was rejected probably because of his mediocre grades. Also, colleges and universities were inundated by war veterans receiving generous education benefits. This made it even more difficult to enter colleges or universities many of which lacked adequate facilities and staff to absorb the sharp increase in applicants. But Jack was determined to continue his education and sought the advice of the Brookline High School principal whom he knew from earlier years when attending Brookline High.

Seated in his office, Mr. Brown looked steadily and sympathetically at Jack. "Look Jack, these are difficult times. Getting into college these days has become very competitive. Your grades are not that high, and college isn't for everybody. Are you sure this is what you want?"

"Yes, Mr. Brown I am sure." Jack replied emphatically. "Can you help me? Isn't there somewhere I could go on to college?"

"Okay, Jack, there is a place, Sampson College in New York State. It's a two year college just set up to absorb spiking applicants. It was a naval training station during the war, and barracks have been converted into dormitories and classrooms. Hesitatingly he added: "It's a desolate place and the winters are very cold and long."

"It's okay. That's where I'll go!" Jack exclaimed.

"Good! Here's the application. Just fill it out, and mail it in the enclosed envelope. You should get a reply in a few weeks."

Jack grasped the paper work, thanked the principal, and left. Later he submitted the application, and within a few weeks received a letter of acceptance.

It was early September when Jack's stepfather drove him to the North Railroad Station. He paid a quick farewell to his parents and boarded the train headed for Geneva in upstate New York. Shoving his suitcases into a storage rack, he slid into a seat as the train crept slowly out of the station. Gradually it gained speed, and Jack began scanning other passengers. Seated nearby were two fellows about Jack's age. One was tall and muscular looking. He had a fair complexion, and his hair was cut very short. The other was smaller and more frail with sharper facial features and curly brown hair. Some time passed before the big, muscular looking fellow looked directly at Jack asking him:

"Are you traveling far?"

"Pretty far", Jack answered, "I'm on my way to Sampson College near Geneva."

"What a coincidence I'm on my way there, too!"

Then the other fellow excitedly joined in: "Hey, that makes three of us !"

They introduced themselves to one another, shook hands, and chatted for much of the rest of the trip. Hal, the big guy was from Manchester, New Hampshire where he had worked as a lumberjack and was planning to study engineering. The other fellow, Jerry was from Providence, Rhode Island, had worked in sales, and expected to major in business administration.

During the conversation, Hal turned to Jack: " Have you decided on any major?"

"I'm not sure," Jack replied. "English, maybe. Hope to be a writer someday."

After several hours, the conductor yelled out, "Geneva, the next stop!" By that time, Jack and his traveling companions had decided to share a room at the college. Inside the station, the train lurched forward and came to an abrupt stop. The three men grabbed their luggage, left the train, and headed for a nearby bus which would take them to Sampson College. It was a short ride of only twenty or twenty five minutes when the bus pulled up in front of the administration building. Stepping off the bus, they viewed the surrounding area.

"Wow!" Hal exclaimed, "This doesn't look very much like a college campus!"

It was a barren landscape except for a collection of drab and gray colored buildings. Farther away were docks stretching out into Seneca Lake. The sun was just beginning to set, and you could barely see the opposite shore. Jack and his companions entered the administration building, filled out some paper work, and were assigned their living quarters. Then they threaded their way to one of the barracks which had been altered into separate living quarters. Their room was small and the furniture limited: one double-decker bed, a single bed, a large table, a lamp, and three chairs.

"Well, this is it guys! Shall we toss a coin to see who sleeps where?" Jerry suggested. Jack and Hal nodded in agreement. Jerry won the toss and chose the single bed.

"Jack, I'll take the upper bed", Hal said smiling. "I have longer legs"

Jack laughed: "That's okay with me."

The next several days were spent at orientation sessions. After that, prospective students were individually counseled on required courses and electives.

Jack found two of his courses especially interesting: European History and Philosophy and Logic. At the beginning of one of his European History classes the instructor announced:

"Today I want to discuss the question who was really responsible for starting World War One?" Then in a cautionary tone he added, "but first I better shut this door."

He took a few steps, closed the classroom door, and began his lecture.

"Many believe that Germany was the major culprit. But I think the facts suggest otherwise. Over time, countries in Europe had developed mutual defense agreements: Russia and Serbia, Germany and Austria-Hungary, France and Russia formed one alliance and finally Britain, France, and Belgium the other. In addition, there was contention among European countries engaged in imperialistic policies or empire building. International tensions further increased with military buildups by Great Britain, Germany, and Russia. Then came the assassination of Archduke Franz Ferdinand by a Serbian nationalist while the Archduke was in Sarajevo, Bosnia which was part of Austria-Hungary. Presumably this was in protest of Austria-Hungary having taken over this region. Serbia aspired to take over Bosnia and Herzegovina. The assassination led Austria- Hungary to declare war against Serbia; and, against the advice of his general staff, the Tsar mobilized the Russian Army, which, in those days was tantamount to a declaration of war. Faced with the threat of having to fight on two fronts, Germany planned a quick strike on France. Subsequently, there was an expansion of the war to include all those countries involved in mutual defense agreements. So, it appears that the responsibility for the deaths of millions must be shared by a number of nations!"

The instructor lectured further, and nearing the end of class he asked if there were any questions. A few were raised, but no one asked why he made a point of closing the classroom door before starting his lecture. There were no disturbances or distractions out-side in the corridor. This somewhat puzzled Jack. Perhaps it was a "red flag", portending growing constraints in higher education?

Jack's course in Philosophy and Logic highlighted the great con-tributions of Socrates, Plato, and Aristotle to Western thought where Plato described the Socratic Method in the "Socratic Dialogues". It was a dialectic method applied to a problem by asking a series of questions ultimately leading to an underlying answer or solution. This type of inquiry later influenced the development of the scien-tific method. Aristotle, considered the father of formal logic, was similarly responsible for the later emergence of the scientific method especially with his emphasis on the role of deductive and inductive thinking. Especially memorable for Jack was Aristotle's quote:

"Man is by nature a social animal; an individual who is unsocial naturally and not accidently is either beneath our notice or more than human. Society is something that precedes the individual. Anyone who cannot lead the common life or is so sufficient as not to need to, and therefore does not partake of society is either beast or god."

The days and weeks passed rather quickly during the first semester at Sampson College. By November, snow began to fall and heavy drifts accumulated. There were sharp drops in the outside temperatures, as strong cold winds whipped across the campus. Jack made sure his hands, head, and ears were well covered and protected from the extreme cold. He even wrapped a scarf around his face to reduce the possibility of frostbite. It was a very isolated environment, and there wasn't much else to do except study. On weekends some students would drive into town and pick up cases of beer and bottles of whiskey or wine. Then many students would imbibe rather freely. During milder weather Jack and other students would patronize the clubs and bars of Geneva generally in search of female company, as Sampson College was not coeducational. Food at the college was abysmally poor. The school newspaper even published a cartoon depicting a couple of gorillas serving food at the college cafeteria with a caption reading: "untouched by human hands". The administration was quick to admonish the newspaper editor. Although college regulations prohibited the use of "hot plates" in the dormitories, their use was commonplace. This helped to remedy the "food problem". Both Jerry and Jack were unacquainted with the culinary arts. Hal, however, assisted in providing much of the cooking expertise.

As the first semester was ending, Jack and his roommates arranged to ride with another student who was driving to Boston. From there Hal and Jerry would continue to their respective homes either by bus or train. While on the road one cold and snowy night, their car had a flat tire. Luckily, they were near an exit around Albany and were able to pull off the expressway and quickly put on a spare tire. It was extremely cold. Close by was a liquor store where they purchased a bottle of Southern Comfort. A few sips of the liquor helped them to thaw out and resume their trip to Boston. After a few weeks, Jack, Hal, and Jerry rejoined each other to begin the second semester. The college was still buried in drifts of snow with cold biting winds blowing across the campus. But if one were dressed properly, he could make his way along the dugout pathways that linked the student dormitories, classrooms, and faculty offices.

Jack's grades for that first semester were above average. He had done well particularly in college algebra. He felt that all his teachers had been very helpful and stimulating. Many had been drawn from leading colleges and universities throughout New York State. But now Jack had to take a calculus course in order to complete his math requirement. On the first day of instruction, the instructor sauntered into the classroom and dropped an attaché case and a few books on a small table. He was a short, slender man with bushy black hair and a conspicuous black beard. He briefly gazed about the room and cleared his throat before speaking.

"Good morning, gentlemen. Welcome to Calculus 101, I am Professor Smith", and in a boasting tone he added, "you may also call me Doctor Smith. I have a PhD from Haaarvard University."

His strong Boston accent was unmistakable, and he continued lecturing in a somewhat condescending manner. Unfortunately,

Professor Smith was inclined to abuse and intimidate his students. He would explain the calculus by running the length of the blackboard and briskly chalk out a sequence of equations. Quickly turning to the class, he would exclaim, "Do you see it?" Then he would run to the other end of the blackboard erasing all computations. "And now you don't see it! But you better remember it!" This essentially was his method of teaching. He had office hours for students seeking help. But often he would discourage any visits, saying, "I'm too busy now. Come back another time."

Jack struggled in the calculus course as did other students. He thought to himself: This guy is a pompous ass, and the worst teacher I have ever had. It was a hopeless situation. There was no avenue of appeal, and he and many other students felt forced to withdraw from the course. But in later years, he would master the basics of the calculus.

One year at the desolate and depressing campus of Sampson College was enough. Jack had been accepted at American University in the nation's capital. As the academic year drew to a close, he was looking forward to leaving the desolate and depressing campus of Sampson College. But he was beginning to feel some pangs of nostalgia. Despite the harshness of the physical environment, he had found the students very congenial and dedicated in their studies. Most came from very diverse backgrounds and tended to show much tolerance and understanding. Hal had been especially friendly. During the spring break, Jack spent several days with him and his family in Manchester. Hal had talked about going bear hunting, but that didn't happen. It rained nearly every day during Jack's visit.

Finally, the academic year ended. Sampson students parted going their separate ways. Jack returned home to Brookline for the summer, and in September he headed south to Washington, D.C. and American University to continue his undergraduate studies.

At Union Station Jack hailed a cab which took him along Massachusetts Avenue and embassy row to American University. The campus was compact and well landscaped. University buildings were constructed in attractively colored concrete or brick. Jack had already been assigned a room in one of the student dormitories: Gray Hall, and he had been sent a map of the layout of the campus. Carrying his two suitcases, he found his way to his dormitory. Once inside, he entered his new room which was spacious and appeared very comfortable. It contrasted sharply with what had been his living quarters at Sampson College. There were two separate double beds, two bureaus, a couple of tables with reading lamps, chairs, and bookcases. The floor was even carpeted and curtains hung in large windows that overlooked a grove of trees and a nearby parkway. As Jack looked out of one of the windows, he heard a voice from behind.

"Hi there! You must be my new roommate."

Jack turned quickly and introduced himself.

"I'm Jack Rubin. Just arrived from Boston."

"Glad to have you here, Jack. The name is Seymour, Seymour Robbins. I just stepped out of the shower." He extended his arm, and the two men shook hands.

Seymour was dressed in a bathrobe with a towel slung around his neck. He was about Jack's height, but older, maybe twenty three or twenty four years old. He had curly brown hair, bushy eyebrows, and fleshy facial features. They chatted incessantly while Jack unpacked his suitcases and arranged his clothing and other paraphernalia in a chest of drawers. As he finished dressing, Seymour asked:

"Say, Jack are you hungry?"

"I certainly am. I didn't have much to eat on the train."

"Okay, let's head for Mary Grayson Center. The cafeteria should be open by now."

It was a short walk to Mary Grayson Center, an attractive red brick building with a flight of wide concrete steps leading to the main entrance. After entering, Seymour led Jack to the lower level where the cafeteria was located. It was crowded and noisy with students either waiting in line for food or seated eating and conversing. They found an empty table where Seymour propped up two chairs.

"That's to let people know the table is taken", Seymour asserted.

They picked up their trays selected their food and returned to their table.

"The food looks pretty good and tastes good." Jack commented. Then glancing about he said, "Seymour, when we entered the building I noticed some booths marked with Greek letters and students who seemed to be soliciting What's going on?"

"Oh, this is pledge week. The fraternities and sororities are out to recruit new members. They run many of the social activities here."

"Are you a member of a fraternity?" Jack inquired.

Seymour was quiet and seemed reluctant to answer. He looked a little uncomfortable and shook his head.

"No I'm not, Jack," he replied. "I'm Jewish, and they don't accept Jews."

"Well, that makes two of us!" Jack retorted.

"What about blacks and Catholics?"

"I'm not sure, but I don't think Catholics are eligible either, certainly not blacks. They're not even admitted to the university. This isn't Boston, Jack. It's a Jim Crow town."

"Well, there isn't that much tolerance in Boston either. By the way, what do you do for a social life?"

"I have a girlfriend, Rita. She's a foreign student from Mexico City. I'll introduce you to her later."

"Is it serious?" Jack asked.

"Pretty serious. We're thinking of marrying in a few years. After we've graduated." At this point, they finished eating, left the cafeteria, and returned to their dormitory.

The next day Jack went to counseling and then to registration. At counseling he was asked if he wished to select a major, and he thought perhaps English, "I want to be a writer," he asserted.

"That's fine." His counselor replied. "But don't you want to earn a living?"

"Well, of course."

"Then I suggest that you major in Journalism. This means that all of your courses will be at the downtown campus at the School of Social Sciences and Public Affairs."

Jack did complete his first semester taking courses at the main campus. The courses weren't especially interesting: Speech, Psychology, Spanish, and Geology. Perhaps the most difficult and boring was Geology. But it had a few redeeming features. First, it was a small class of perhaps ten students; but, more importantly, one of the students was a very attractive blond. He would sometimes stare at her and try to catch her eye but was unsuccessful. He tried to accost her at the end of class, but she always slipped away hurriedly disappearing into the night. An opportunity arose when the class was going on a field trip to caverns in Virginia. It was early morning. When Jack boarded the bus, he spotted an empty seat next to the elusive blond. He made an obvious maneuver, passing several empty seats, and sat down beside her. As the bus began to move, Jack introduced himself thinking that perhaps she didn't know his name. She responded and said her name was "Alice." They talked for a while, and she spoke very slowly as if she were measuring every word. It seemed to be a strained conversation. Then it was quiet, and Jack became drowsy. This was too early in the morning for him. Soon, he actually fell asleep. Some time passed, and suddenly Alice was shaking him.

"Get your head off my shoulder!" she cried out angrily.

Jack, of course, apologized. But that didn't help. When the bus arrived at the caverns, he and Alice went their separate ways.

As the semester progressed, Jack felt increasingly isolated. He didn't see too much of Seymour who spent a good deal of time with Rita. When he and Seymour were together, the latter liked to relate tales of his war experiences He had flown bombing missions over Germany, during World War Two and said that on one mission he had been ordered not to bomb certain targets. He believed they were armament factories owned by U.S. companies. Also, he bragged that he had slept with a well-known actress he had met at a Hollywood party for servicemen. Seymour had grown up in New York City and claimed that, in those years, he came to know members of the Italian Mafia and Murder Incorporated. He had a lot of stories to tell, and Jack wondered how many were credible.

Usually Jack ate alone at Mary Grayson Center. He would try to join students at other tables but was often snubbed; and if he sat alone, other students would generally pass by him. Once he went to a dance hosted by a sorority; but, not being a member of a campus fraternity, he was made to feel like an intruder. Wherever he went on the campus, people seemed to cohere in small impenetrable cliques. What he felt especially offensive was the requirement that all students attend church services once every week. Attendance was monitored with a sign in sheet. But Jack simply refused to attend. He remembered that a somewhat like situation arose during his high school years at Augusta Military Academy. The commandant had issued an order for all cadets to attend sermons given by a religious revivalist. After a few sermons many cadets, including Jack, had sent a petition to the commandant claiming that the order was an infringement on religious freedom and they would not attend any additional sermons. Subsequently, the commandant rescinded the order. The cadets had "taken a stand", and Jack was always proud of that. He shared his feelings and past experience with his roommate, but Seymour simply shrugged his shoulders, saying:

"Look Jack, the students here aren't going to raise objections to something like this. Why make waves? Besides, church attendance is a rule for students living on campus."

"Okay, Seymour, I'll be out of here in another month anyway. So it doesn't really matter."

"Why are you leaving?"

"Perhaps I should have mentioned it earlier. My major will be journalism, so my courses will be at the downtown branch."

"You'll be missed."

A few days later as Jack was heading for class, he heard someone shouting from behind him.

"Hey, Jack!"

He turned, and saw a familiar figure approaching. It was an old friend from Brookline High School, Howard Levy. "Hello, Howie," Jack exclaimed, "What a surpise! It's a small world! What are doing here?"

"I'm a student here ", he replied, "visiting the main campus to take care of a few matters. I'm enrolled at the downtown campus and living at a rooming house within walking distance of my classes."

They talked for a while. Jack told Howie that he would also be taking his courses downtown at the School of Social Sciences and Public Affairs and planned to move downtown. But he wasn't sure where he would relocate. Howie suggested that Jack join him and hastily wrote down the address and phone number of his rooming house.

"There's plenty of space at the house, Jack. The guy who runs it is called Pappy. I think you'll like it. Your life will be a lot different from what it is here."

"Thanks, Howie. I've got to run now. Good seeing you again."

It was a few weeks later that Jack packed up, said good bye to Seymour, and happily left the main campus of American University. A cab took him to the rooming house in the northwest area of the city close to Dupont Circle. Carrying his suitcases and some books he entered the rooming house. Off to his left was an office. A very plump, bald headed man sat inside behind a large desk. He arose immediately and greeted Jack with a broad smile and a clasped hand.

"Welcome! You must be Jack Rubin. Howie Levy said you were on your way here."

"And you must be Pappy. I'm glad to be here," said Jack.

"Let me help you with your bags and show you to your room."

Pappy led Jack up a flight of stairs to his new living quarters, adding: "We have men and women living here but in separate sections of the building. Downstairs there's a lounge and a recreation room with a ping pong table."

The room was fairly large. There were two double decker beds, four bureaus, closets, chairs, some bookcases, and tables with reading lamps. Two large windows overlooked a small patio and a clump of trees.

"Get settled, and make yourself comfortable," suggested Pappy. "Your bunk is over there," he pointed at one of the double decker beds. "See you later about the rent," he added.

Jack had three roommates. One was Howie Levy. Another was George who was also a student at American University. The third named Sam worked full time as a government employee. They were all young people living in the house, and most were either working for the federal government or attending American University. Jack's classes were in the evenings, and generally he would walk almost a mile to the downtown branch of the university. In bad weather he would ride a bus that ran along nearby Connecticut Avenue. There wasn't much of a campus. Classes were held in a stretch of old wooden buildings with stairs leading up to the entrances. A couple of blocks away was George Washington University, and several blocks in the opposite direction was the U.S. Treasury building and the White House. There was much reading and writing involved in his courses. Instructors distributed extensive lists of supplementary readings; and essay questions made up the bulk of the content of examinations. He took a number of journalism courses focusing on aspects of newspaper layout, news reporting, feature writing, and ethics. Other courses were principally in the social sciences. Especially enlightening was "Introduction to Sociology". For Jack this was a whole new way of thinking in terms of understanding human behavior. He drew a grade of "A" in the course and then went on to take more sociology courses. Eventually he added sociology as another major. Many of the students in his classes were working during the day as government employees. Most were older than students he had encountered at the main university campus and more committed to their studies. Also, some were World War Two veterans.

Life at the rooming house was much different. In contrast, to the main campus of American University, people were quite friendly. House residents had very diverse and interesting backgrounds, and Jack became very friendly with several of them. There was Aarif, a student from India, who had fascinating tales to tell. He would describe in detail strategies involved in tiger hunts in India. Also, he related a story of a gardener discovering a cobra in the backyard of his home; and described how the gardener, despite being bitten, carried the snake away and later returned unharmed. One of Jack's close friends was Tom Carusso, a student at American University and a World War Two veteran. They were together often, and sometimes Tom talked reluctantly about his war experiences. Race, religion, politics: All kinds of controversial subjects were open to discussion between Jack and his new friends.

About this time, Willie McGee, a Negro from Mississippi was accused of raping a white housewife and sentenced to death in Mississippi by an all-white jury. The verdict won international attention. William Faulkner, a prominent Southern writer, wrote a letter claiming that the case against McGee was unproven. The case was appealed by Bella Abzug all the way to the U.S. Supreme Court. President Harry Truman was even pressured to grant McGee a pardon. A demonstration against the sentence was scheduled to be held in front of the White House, and Washington residents were invited to participate in a supposedly spontaneous protest. Jack asked Tom if he would join him in the demonstration, but he declined. Tom did agree that McGee had been treated unjustly but that he was apprehensive about being involved in any demonstration. This was the time when the "witch hunt" for Communists and Communist sympathizers was underway spearheaded by Senator Joe McCarthy. So Jack headed down to the White House alone. A circle of protesters was already present carrying a variety of printed signs. One of the signs read "Georgia Fascists" in large black letters. This somewhat troubled Jack, as his mother had grown up in a small town in Georgia making him half "Johnny Reb". Nevertheless, he joined the circle of protesters some of whom were chanting outside the White House gate. And he tried to talk with a protester walking in front of him.

"Hi", he said, "do you live here in the city?"

"No," she replied, "I'm from the Bronx. Do you live here?"

"Yes," Jack continued. "You're a long way from home."

Strangely the woman wouldn't talk further, and Jack thought her silence was odd. Then a tall, slender man with a megaphone announced: "Our bus will be leaving the city in a half hour." A half hour later all the protesters filed into a waiting bus. It was clear that the demonstration was well organized and hardly spontaneous. A few weeks later Jack discovered that a photographer from Life Magazine had been present at the demonstration. A picture of some protesters appeared in the magazine with a caption reading: "Communist front organization stages protest in death sentence of Willie McGee". However, Jack did not appear in the picture. On May 8, 1951 Willie McGee was executed. It was reported that the night before the execution the son of the prosecutor drank whiskey with Mcgee and that the latter admitted having sexual relations with Willette Hawkins but that it had been consensual. According to Mcgee, the white housewife feared that if this became known she would be stigmatized; consequently she accused him of rape.

In June, 1950 Jack, Howie, and two other students traveled to Mexico City where they planned to spend most of the summer. They found a scantily furnished apartment and arranged for their meals at a nearby sidewalk cafe. Jack enrolled in a Criminology course at Mexico City College only a few blocks away from their apartment. Shortly after their arrival he saw the headlines of an English language newspaper. America was at war again! The military forces of the People's Republic of Korea had crossed the 38th parallel and invaded the Republic of Korea. Under the auspices of the United Nations, the United States was to provide almost ninety percent of the troops needed to repulse the aggression. President Harry Truman was to describe our participation as a "police action". The summer passed by quickly. In late August Jack and his companions returned to Washington, D.C. and his last year of college. When June came, he donned the traditional cap and gown for the graduation ceremonies. Following that, his draft board in Brookline notified him that he was scheduled to report to an induction center in Alexandria, Virginia the following September. He returned home to Brookline for the summer; and in September he packed a small suitcase and boarded a train heading south out of Boston. As he sank back in his seat, he recalled Tom Carruso's last words as the two men parted.

"Jack, at induction you'll be asked if you want to serve in the marines. Don't do it," he advised. "You're not the killer type. And don't be quick to volunteer for anything." Tom was speaking from experience. He had served in the U.S. Marine Corps during World War Two and had seen combat in the South Pacific.

CHAPTER THREE:
YEARS OF UNCERTAINTY

At Union Station Jack entered the bus that would take him and other recruits to the induction center. After arriving, they were led into a large hall and told to be seated. There was a brief orientation, and volunteers for the U.S. Marine Corps were ordered to leave the room. Then the rest of the men rose from their chairs and were sworn into the U.S. Army.

"Attention, men!" One of the sergeants bellowed. "You're no longer civilians! You'll now be issued your uniforms. Use those rooms in the back of the hall to change your clothing. We'll be heading out of here in a half hour for boot camp."

"Where are we headed?" one of the men asked.

"Camp Breckenridge, Kentucky."

In about a half hour the soldiers boarded the waiting bus. It was a ride of several hours, and night had fallen by the time they reached the camp gates. Inside they got off the bus and marched to their assigned barracks.

"How many of you men know how to type?" shouted one of the cadre. "We need some volunteers!"

Many of the men probably believed that this sounded like a good deal and raised their arms but not Jack. As it turned out, several of the volunteers were told to carry typewriters from one building to another. Afterwards, the men were ordered to fall out and find their respective bunks in the barracks.

Jack spent a restless night tossing about in his bed. At 6 a.m. reveille sounded. Lights in the barracks went on, and the first sergeant came out of his room shouting: "Everybody up! Rise and shine!" You could hear the moans and the groans throughout the barracks. Reluctantly everyone rose, headed for the bathroom, dressed, and marched to the mess hall for breakfast. Later the men were issued M1 Garand rifles, semi-automatic and gas operated, which had proven very effective during World War Two. Repeatedly they were told to give their rifles the greatest of care, as their very lives would depend on it. They even learned to strip and reassemble them blind-folded. Basic training was to begin after some processing related to future assignments. At first there was some enthusiasm among the men to continue on to Officers Candidate School (OCS) after basic training But their enthusiasm would later dissipate as their training progressed. Jack was considered especially eligible for OCS since he was a college graduate. But he was not eager for any such appoint-ment. During the course of an interview, an officer tried to coax him into applying for OCS.

"As an officer you'll have higher pay, more prestige, authori-ty,and other benefits. Don't you want these things?" he pleaded.

Jack shook his head: "Not really.Look, I'm here because my country says I have to serve. It's my duty. But I don't want the respon-sibility of leading men into battle."

"Well, you'll have to take the test for OCS anyway."

Jack was well aware that the war in Korea was intensifying and casualties were heavy. More second lieutenants were needed as platoon leaders to replace the fallen. All he wanted was to increase his likelihood of staying alive. But a few days later, he was awakened about 4 a.m. by one of the cadre who shook him, exclaiming: "Wake up soldier! You have to get up to take a test for OCS!" Jack mumbled incoherently, rose, hastily threw on his clothing, and followed the other soldier. Inside a well-lit building, he was ordered to sit at one of the empty tables. Examination booklets were distributed to all the men seated. Then an officer in the front of the room spoke.

"Good morning, men. You've all been considered eligible for OCS. But in order to completely qualify for acceptance, you must pass this examination. When I tell you to begin, open your booklet and start answering the questions. Pencils are on the table. You have one hour to complete your examination. Okay, begin and good luck!"

Jack yawned and rubbed his eyes. This was too early in the morning, he thought. But he opened his booklet and started to answer the questions. Deliberately he selected all the wrong answers and was finished within a half hour. Still yawning, he stumbled to his barracks and slipped back into bed. There he slept until reveille. It didn't make any difference that he had selected all the wrong answers. A week later he was notified that he had passed the test for OCS.

Basic training began, and it was rigorous. Every week the company went on five mile marches clutching their rifles with full packs on their backs. They ran or "double timed" much of the way. There were the bayonet drills. Screaming at the top of their lungs and with fixed bayonets, the soldiers would charge along a muddy trail, sticking dummies, falling down on their backs, and crawling through mud and under a mesh of barbed wire. Rising on their feet again, the troops would charge the rest of that muddy mile. The cadre stood along the trail. "Scream, soldier, scream!" they would yell. When the troops were finished and covered in mud, they were ordered to clean their rifles, change clothing, polish boots and prepare for inspection. The cadre were all Korean War veterans wearing awards and campaign ribbons. They were tough and pushed the company hard. On occasion, a cadre would stand in the middle of a ring of fixed bayonets and order the men to move in against him. Their bayonets came so close that they nearly touched. Sometimes soldiers would doze off in training sessions. When that happened, the cadre would shake them and shout in their ears.

"Wake up soldier! Pay attention! Learn what you can now to stay alive tomorrow!"

The men were often reminded that their destination was Korea. Films were shown of the mountainous and rugged terrain where they would confront a resilient enemy. There were the night maneuvers when the company would divide up into two forces and take up positions in the surrounding hills. One force was ordered to infiltrate and attack, the other to defend; and the cadre participated. One time Jack was part of the defending force and on guard at the perimeter. Suddenly, one of the cadre appeared from out of the darkness.

"Hello, soldier", he said. "Do you have a light?"

"Sure," Jack replied, digging into his pocket for a book of matches.

"Soldier! You are dead!" exclaimed the cadre.

Jack had failed to challenge the infiltrator. The password was "Bronx", the counter password was "Bombers". Infiltration was a frequent tactic of the enemy. It had been effective especially when North Koreans wore South Korean uniforms. In which case, friend and foe were indistinguishable.

It was only after several weeks that the troops were permitted to leave the camp. Jack and some others headed for Evansville, Indiana. It was the nearest city just a few miles across the state line from Kentucky. For a while they drifted about the city streets trying to decide where to go and what to do. They stopped briefly at a small restaurant for hamburgers and beer and then moved on in search of female company. Jack and his companions whistled and cast flirtatious glances at a few passing women who were usually unresponsive. They peered into a number of bars, and finally entered one that looked inviting. It was dimly lit, some couples were dancing to soft music played by a small band, and several unescorted women were seated at the bar or at nearby tables. Most of the soldiers, including Jack, took seats at the bar and ordered drinks. The music stopped and the band of three players took a break. Gazing about the room, Jack noticed a rather attractive woman seated alone at one of tables. He managed to "catch her eye" and she smiled back at him. The band returned, the music resumed, and Jack waited with his eyes still fixed on the woman. He wanted to be sure she was unescorted. Finally, he rose and walked to her table.

"Would you like to dance?" he asked.

"Oh, yes, of course," she answered without hesitation.

He led her to the dance floor. She was slender and well proportioned. She had large brown eyes, a smooth complexion, and long black hair that fell down over her shoulders. As they swayed to the slow music, she pressed her supple body against Jack. He was becoming increasingly aroused and spoke bluntly.

"Listen, why don't we get out of here" he suggested. "Get a hotel room." It had been a long time since he had been with a woman.

"Yes", she replied trembling slightly and somewhat breathless.

Suddenly someone grabbed Jack by the arm and spun him completely around. Two men confronted him, and the shorter one shouted: "That's my wife you're dancing with! Let's go outside and settle this!" Jack's companions, as well as other soldiers, immediately moved to Jack's side

"Okay, let's go!" Jack exclaimed. He felt ready for a fight.

Out of a dark corner of the room a familiar voice bellowed.

"Listen, you guys! Break it up!"

It was Jack's first sergeant. Either he had been following the men, or this encounter was coincidental. He shook his finger at the soldiers.

"Calm down! Don't be fools! The MP's will be on you!"

"And you!" The sergeant turned shouting in the face of the man claiming to be the woman's husband! "Get your wife the hell out of here! Keep her home away from my men!"

The incident was closed. But it did signal a sense of group cohesiveness, a bonding where each soldier learned that he was his brother's keeper. And, in the days and months ahead, men who had been displaced civilians were becoming hardened, aggressive soldiers. On occasion, they would taunt the cadre who would simply smile in response. Perhaps this was part of the process of preparing the men for combat. As more time passed, the snows of winter receded, spring came, and nearly six months of basic training was close to ending. Casualties in Korea were high. There were reports of troops with just a month of basic training ordered into battle. In contrast, Jack and his company were much better prepared for combat; their cadre had seen to that.

When basic training ended, the company anxiously awaited orders from higher headquarters. It is difficult to describe the emotions felt and expressed on the night that the orders came down. In 1948 President Harry Truman issued an executive order calling for the racial integration of the U.S. Armed Forces, and the integration process had been gradual. Jack's company was an integrated one: white and black men, who had trained together, ate together, shared living quarters, and were "brothers in arms". When the orders came down, a shock wave rippled through the company. All black soldiers, with the one exception, were on orders for Korea. The one exception was assigned to army intelligence school. The remainder, all white soldiers were on orders for Germany. Jack had never witnessed such an outburst of feelings of resentment, remorse, and bitterness. It was as if lightening had struck the barracks. Some of his black comrades were sobbing:

"Why just us? Why just us?" they cried out.

Jack and others tried to console them with expressions of sympathy and regret. But it didn't seem to help. That night Jim Crow appeared to be very much alive. It seemed like a flagrant act of racial discrimination. Although white troops were relieved that they had not been ordered to Korea, they still felt a sense of shame and betrayal. Also, it could have been considered dysfunctional since research evidence suggested that the breaking up of infantry units after basic training could undermine group cohesiveness and hence combat effectiveness. In 1949 Samuel Stouffer's study, the *American Soldier* was released. The study, originally sanctioned by the U.S. Army in 1945, involved interviews of more than a half million of World War II soldiers. In these interviews soldiers emphasized that they felt responsible for their group's success, the importance of someone watching their backs, and that they were fighting to protect their buddies or guardian angels.

During the company's last night together, a few of the men knocked on the door of the first sergeant's room. The door opened, and the sergeant grumbled: "Yeah, what do you guys want?"

"Sergeant," said one of the men, "the company wants to say good bye to you."

The sergeant stepped out of his room, and the company gathered around him.

"Sergeant, this is a gift from us," the soldier continued, "to thank you for the training you've given us." He handed the sergeant a small box containing a wrist watch. When the sergeant opened the box and held up the watch, he smiled broadly and spoke in a stammering voice choked with emotion:

"Thank you, men. I think I've - given you my best. Take care of yourself and each other."

Jack had never seen this man smile before or hear him speak so softly. For a moment, it seemed a tear rolled down the sergeant's cheek. The next morning the men packed their duffle bags. White and black soldiers bade farewell to each other, as they were going to very different destinations. Jack and others alighted a bus taking them to Washington D.C. and Union Station. From there he took a train to Boston for a furlough of two weeks. After that, he was scheduled to ship out to Germany.

It was an early morning in March. A canopy of grey clouds hovered over one of the many harbors extending along the New York and New Jersey coasts. There was no wind. A calm great ocean stretched out to the far horizon like some massive sheet of glass. A long line of infantrymen, with duffle bags slung over their shoulders, slowly moved up a gangway and boarded the moored troop ship. It was an exciting experience for Jack Rubin. It was his first time on an ocean going ship, and one that would take him far away from home. The troops were directed to the bottom level in the bow of the ship. Their living quarters were cramped: the men's beds were hammocks next to which were lockers where they could store their clothing and other personal possessions. Jack unpacked his duffle bag and ascended a stairway to the top deck. The ship had pulled up anchor, and a couple of small of tugboats had begun to draw it out into the open sea. As they passed the statue of liberty, a gleam of sunlight fell upon the upheld torch. Once the ship cleared the harbor, the tugboats departed. Jack leaned over the rail and looked back at the shrinking shore line. He heard a voice next to him. It was one of the men in his company.

"Well," he observed, "we're on our way to Germany. They're a very smart people."

Jack said nothing. He only wondered: Smart? They lost the war, inflicted a lot of suffering, and suffered a lot as well.

The ship's destination was Bremerhaven, Germany a port on the North Sea. The weather was favorable and the ocean calm, as they began the long voyage across the North Atlantic. They had been at sea nearly a week when Jack and his company were awakened early one morning by a chorus of loud voices.

"Wake up, you guys! You're needed in the kitchen! It's KP duty today!"

It was not the most pleasant duty. Some of the men prepared the food, others did the cooking, and cleanup chores. Later in the day it was rumored that the same troops would be called for KP duty the following morning. Before taps sounded, Jack and others huddled together to plot a strategy to avoid a repetition of KP duty. What could be done? Very early the following morning, they all slipped out of their hammocks and hid in dark corners and holes of the ship. Shortly, you could hear loud voices.

"Hey, you guys wake up! It's KP time again!"

They shuffled about the empty hammocks, one soldier saying: "What do you know! These guys have vanished! Oh, well we'll find some other men." A few of the searchers laughed, and then they all disappeared. With sighs of relief, Jack and the rest of his troop emerged from their hiding places.

A few more days passed. When an announcement was made over a loudspeaker, "Now hear this! All soldiers report on deck! Bremerhaven is ahead!" The troops packed up their gear and clambered up to the main deck. Flocks of sea gulls were flapping their wings and circling noisily overhead. Tugboats were waiting alongside, and gradually drew the ship into a berth of the harbor. Other ships were moored nearby with flags flying: American, British,

Russian. The vessel dropped anchor, the gangplank fell, and the troops prepared to disembark. With duffle bags slung over their shoulders, the men filed down the gangplank and boarded a waiting train. Jack found a seat in one of the cars; and as he gazed out of the window, he saw a troop of armed British soldiers briskly marching by. Shortly, the train lurched forward and began to accelerate south toward the American occupation zone. A panorama of the German countryside flashed by: small towns, neatly trimmed forests, rivers, and medieval towers of bygone eras. Hours passed, and the terrain changed as the train plunged forward up and down hills and through a stretch of tunnels. The sun was beginning to slip behind a range of distant mountains. Twilight was approaching followed by a curtain of darkness. Shrill sounds of the engine pierced the stillness of night. After a few more hours, the train gradually slowed and came to a complete stop. The troops disembarked and climbed on to some waiting trucks which took them to a nearby military depot where they spent the rest of the night.

Reveille sounded at daybreak. The men rose from their beds, hurried into the bathroom, dressed, and assembled outside the barracks. A sergeant greeted them, speaking loudly. "Okay, men. Follow me! The mess hall is just up the hill!" The troops looked around in awe. at the high snowcapped mountains surrounding them.

"This must be the Alps!" One soldier gasped.

"That's right!" the sergeant shouted back. "The Bavarian Alps!"

Following breakfast the company was led into a large hall where an officer addressed them. "Good morning, men," he began. "This is Sonthofen, a replacement depot. We have a surplus of infantrymen here in Germany, so you will all be reassigned. Actually you should've been shipped to Korea. But somehow your orders got scrambled, and it's too expensive to send you back."

Within a few days the remainder of Jack's company was broken up, and he was assigned to a field artillery battalion in the town of Schwabisch Gmund about fifty kilometers east of Stuttgart. The battalion was equipped with 155 millimeter cannons left over from World War II, and Jack's job was to assist loading shells into one of the cannons. The battalion was quartered at the Hardt Kaserne on a hill overlooking the town. The kaserne was unlike typical U.S. Army barracks. The buildings were constructed of solid concrete and the interiors were partitioned into separate rooms. For a few weeks Jack worked with other soldiers loading and unloading cannon shells before he was ordered to report to his company commander, Lieutenant Callahan. Stepping into the lieutenant's office, he saluted: "Private Rubin reporting as ordered, sir."

Lieutenant Callahan looked up from a personnel file on his desk: "At ease soldier. Jack, I've been looking at your records. You're a college graduate. I understand you've been assigned to work on one of our cannons. It seems to me that we can make much better use of you, unless you like what you're doing."

"No, sir", Jack replied smiling and shaking his head. " I really don't like what I'm doing. What do you have in mind?"

"Well," the lieutenant continued, "Every month we have to submit medical reports to Seventh Army Headquarters in Stuttgart. Making up these reports is rather complicated. One mistake, and they bounce back to us. The soldier who's been taking care of these reports is leaving us. Would you be interested in the job? First, you would go to medical records school in Stuttgart."

56

"Yes, sir," Jack replied. "I would be very interested!"

"Good! There will be some additional duties such as interviewing soldiers diagnosed with venereal diseases and getting information on their contacts. Also, you'll be reassigned to our medical detachment."

"Thank you very much, sir." Jack saluted and departed.

Within several days Jack joined the medical detachment which comprised a commanding officer who was a physician with the rank of captain, a first sergeant, two lower ranking sergeants, and twelve privates including Jack. The captain resided in officer quarters, the first sergeant was married and lived off the post. The other two sergeants shared a private room in the kaserne next door to the rest of the detachment who occupied a large and fairly comfortable room. Almost immediately Jack was gone for about two weeks attending medical records school in Stuttgart. When he returned he was adequately trained to prepare and submit monthly medical reports to higher command. He enjoyed a special status; for he was the only one in the entire battalion who knew how to compile the medical reports and spent most of his days in the post dispensary. Occasionally he injected soldiers with needed medications, but more often he interviewed those who had contracted either syphilis or gonorrhea. The obtained information would be recorded and subsequently sent to the U.S. military and German police. Any syphilis case received high priority in that immediate action would be taken to locate and apprehend the female contact. One morning Captain Cain, the detachment physician called Jack into his office. Seated there was a soldier naked from the waist down with his genitals fully exposed.

"Jack," the captain began pointing at the soldier's infected genitals, "take a good look! This is syphilis in an advanced stage. We can't cure it. All we can do is slow it down. If you must have a woman, take the proper precautions!"

It was a revolting sight, leaving Jack well impressed. He would certainly take the necessary precautions. The captain invoked similar caveats to the troops but often to no avail. In interviews, Jack would ask infected soldiers if they had used issued contraceptives and prophylactic kits. Their answers were always: "No".

Generally the troops were allowed to take passes almost every week-end. Jack would usually leave the post on a Friday evening or Saturday morning alone or with one or more other soldiers, and the troops had to return to the post before midnight on Sunday. There was no transportation down the hill to the town and the railroad station. Sometimes soldiers could get a ride in an army ambulance or other vehicle that was going to the battalion dispensary in town; and if they were really lucky, they might catch a ride back up the hill when returning to base. None of the soldiers were allowed to wear or even possess civilian clothes, and the fact that they had to be in uniform at all times didn't endear them to the local population. They were, of course, occupation troops whose presence was naturally resented. For example, Jack found that whenever he tried to accost young women publicly on the streets of Swabisch Gmund, they hurried past him.

The train ride to Stuttgart was less than an hour. Once there Jack would wander about the city for a while. Unlike Schwabisch Gmund and other parts of the German countryside, there was extensive evidence of destroyed buildings and other wreckage from the war. Eventually, he became hungry and stopped at a restaurant where he ordered his favorite meal: a schnitzel or thick veal steak coated in bread crumbs along with some thin sliced browned potatoes smothered in onions, and a stein of beer. Afterwards, he returned to the railway station or bahnhof the latter, frequently used by American soldiers, was an abbreviated term for the German word hauptbanhof. Inside the station, he entered a small restaurant, sat down at an empty table, and ordered a mug of beer. Several young women were seated at surrounding tables sipping on cups of coffee or tea. The women were known to be available for sexual encounters. Finishing his beer, he rose from his table and approached one who was fairly attractive. He spoke a few words to her. She smiled back at him, they left together in cab, and the woman gave the driver directions to a nearby gasthaus or inn where she and Jack spent the night together.

Jack made quite a few trips to Stuttgart. One involved what Jack referred to as the "cognac and cola" incident. It was late Sunday night as he sat in the Stuttgart station restaurant drinking a glass of cognac mixed with Coca- Cola. His train connection to Schwabisch Gmund was running about an hour late. He looked at his watch; it was a few minutes past midnight. Two soldiers entered the restaurant and asked Jack if they could join him. He assented with a nod, and they ordered bottles of beer. As they sat talking and drinking, a trio of American military police entered the restaurant, gazed about, and quickly approached Jack's table. One of them spoke in a reprimanding tone:

"Hey, you guys! Don't you know it's past curfew? What are you doing here?"

"The train back to my post is running late," Jack answered.

The two other soldiers also explained that they were waiting for train connections.

"That's okay," another of the military police commented, "but you guys are drinking alcoholic beverages in a public place! That's prohibited after curfew! Sorry, we have to take you in. "

Jack and the other soldiers were led out of the hauptbanhof, directed into a paddy wagon, and driven to a military police station. Jack was told to wait in a separate room while the other soldiers were taken before the desk sergeant.

"You men are in trouble," said the sergeant. "Drinking alcoholic beverages in a public place after midnight is a curfew violation. Your company commander will be notified, and you'll be spending the night here."

Then the sergeant addressed one of the military police. "Hank, bring the other soldier here."

Even though Jack was in the next room he could overhear all that was said. The room door swung open, and he walked forward facing the desk sergeant.

"Soldier," the sergeant began, "We apologize for inconveniencing you. I understand you were drinking Coca Cola. You shouldn't have been brought here with these other men. We have a jeep waiting outside to take you back to the railway station. Do you need a note to your commanding officer because of any delay reporting back?"

"No," Jack replied. "I don't think a note will be necessary. But anyway, thank you."

Jack was driven back to the station where he took his train and returned to his post before reveille. In the weeks that followed, leaving the post became more difficult with the beginning of the rainy season and reduced availability of transportation to the town. But Jack saved a few hundred dollars which he used to purchase an old Chevrolet from his first sergeant. He thought this would eliminate any transportation problem. However, he learned later that the car was more of a problem than an asset. Periodically it proved unreliable, failing to start or stalling. But with his first sergeant's assistance he took his driver's test in Stuttgart, qualified for a license, and off he went driving about the German countryside. One afternoon he had driven to an inn just outside of town and sat alone at a table. Three Germans were sitting nearby, an elderly man and two young women. One of the women was rather stout and not particularly appealing. The other, however, was very attractive, slender with wavy blond hair, soft blue eyes and a fair complexion. Jack kept staring at her, and she looked back smiling flirtatiously. The elderly man and the two women spoke in English, and Jack could clearly overhear them. It sounded like they were complaining about the American occupation. At that point, Jack walked over to their table where there was an empty chair. Politely, he asked:

"May I join you?"

"Yes, of course", the elderly man replied. The two women nodded agreeably and smiled.

Jack introduced himself, indicating that he was not a career soldier, that he had been drafted. He would serve his stint of two years and return to civilian life. The Germans then seemed more at ease and introduced themselves

"Oh, then you're just a citizen soldier," Lola commented. She was the very attractive woman probably about Jack's age.

They talked for perhaps an hour. Then the elderly man looked at his watch.

"I think it's time for us to go." He shook Jack's hand. "It was nice meeting you", he added.

Jack took Lola's hand and drew her aside: "I want to see you again," he said softly.

"Oh, yes." She replied, squeezing his hand: "Meet me at the Schwabisch Gmund railway station Saturday about noon?"

"I'll be there".

They parted. Jack had been lonely despite encounters with other women which had been purely sexual. Perhaps Lola would help fill his void of loneliness. Her appearance reminded him of a girl he had first met when he was still in high school. Later she was a student at Wellesley College, and they became somewhat infatuated with each other. But they were never really intimate. Jack saw her just before he shipped out to Germany. At the end of their last time together he tried to kiss her; but she moved her head aside. It's over, he thought. As he started to walk away, she said:

"Please, Jack, call me before you leave."

Jack shrugged his shoulders: "Why should I? What's the point?"

"Please call me", she entreated.

But he never called her. It seemed she had put on some weight. Maybe she was pregnant. He suspected she was involved with somebody else. These were uncertain times, and it was probably better to break off the relationship. Maybe later he would try to write her. Later he did write, but she never answered.

It was Saturday, and Jack was waiting at the railway station. Lola appeared shortly before noon; Jack met her as she stepped off a train that came from a neighboring town. She took his arm, and they went to his car parked near the station. He drove several miles outside of Schwabisch Gmund to an inn where they ate lunch, drank a few glasses of wine, and talked almost incessantly. Lola's English was flawless, and her German accent was barely noticeable. Jack asked her many questions. She had grown up in a city near the French border. Her parents had sent her to a church school out in the country where she escaped Nazi indoctrination. Her father had designed aircraft during the war. Her family wanted to leave Germany when the Nazis took power, but it was becoming increasingly difficult to leave. Also, where could they go?

"Where are you parents now?" Jack asked.

Lola was quiet for a few moments and then sadly replied, "They're both dead: killed in an air raid. The planes kept coming, bombing day and night."

"I'm sorry," Jack said. "War is a terrible thing. For a moment he thought about a father he never knew because of the First World War. "But we Americans had no choice", he added. "Look what your country did to Warsaw and Rotterdam."

Lola was silent. The conversation seemed strained, so he began talking about other things: his experiences growing up in Boston, his college days. They talked further, and the time passed quickly. Jack looked out of a nearby window. The sun was already beginning to set, and the sky was taking on a reddish hue.

"I think it's getting late," Lola observed. "I'll have to take the train back to Aalen soon. But I hope I'll see you again. Then we can spend more time together."

Jack paid for the food and drinks, and they walked back to his car. Inside they drew close to each other. His arms went around her, and he began kissing her. She returned his kisses passionately. His hand stroked her firm breasts, and then caressed her smooth legs and thighs. He was becoming more aroused and more aggressive. Lola began breathing heavily and blurted out, "Please, Jack! That's enough! There will be other times."

He relented, took a deep breath and kissing her again, he murmured: "It's okay. I better get you to the station so you don't miss your train." Then he suggested: "I could drive you back to Aalen."

"No, no," she insisted. "I have my ticket. It's better that I take the train."

They parted at the railway station. He kissed her, and they agreed to meet again the following Saturday at the same place and time.

The week seemed to pass so slowly. But, finally it was Saturday again; and Lola was waiting for Jack at the railway station. They went to the same gasthaus where they had been before. They had lunch, a few glasses of wine, and talked. It was twilight when they went back to the car. Jack began kissing Lola as they climbed into the back seat of the car. She put her arms around him, drew up her legs, and with one hand she pulled down her underpants. Jack dropped his trousers. Clutching each other tightly, they continued kissing and caressing each other. After that, they spent the night together at the inn.

During the days that followed, Jack shared more of his past with Lola. He talked about his father who sailed from Germany to freedom in America, and served in the American Expeditionary Force in the trenches of France, enduring unsanitary conditions and eventually dying from dysentery years later,. Then in a choking voice, he spoke about his older sister who died slowly from leukemia at the age of twelve. The death of his sister had been especially hard on his mother who desperately struggled to support them both through hardships of the Great Depression. At one point, he told Lola he was Jewish. He thought that might shock her. But she didn't even blink; it didn't seem to matter to her. Sometimes he did wonder why she didn't want him to visit her in Aalen. He never pressed for an explanation. But he did speculate that her life might be made more difficult if she were seen in Aalen with a uniformed American soldier. Of course, he could not wear or even possess civilian clothing, as it was prohibited by military regulations.

Nearly every weekend Jack and Lola would spend days and nights together. Sometimes he would get a three day pass in which case he would take her to Stuttgart or other places. Being so intimate with her was a novel experience for Jack since his relationships with other women had always been short-lived and superficial. He mentioned Lola in letters written home. That might have been unwise, for later he received a letter from his stepfather's rabbi who had served as a chaplain in the U.S. Army in France and Germany during World War Two. He harshly criticized Jack for fraternizing with a German girl. As army chaplain he had toured the concentration camps throughout Germany and witnessed the surviving emaciated inmates, piles of unburied corpses, gas chambers, and ovens designed to cremate the dead. He wrote that the inhabitants of nearby communities were often ordered to bury the rotting corpses. It was estimated that six million Jews were executed, but the true figure would never be known. But, Jack felt that the rabbi's harsh criticism was a non sequitur. What did this German girl have to do with the Holocaust? Surely, he thought, the sins of the fathers should not be visited upon their children. The principal perpetrators of this horror were tried and sentenced at Nuremberg. But weren't there many others who shared in the responsibility of what happened, who simply stood by, turned their backs, and waited until it was almost too late? That was Jack's rejoinder to the rabbi and his parents. He did not have to be reminded what it meant to be a Jew. He questioned the existence of some communicable and benign Creator. But he did try to live by a moral code, taking pride in his Jewish legacy, and had even developed a "chip on his shoulder". One night he was somewhat intoxicated.; and returning to the post, he and a friend stopped in the cafeteria for coffee. As they stood in line the soldier in front of Jack made a remark that Jack misunderstood. He grabbed the soldier and shook him.

"What did you say about the Jews?" he blurted out.

Jack's companion was surprised and pulled him back, exclaiming: "Jack, calm down! He didn't say anything about the Jews!"

Although Jack continued seeing Lola, their encounters became less frequent. She had helped to fill his void of loneliness, but he still felt there was much he didn't know about her. He never visited her home in Aalen. Did she have any family at all? Who were her friends? She claimed to be a social worker but never divulged details of her work. Then there was another German girl, Edith who dated Tony, Jack's friend and a member of his medical detachment. Edith's family operated an inn near Schwabisch Gmund, and Jack would visit the inn occasionally. Edith claimed that she knew Lola and cautioned him "to be careful". Jack pressed her for an explanation, but Edith refused to say anything further. Much about Lola would forever remain a mystery.

At least once a month the battalion went on maneuvers to Grafenwohr. This was an extensive hilly and forested area that stretched from the American occupation zone across the border into Czechoslovakia. It was an area used by both the American and Russian or Warsaw Pact forces. The battalion would depart the post shortly before dawn and head east along the autobahn, a trip taking several hours. The 155 millimeter cannons were mobile but moved very slowly. The night before the battalion moved out on maneuvers, it was customary for the troops to imbibe rather freely even though the drinking of alcoholic beverages on post was officially prohibited. It was on such a night that one of the medics, Harry had too much to drink. Shortly after midnight, Harry burst into the sergeants' quarters and almost shook Sergeant Brown out of his bed.

"Wake up! Wake up, sergeant! "Harry yelled. Except for Sergeant Brown, relations in the detachment were congenial. Brown had failed to make it in the paratroops which left him somewhat frustrated and embittered. He was an irritant often harassing members of the detachment. The sergeant leaped from his bed shaking his fist at Harry.

"I'll report you for this!" He shouted.

At that point, Harry departed the room. There were only a few more hours to sleep, as reveille sounded at 4:00 a.m. sharp. Within a half hour, the troops moved out traveling along the autobahn. By daylight they reached Nuremberg. Much of the city, devastated by day and night bombings, was still in ruins. Sometime later the battalion arrived in Grafenwohr where the troops pitched large tents: their living quarters for the following week. In the meantime Sergeant Brown had carried out his threat. He reported Harry as drinking alcoholic beverages on the post, drunk, and engaging in disorderly behavior. In response, the battalion adjutant merely denied Harry any leave while the troops were on maneuvers which was rather meaningless since generally no leave was permitted while the troops were on maneuvers. This leniency infuriated Sergeant Brown who continued to threaten Harry:

"You got off easy this time, Harry! But watch it! You get out of line again, and I'll run you into the stockade!"

One late night or early morning, Jack was awakened abruptly by what sounded like bellowing artillery fire. He leaped to his feet thinking the worst Perhaps another war had begun. These were the years of the Cold War, and tensions were running high in Europe. A mere spark could lead to armed conflict. He was relieved later to hear that the firing only came from the Warsaw Pact forces or Russians simply engaged on maneuvers some distance away.

After the battalion returned to Schwabisch Gmund, Jack and the other medics began to discuss what action they should take in dealing with Sergeant Brown. They were a tightly knit group strongly supportive of each other. It was agreed that whatever action was taken, they would act as one. There was some discussion about what course to follow. It was Jack who suggested a strategy.

"Listen, you guys we need to get rid of Sergeant Brown; and whatever we do, we have to go all the way. We need to do something that will really work, or this sergeant will try to run us all into the stockade. Here's what I suggest: Every week Brown and the other sergeant, Montero, leave the post claiming that they are picking up medication at the main dispensary in town. But instead, they go to a local gasthaus. Remember, before they leave they always ask us if we want them to bring us back any food or drink. This is how we can nail the sergeant. We report him as AWOL."

"But, wait a minute," Tony interrupted, "if we turn Brown in then we have to report Montero AWOL too; and he hasn't been much of a problem for us."

The others nodded and murmured in agreement.

"I know," Jack acknowledged. "I'm not too happy about that. But what other choice do we have? Can anyone come up with another plan?"

Harry, Tony, Smitty, Glen, and some of the others discussed the matter further. Finally, Harry said: "I don't think there's any other way. Let's vote on it. How many want to go with Jack's plan?"

There was unanimity. All twelve men raise their hands.

One evening, almost a week later, the sergeants stopped by the medics' room. "We're going into town for a beer," Montero said. "Do any of you want anything?" They all declined; and from their window, they watched the sergeants stop at the guard house and drive off the post.

"Okay, this is it guys!" Jack said excitingly.

But who would report the sergeants as AWOL? The men had already decided they would draw lots two of which were marked. Also, it was agreed that those drawing the marked lots would report the sergeants as AWOL. Jack and Glen drew the marked lots. The two walked slowly to the guard house. There they reported the sergeants as violating military regulations: making an unauthorized trip off post. Jack and Glen then rejoined the rest of the medics.

"Where do we go from here?" one of them asked.

Jack reflected for a few moments and then spoke forcefully. "We must have documentation to support the AWOL charge." Turning to Harry, he asked: "Harry, don't you make a trip to the main dispensary tomorrow?"

"Yeah," Harry replied. "I have to pick up some medical supplies."

"Good! Then get a copy of the sign in sheet from last night. That will be hard evidence to show that the sergeants never showed up at the dispensary. Also, if you can, get a signed statement affirming that the sergeants didn't check into the dispensary last night."

"I'll take care of it, Jack."

Almost two hours passed. Suddenly there was a loud commotion at the guard house. All the medics peered from the window and watched as the two sergeants and the corporal of the guard came walking hastily toward the barracks. Quickly they burst into the room confronting the medics. Looking at the corporal of the guard, Sergeant Brown demanded, "Which men turned us in?" The corporal pointed at Jack and Glen.

The sergeant's face became flushed and contorted with anger. "I'm going to get you two guys!" he threatened, shaking his fist at them.

Jack answered calmly. "Sergeant, you'll have to come after all of us. If I were you I would think about transferring out of this outfit."

The medics acted quickly. Harry obtained the desired documentation. They showed the evidence to their first sergeant and insisted that the two sergeants, Brown and Montero, be transferred as soon as possible.

The first sergeant balked at first saying, "Calm down. You guys really don't want to do this."

But the men continued to insist that the two sergeants had to go. If not, then all of them would request a transfer out of the battalion. At that point, the first sergeant capitulated. The AWOL evidence was forwarded to higher command, and within a few weeks sergeants Brown and Montero were gone.

A new year had begun. It was January, 1953, and Jack parted with his car which had been very unreliable. He had the car repainted and sold it to another soldier. Fortunately he was able to recover what he paid for it. After that, he planned a trip to Frankfurt. He took the train to Stuttgart and sat alone in the station restaurant waiting for his connection to Frankfurt. A young man dressed in a heavy coat and smoking a cigarette approached his table

"Hey, soldier, where are you headed?"

"Frankfurt," Jack said.

"Oh, I know the city well, and can show you the sights."

Nearby two other men sat sipping their mugs of beer. One of them waved to Jack motioning him over to their table. The man who waved spoke in a low voice: "Soldier, that man who was speaking to you is no good. Stay away from him. He'll try to steal your money."

"Thank you very much," Jack replied. When he returned to his table, the other man was gone.

The train ride to Frankfurt was a few hours. Leaving the station, Jack spent time wandering about the city. As darkness fell, he stopped in a café, ate dinner, and had a few beers. He dropped into a number of night clubs where he imbibed too freely. He lost count of the boilermakers. Realizing that he had too much to drink, he stepped out on the street and flagged a cab.

He opened the door of the cab and fell into the back seat. "Driver," he groaned, "I've had too much to drink. Please take me some place where I can sleep."

The driver obliged. He drove several miles to an open area where there was a large building. Pointing at the structure, he told Jack: "Go in the front door and up the stairs. Find an empty room. There are mattresses and pillows on the floors."

Jack paid the driver and profusely thanked him. Walking a short distance, he entered the building, climbed a flight of stairs, and stumbled inside an empty room. He collapsed on a mattress and laid his head on some pillows. Within moments he was sleeping soundly.

He awoke in a flood of daylight pouring through a large window. Voices could be heard outside his room. People were not speaking German but perhaps Russian or Polish. Rising to his feet, he smoothed his uniform, put on his overcoat, and exited the building.

He shuddered, as it was chilly outside. Then in the bright sunlight he could clearly see a large sign in front of the building. The bold black letters read: "Displaced Persons Camp". Jack chuckled thinking it had been an appropriate place for him to have spent the night. He hailed a passing cab, returned to the railway station where he boarded a train to Stuttgart and then another which took him back to Schwabisch Gmund.

It was April. Jack and one of the medics, "Smitty" were going on a ten day furlough touring as many places as they could. The first stop was Paris. From there they would travel to London where it was coronation time: England was to have a new queen. Sitting next to the window of his plane, Jack peered down at the green fields of France, the farm houses, and small villages. In World War One all this had been a "no man's land" of barbed wire and trenches where men had fallen in the face of enemy fire. It was so peaceful now. He thought of his father who had been there His eyes became moist as poignant emotions gripped him. But he was heartened knowing that in a few months he would be going home to America.

In July the fighting officially ended in Korea. There was no peace treaty; but a truce was signed. Jack remembered the black soldiers with whom he trained. He wondered if they survived. He hoped so. When September came he was on his way back to Bremerhaven: port of embarkation. Within the week his troop ship sailed out into the North Sea and toward the North Atlantic. After about ten days, the New York skyline became visible. Flocks of sea gulls noisily circled above flapping their wings. As the ship neared the harbor, soldiers excitedly gathered at the rail of the main deck. One shouted: "There she is, lady liberty!" The statue of liberty stood high in the bright autumn sunlight: her inscription, a message to the world:

Give me your tired, your poor, your huddled masses, yearning to breathe free, the wretched refuse of your teeming shore. Send these the homeless, tempest tossed to me. I lift my lamp beside the golden door.

Small tug boats were waiting to draw the ship into the harbor and to the docks. Once there, the gangplank dropped; and the troops, gripping their duffle bags, disembarked.

CHAPTER FOUR:
THE SEARCHING YEARS

The troops moved to Fort Dix, New Jersey for a few days of processing. Jack chose to remain in the inactive army reserve, so he was only separated from the armed forces and would have to wait several years before receiving an honorable discharge. A bus transported him and other soldiers to Fort Devens, Massachusetts where he joined his mother and stepfather. For some time he lingered at home in Brookline. He had been living one day at a time. But now the years of uncertainty had passed, and he began to speculate about the future. Should he pursue a career in journalism or a graduate degree in sociology? As a Korean War veteran, he would be entitled to generous educational benefits. After deliberating a few weeks, he decided to return to Washington D.C. and hopefully find work on one of the major newspapers: either the Washington Post or Washington Evening Star. He contacted an old friend, Al Shine who was sharing an apartment with his brother Sidney in the southeast area of Washington, and the brothers invited him to join them. Once resettled, Jack began his job search. There were no positions open at the Washington Post. But the Washington Evening Star did offer him a job as a copy boy. In the newspaper business you had to start at the bottom. But he would have the opportunity to do some news reporting and quickly accepted the position.

Jack's working hours were from 6: 00 a.m. to 2:00 p.m. five days a week. He rose quite early in order to catch a bus about five in the morning. Arriving at work, he found the newsroom already buzzing with activity. The reporters and columnists were busy at their desks, adjusting their headphones, speaking into mouthpieces, and typing assiduously.

"Copy boy!" hollered one of the reporters, waving some copy in the air.

Jack hurried over, snatched the sheets of copy, and took them to the city editor's desk. Then another reporter, with a dollar bill in his hand, motioned to Jack: "Hey, copy boy! Get me a cup of coffee and a Danish pastry from downstairs!" Jack obliged. These chores were routine in the newsroom. However, on one occasion, a reporter called in and asked Jack to take dictation. He slipped on a pair of headphones and began talking into a mouthpiece. The reporter on the other end of the line spoke in an urgent tone:

"Listen!" he exclaimed, "I'm in the basement of an apartment building, and have to talk fast before they throw me out of here!"

Jack was already fingering the keys on a typewriter. The reporter talked rapidly, but Jack had difficulty following the dictation. He simply couldn't type fast enough.

The reporter grew impatient. "Hey, you're too slow!" he shouted. "Get somebody else on the phone!" Jack handed the headphones to one of the other workers in the newsroom. Following that incident, he became reluctant to take any dictation.

Nearly every week the copy boys reported on certain news events which were citizen association meetings held in evenings throughout the Washington Metropolitan Area. Jack would attend these meetings, take notes, and write up his reports while sipping a beer at a bar across the street from the Star building. Then he would submit his copy to the city editor. At a number of these meetings, a guest speaker appeared advocating racial bigotry and segregation. This was about the time of 1954 United States Supreme Court decision to overturn the Plessy versus Ferguson decision of 1896 which allowed state supported racial segregation. The "separate but equal" doctrine was struck down by the Court and considered in violation of the Fourteenth Amendment of the United States Constitution. It was a major victory for the Civil Rights Movement. During this time, a racial bigot and advocate of racial segregation was appearing as a speaker at citizen association meetings; and Jack happened to cover one of these meetings. He arrived early and stood in the back of the meeting room holding a pad of paper and pencil. The invited speaker approached him, inquiring:

"Are you from one of the newspapers in town?"

Jack nodded: "The Evening Star."

"Great! Give me good coverage."

Jack left quickly after the meeting to write his article which included a detailed description of the bigoted remarks made by the speaker. But the city editor deleted much of his copy applying his red pencil like a razor. At first Jack was somewhat dismayed. The editor, sensing Jack's reaction, turned to him, saying:

"Look, Jack we don't want to give this guy the publicity he wants. We'll just mention that he addressed the association." Jack nodded in agreement. He quickly understood this was good journalism and that intolerance flourishes on publicity.

From 1950 to 1956 McCarthyism: the practice of charging people with national disloyalty or subversion without supporting evidence was gripping America. This was the Second Red Scare, the first having occurred in the 1920's. The term "McCarthyism" had been coined by critics of Senator Joe McCarthy of Wisconsin who had encouraged investigations of suspected Communists. Unfortunately, many of his efforts destroyed the reputations and even lives of innocent people. In the spring of 1954, the McCarthyism culminated in Army-McCarthy hearings were being televised. Senator McCarthy had charged that the U.S. Army high command had been infiltrated by Communists.

On a rainy day in April, 1954, Jack was sent up to the capitol to pick up some photographs taken at the Army-McCarthy hearings. He emerged out of the rain, his head soaking wet, and found his way to a Senate hearing room. The Star photographer motioned for Jack to sit down. He took a seat only several feet away from Senator McCarthy, and listened to the attorneys and the Senator exchange barbed remarks. The soft but incisive speaking attorney, Joseph Welch was there representing the Army. For a while Jack reminisced. It was during those first months in the Army at a troop information and education session when an officer asked for comments related to his lecture. Jack had raised his hand, stood up, and criticized the tactics of Senator McCarthy. The troops booed and tried to drown him out. But the officer shouted: "Shut up, let the soldier speak!" Later some of the troops came to Jack privately expressing their support of his criticisms.

Suddenly, the Star photographer nudged Jack and handed him some photographs. Jack departed and returned to the newsroom. In December, 1954 the United States Senate censured Senator McCarthy.

By June Jack left the newspaper and returned to Brookline for the summer. His stint on the Washington Evening Star had been very enlightening. He learned to apply Occam's Razor: to write clearly, simply, and concisely But he felt a career in journalism was not for him, and instead he would take advantage of the Korean War Veteran educational benefits and pursue a graduate degree in sociology. In September Jack began graduate studies in sociology at New York University, renting a room in Greenwich Village in lower Manhattan within walking distance of Washington Square and the university. He had a car, but driving and parking in Manhattan was extremely difficult. His classes were at night; and one evening while heading to the university, he heard someone shouting from behind. He turned to greet an old friend.

"Hello, Howie!" Jack cried out. "So, we meet again!" Then jesting he asked, "Have you been following me?"

"Not really," Howie replied laughing, and the two men immediately shook hands. "I've been working here in the city the past year," Howie continued. " Discharged from the Marine Corps about a year ago."

"I got out of the Army at about the same time," Jack said. " Spent over a year in Germany. Were you in Korea?"

"Yeah." Howie grimaced slightly.

"Was it pretty bad?"

"Yeah. One night the squad went out on patrol. I was the only one to make it back." Then Howie quickly changed the subject. "What are you doing here, Jack?"

"I'm renting a room in the Village and taking some graduate courses in sociology at New York University. On my way to classes now."

"Look, Jack. Another fellow and I are renting a place up on the West Side near Central Park. Why don't you move in with us?" Howie wrote a phone number and address on a slip of paper and handed it to Jack.

"Thanks. I'll call you. Good seeing you again." He waved back at his friend as he resumed walking the few blocks to Washington Square and the university.

Within a week Jack had moved into the apartment shared by Howie and his friend. He could no longer walk to his classes. But the subway was nearby, and it was a short ride to Lower Manhattan. All was well until the beginning of January, 1955. The three men had been away during holidays in December. When they returned, they found that their apartment had been burglarized. Some of their clothing had been stolen, and Jack had lost a typewriter. They separated after that. Howie and his friend moved out to Long Island and Jack returned to the Village to complete his studies for the semester. He had taken three courses one of which really aroused his enthusiasm for sociological research: Social Science Research Methods. His instructor, Matilda White Riley would later become a president of the American Sociological Association. She provided students with a research paradigm that proved invaluable to Jack in future years. Another course, Industrial Sociology would later influence Jack's research interests. As the semester drew to an end, he decided to leave New York University and continue his graduate studies at Catholic University of America in the nation's capital. It was inconvenient having a car in New York City, and living in Greenwich Village was rather expensive. He contacted an old friend, Sidney Shine who was sharing an apartment with a government worker in the northwest area of Washington; and they invited Jack to join them.

The apartment was unfinished and in a relatively new building. Sidney had brought in some old furniture and he and his roommate Kevin had the put up blinds on the windows. Jack and Kevin shared the one bedroom, and Sidney slept on a couch in the living room. Jack's course credits from New York University were transferable to Catholic University of America which helped to reduce the amount of course work required for his Master's degree in Sociology. Academic standards were high, and Jack spent a good deal of time in the university library poring over notes and other reading materials. Most of his teachers were priests, and he was the only Jewish student in the Sociology Department. A minor in Catholic Social Principles, comprising three courses, was required in the graduate program. Jack took one of the courses, Papal Social Encyclicals, which described the views of the Catholic Church on a number of issues such as marriage, the family, capitalism, and communism. From a sociological perspective, the course was interesting dealing with the values and norms or prescribed rules of a social institution. However, when he completed the course, he desired to satisfy his minor requirement by taking two courses in psychiatry: Psychoanalytical Theory and Clinical Psychiatry.

Before the beginning of the following semester, Jack called on the Dean of the School of Social Sciences to request a change in his minor. They sat and talked for some time. It was a very congenial exchange, and Dean Nuesse tried to persuade Jack to take additional courses in the Catholic Social Principles sequence. But Jack had made up his mind and was pretty adamant.

"Okay, Jack," the dean conceded. "You seem to be quite decided about this But it's not up to me to authorize the change. You will need to see your department chairman."

A few days later Jack entered the office of the chairman, Father Paul Furfey who immediately recognized Jack as one of his students.

"Sit down, Jack," he said motioning to a nearby chair. "What can I do for you?" he asked seated behind a large desk littered with some papers.

"Well, well, Father," Jack began, stammering a bit. "I'd like to request a change in my minor. I've taken one course in Catholic Social Principles, but I would like to complete the minor with two courses in psychiatry."

The chairman stroked his chin, pursed his lips, and spoke in a very serious tone. "But Jack, we expect all of our Catholic students to take all three courses in Catholic Social Principles."

"But Father, I'm not Catholic. I'm Jewish.."

The chairman tilted his head in surprise, and a broad smile spread across his face.

"Well, that's different!" he exclaimed. "You go ahead and take those psychiatry courses!"

By the beginning of 1956, Jack had completed his course requirements and passed comprehensive written examinations for the master's degree. Subsequently, it was time for him to begin his dissertation: the final requirement for his degree. Two factors influenced his choice of a dissertation topic. First, he had a strong interest in Industrial Sociology. Secondly, Sidney Shine was owner and supervisor of a laundry and dry cleaning plant in the Washington, D.C. area. Jack discussed with Sidney the possibility of his working part time at the plant where he would conduct his dissertation research as a participant observer. This meant he needed to be on the payroll performing some simple task for a few months in order to gather sociological data for his dissertation Also, it was essential that his true identity and purpose in working at the plant be concealed from other plant employees. Sidney consulted his brother-in-law, the other owner of the plant and they both granted Jack's request.

Jack submitted a research proposal to his department at the university. It was quickly accepted; and a faculty member, Father Bernard Mulvaney, was appointed as his dissertation adviser. The major objective of his study was to test the hypothesis that: A work group in a laundry and dry cleaning plant had a dynamic informal structure as distinct from the formal structure specified by an explicit table of organization. The primary method of research was "participant observation". Before he even began his research, Jack practiced the method in a number of social gatherings and settings. He spent nearly two months working in the plant accumulating data on the nature of social relations among workers as well as the kind of relationships prevailing between management and the workers. His enthusiasm for sociological research increased steadily during this time. Later he even presented a paper, based on his findings, at meetings of the District of Columbia Sociological Association. As Jack was completing the dissertation, he decided to go further in academia and pursue a PhD in sociology. He sent out applications to a number of graduate schools: University of Chicago, Harvard, University of Minnesota, and Stanford. Only the University of Chicago requested a copy of his dissertation; and it was only the University of Chicago that accepted him. Excitedly he shared the news with Father Mulvaney who tried to persuade Jack to remain at Catholic University to pursue a PhD.

"I know Jack", he said. "It's a great opportunity. Their sociology department is probably the most famous and accomplished in the world." Then in a cautionary tone, he added: "But it will be more difficult there and take you longer to finish."

Jack deeply respected Father Mulvaney, but this was an irresistible opportunity to enhance his knowledge of sociological research. He would go to Chicago.

In June he received his degree and rejoined his parents who had moved to a new home in Portland, Maine. The summer months passed quickly; and when September came, Jack loaded his car and started his trip to the Windy City. He had a passenger who was going to the University of Illinois and would take the train out of Chicago to Champagne. In a few days they passed the steel mills of Gary, Indiana. The mill fumes were stifling forcing them to close the car windows. Shortly, they reached Chicago. The city extended along Lake Michigan from the South Shore, past the Museum of Science and Industry, the Planetarium, the high rise buildings of the Loop and across the Chicago River to the Gold Coast and the far Northside. The traffic was heavy, moving swiftly along Lake Shore Drive. Jack exited at Jackson Boulevard, turned left on to Michigan Avenue and dropped his passenger off at Union Station. Then he drove south to Hyde Park and the University of Chicago area. He parked close to International House along East 59th Street, just a few blocks from the university, and across from the Midway Plaisance, a large linear park stretching several blocks to the west and separating the north and south parts of the University of Chicago campus. Carrying his suitcases, he entered International House and paused at the information desk, where he was greeted by an employee who verified his room reservation. He looked about as he walked along a short corridor. On one side was an expansive lounge filled with couches, chairs and a piano, on the other a doorway leading to an open courtyard. Farther down the corridor and to the left was a snack shop, and beyond was the cafeteria. There was an elevator at the end of the corridor and a flight of stairs leading up to the living quarters. Only graduate students, most of whom were attending the University of Chicago, resided in the House. Jack took the elevator up to his floor and walked down a hallway to his room. It was small but adequate with the basic necessities: a single bed, a table and reading lamp, some chairs, a chest of drawers, and a book case. There was a single window with a shade. Pulling up the shade, he could see his room was diagonally opposite another. As he continued looking, the window of the other room slowly opened, a face appeared, and a hand reached out into a wooden box fastened to the window ledge. The man at the window drew a bottle from the box. He had thick black hair, bushy eyebrows, rather sharp features, and a thin black mustache. It was a curious sight. But he smiled and waved at Jack. Later, the two men again encountered each other in a shared bathroom. Jack quickly introduced himself. They shook hands, and the other fellow responded.

"Glad to meet you, Jack! I'm Joseph, Joseph Matras. You just arrive here?"

"Yeah. Drove in from Portland, Maine. Going to work on a PhD in sociology."

"At the University of Chicago?"

"Yeah", Jack replied. "What about you? Where are you from, Joseph?" He noticed a slight accent.

"I'm from Israel studying for a PhD in economics at the University of Chicago. Say," he said, looking at his watch. "I've got a few errands to run. But let's talk later, Jack."

"Right!"

Downstairs in the cafeteria, Jack and Joseph talked extensively over cups of coffee, exchanging information about their respective backgrounds. Joseph had been born in Palestine, grew up on a farm, and following World War II, he joined the Haganah, a resistance organization of Palestinian Jews. When the United Nations voted for partition and the creation of the State of Israel in 1948, the armies of five Arab nation vowed to drive the Jews into the sea. Then he served as an officer in the ensuing Arab-Israeli War. Especially interesting to Jack was Joseph's description of the Pal-Heib Unit. These were Bedouins with strong ties to Jewish communities and fought with the Haganah in the Upper Galilee against Syrian encroachments. He listened intently as Joseph talked on.

"It must have been difficult raising an army to resist annihilation," Jack remarked.

"Well, yes it was. First of all the two Jewish resistance groups, Haganah and Irgun had to unite. The latter was a rather extremist group. And then we had problems with Jews who immigrated from Arab countries. Many of them didn't even speak Hebrew, and some were very undisciplined refusing to take orders."

"What did you do about that?" inquired Jack.

"Most of us could speak Arabic, so that wasn't a problem. But getting them to take orders was an issue. What you needed to do sometimes was to figure out who was the leader of any group of Arab recruits and subdue him physically. That way you won their respect, and they were ready to follow your orders."

After the war Joseph immigrated to America, and with the help of a scholarship and working part time he attended Boston University where he completed his undergraduate education. Subsequently, he entered the PhD graduate program in economics at the University of Chicago and had been in Chicago for just a few years.

Jack walked several blocks from International House to the Social Science Building for his classes which were now more accelerated than they had been in his earlier college years, as they were now on a quarter rather than semester system. During his first quarter he took a required statistics course and a few electives. The latter included Introduction to Population, a course taught by Philip Hauser who was the Chairman of the Sociology Department. He wasn't sure why he took Hauser's course. Maybe it was intellectual curiosity since he was completely unfamiliar with the area of population studies. However, later this would prove an asset. Also, the PhD program required students to qualify on eight hours of comprehensive written examinations which subsumed the area of Population and Human Ecology as well as the areas of Theory and Methods, Social Organization, and Social Psychology.

The fall quarter was drawing to an end, and winter was fast approaching. It was becoming very cold and damp with strong frigid winds blowing snow and ice across the white capped waves of Lake Michigan and the city's level terrain. Roofs were covered with blankets of snow, and tapered rods of ice hung from building gutters.

Lengthy lists of assigned readings had been common in Jack's courses. He had found it nearly impossible to digest all the readings, but he quickly learned that some were more important than others. Attending classes regularly and recording detailed lecture notes helped a great deal and were critical in preparing for course examinations. The atmosphere of the university was quite different from what he had experienced elsewhere. Academic ambience was intense, and students seemed pretty aggressive. In one class a young instructor, a fresh PhD from Harvard, working through statistical problems at the blackboard, was caught making mistakes and was rather embarrassed when a number of alert students quickly pointed out his errors.

After classes Jack would usually leave the social science building and walk through a large quadrangle. Passing the business school and administrative buildings, he would stop at the C Shop for a sandwich or Hutchinson Commons for a more complete hot lunch. Space was limited in the C Shop where he could overhear students intensely discussing academic matters. Hutchinson Commons, in contrast, was spacious and much quieter. On the walls hung an array of portraits of University of Chicago Presidents and different Heads of the Board of Trustees. Perhaps most impressive for Jack was the portrait of Robert Hutchins, the fifth president of the university who abolished varsity football and placed more emphasis on academics. Growing up in Boston, Jack had heard a great deal about the University of Chicago and Robert Hutchins who had been a major innovator at the institution. Many of the older university buildings were characterized by collegiate Gothic architecture similar to that of the University of Oxford. Their tall spires, archways, and protruding gargoyles conveyed an almost medieval atmosphere. When the weather was warmer and more tolerable, Jack spent time exploring the main campus which included the neighborhoods of Hyde Park and Woodlawn as well as a stretch across the Midway along East 60th Street. Sometimes he felt overwhelmed by the intense intellectual ambience of the university. On such occasions he might get into his car, drive along Lake Shore Drive, and stop at the Planetarium which jutted out into Lake Michigan. There he experienced a sense of relief, walking about, and surveying the Chicago skyline. At other times, he would drive up to Evanston and stroll around the Northwestern University campus which was a more casual and relaxed environment.

One spring day Jack emerged from the Social Science Building and headed along East 59th Street toward International House. He had not gone far when he heard footsteps and a voice from behind.

"Hello, there. Walk with me."

Jack turned quickly. It was Philip Hauser drawing up beside him. He had done very well in Hauser's Introduction to Population course. He was one of the few students who had earned an "A" grade, and was currently taking another course with Hauser in Sociological Theory. The chairman was a short man just a little over five feet tall, but he was an intellectual giant. He had earned his PhD in sociology at the University of Chicago during the years of the ascent of the Chicago School of Sociology and had been employed as Assistant Chief Statistician for Population and Deputy Director of the U.S. Census Bureau from 1938 to 1947. He was the founder of the University of Chicago Population Research Center and had numerous scholarly publications and was a very prominent demographer and sociologist.

"Hello, Professor !"Jack responded Then as they walked along together, Hauser asked:

"Where are you from Jack?"

"Boston, sir." He was somewhat deferential and awed. Hauser was in his late fifties about twice Jack's age, and he had never encountered the chairman so informally.

"I thought you were from somewhere back East. Your accent gives you away," Hauser noted smiling. "Where are you going now, Jack ?"

"Well, I was on my way to International House."

"But if you don't have anything pressing to do, why don't you come along with me. Talcott Parsons is speaking to the sociology faculty and students. You might find it interesting."

By this time the two men had passed Rockefeller Chapel where graduation ceremonies were regularly held. Jack followed Hauser into a nearby university building and a large auditorium already filled with faculty and students. Inside the two men parted. Hauser joined a group of faculty, and Jack slipped into a seat next to some sociology students. Shortly a graduate student introduced Talcott Parsons, a renown faculty member in the Harvard Department of Social Relations and an advocate of structural functionalist theory. Parsons had received his PhD degree in sociology and economics at the University of Heidelberg, and it was there where he first became involved in the sociological work of Max Weber.

Parsons spoke for almost an hour describing some new grand sociological theory that he was developing. Then he inquired,

"Are there any questions?"

A number of faculty and students raised their hands, and several questions were asked including one by Philip Hauser.

"Your theory is quite interesting" Hauser asserted. "But can you tell us how you would go about operationalizing your theoretical concepts? Development of measures of the concepts would, of course, make your theory more amenable to research."

Parsons appeared somewhat miffed; and ignoring Hauser's question, he simply continued responding to questions asked by other faculty and students.

"The man is very rude," Jack muttered to himself. "Maybe he just didn't understand Hauser's question."

Talcott Parsons was noted for building theories which had limited connections with empirical research. And he was strongly influenced by the sociological perspectives of Max Weber and Emile Durkheim, The former took more of a social psychological approach in understanding social phenomena emphasizing the importance of social action in ongoing social relationships between or among individuals or groups as well as action taken toward specific values. An example of the latter would be the captain, who in observing the "code of the sea", is the last to leave his sinking ship. A salient aspect of Weber's theorizing and methodology is the concept of "verstehn" loosely translated as "understanding". According to "verstehn" it behooved the observer or sociologist to ascertain the motivations and intentions of the social actors, and this should be accomplished by interrogating the social actors and not be imputed by any observer. But this could have certain limitations inasmuch as those engaged in social action may be reluctant to divulge or be aware of their true motivations or intentions.

In contrast Emile Durkheim, a disciple of Auguste Comte the founder of sociology, took a more macro approach in describing social phenomena and adopted what became identified in modern sociology as a structural functional perspective. In his *Rules of the Sociological Method* he focused on the nature of "social facts" equivalent to social norms: approved and disapproved ways of acting, thinking, and feeling which facilitate or constrain individual and group behavior reinforced by means of sanctions comprising rewards or punishments. In Durkheim's view, social facts were embedded in social institutions and larger society facilitating social practices which promoted group cohesion, stability, and adaptability. For Durkheim, social groups or social institutions were somewhat independent entities something more than just the sum of their individual parts. Participants of groups or social institutions come and go, that is there is generally turnover in group membership. But the "social facts" or social norms persisted, and existed anterior, exterior, and coercive in relation to individual group members. Some critics of Durkheim charged that this suggested that groups or social institutions were some kind of metaphysical entities existing without individual members. Other critics contended that the coercive nature of Durkheim's social facts ruled out individual autonomy or voluntarism. But Durkheim asserted unequivocally that no group or social institution could persist without participants and that group members were certainly free to deviate from group norms; but, in deviating they risked the imposition of punitive sanctions.

Talcott Parsons synthesized many of the theoretical concepts of both Weber and   Durkheim and developed an action theory based on structural functionalism which discerned society as a system made up of interdependent parts coordinating to promote social unity and stability. The starting point of Parson's approach was the voluntary action of individuals within the context of total social systems and subsystems. For example, we can consider a family as a total social system made up of four persons: husband, wife, son, and daughter. In addition other statuses and associated roles need to be taken into account: father, mother, brother, and sister. The questions arises: How many subsystems are possible ? If the ramifications or number of combinations of two person and three person relationships are calculated, then eleven relationships are discernible including the entire family and all subsystems. In addition, Parson's major attention focused on the interaction process between and among group participants engaged in normatively regulated roles. He saw roles as comprising social structures and helping to fulfill the functional needs of various social systems and larger society. Moreover, he indicated that social processes of socialization and social control were indispensable for the transmission of social values and social norms and that in the socialization process normatively regulated role behavior was supported by negative and positive sanctions. But, like Durkheim, Parson's theorizing allowed for incomplete socialization and deviant behavior.

Soon after Jack began his studies at the University of Chicago, he learned of a student grapevine providing information or rumors about the Sociology Department faculty. One rumor was that Herbert Blumer, who had taught in the department for about twenty five years, had been "banished" to Berkeley. It sounded like Blumer was pressured to leave the department, but this was never verified After leaving in 1952, Herbert Blumer helped to develop the first Sociology Department at the University of California, Berkeley.

Some years before, Blumer had earned his doctorate at the University of Chicago and was strongly influenced by the social psychology of George Herbert Mead and the sociological perspectives of William. I. Thomas and Robert Park. He was a strong proponent of symbolic interactionism: a theory emphasizing a process, rather than structure, arising from the joint social action of individuals. According to Blumer's thinking the meanings of things or objects in the real world were defined and interpreted by social actors. He was very critical of structural functionalism and the growing influence of survey research and advocated direct observation and interviewing as major research tools which were very popular during the years of the advent of the Chicago School of Sociology. His departure from Chicago was perhaps a harbinger of impending changes in the University of Chicago Sociology Department. Quantitative research, reflected in the use of survey data and statistical methodology, was becoming much more prevalent. And Jack recalled a comment made by Hauser questioning the meaningfulness of a distinction between quantitative and qualitative research. He claimed the two overlapped :an example being the consideration or recording of the frequency of observed social events in qualitative research. In his Master's dissertation Jack had supplemented participant observation with a sociometric test which noted the frequency of friendship choices.

During Jack's first year in Chicago momentous events occurred in America and abroad. The Hungarian uprising against Soviet domination began in October, 1956. Sometime later, refugees from the uprising gathered at a rally at the University of Chicago. Just after starting classes, Jack became friendly with a graduate sociology student, Henry who had fled from Czechoslovakia after the Communists had seized power. Henry had been a student at Charles University in Prague and described how the Communists infiltrated the classrooms posing as students, and how student and faculty purges commenced. Freedom of expression was suppressed. Also, in 1957 Arkansas governor Orval Faubus called out the state's National Guard to prevent the entry of black students to Little Rock Central High School. This was aborted by President Eisenhower who responded by dispatching an Airborne Division to Little Rock and by federalizing the Arkansas National Guard marking another victory for the Civil Rights Movement.

At International House, Jack became acquainted with a number of graduate students attending the University of Chicago. He had already met Joseph from Israel, and there were: Pierre, a Frenchman working on a graduate degree in the Business School, Aladdin from Yemen who was pursuing a graduate degree in Economics, Omar who was from Egypt and a graduate student in International Relations. Omar was rather extraordinary. Whenever Jack encountered him in the hallways of International House, he would insist that Jack join him in the cafeteria for coffee and would've been offended if Jack declined. But, at the same time, Omar would make an odd request.

"Please," he would say: "Let's not sit with any Israelis."

Jack felt this was peculiar, especially since Arab and Israeli students frequently sat together at tables and even discussed Middle East political issues. But he reluctantly acquiesced, responding: "Okay, Omar. But you're not home in Egypt now. This is America."

The Egyptian was aware that Jack was Jewish, and they were together one time at a social gathering. Omar may have imbibed a little too much wine and began patting Jack affectionately on the back.

"Jack, I really like you", he said. "You're a great guy. But there's one thing that bothers me. It's a problem for me."

"What's that?" Jack asked.

"Your being Jewish."

Jack patted Omar on the shoulder and replied: "My friend. I like you, too. But I think you do have a problem."

Also, there was this very tall, slender fellow with curly blonde hair. Generally he was impeccably dressed wearing a coat and tie. He walked very erect; and as he gazed about, he seemed to be very self-assured and aware of his surroundings. At first, Jack thought he was an Englishman. His name was Edward, a graduate student in Political Science, a native Chicagoan, and someone Jack would get to know quite well.

Jack did become acquainted with a few of the women residing in International House. Alice, was a very bright and dedicated student pursuing a PhD in sociology with a concentration in population studies. She encouraged Jack to specialize in population, an area where related faculty, specifically demographers, were more supportive of students trying to meet the dissertation requirement. Another House resident whom Jack dated was a student in the School of Social Administration. However, he dated her only once. She was quite attractive, but very assertive and contentious. She would jump very quickly in and out of Jack's car before he could open the car door for her. Also, when they went dancing, she tried to lead him on the dance floor and argued intensely about the application of Freudian psychoanalytical theory.

Near the end of the academic year, Jack left International House. Living there had become too hectic and distracting. In addition, he had tired of cafeteria food. He moved into an apartment building: the Sylvan Arms located along Kenwood Avenue near East 55th Street. Although his apartment was small, it was adequate. It had multiple windows overlooking South Kenwood Avenue, a large room with a bed, couch, chest of draws, a bookcase, and a table with a reading lamp. There was a bathroom and a small kitchen with a stove and refrigerator. The kitchen came equipped with all the basic necessities: eating utensils, plates, cups, glasses, pots, and pans. His earlier college experiences had taught him sufficient culinary skills enabling him to prepare his own meals. Soon he discovered that some of his friends and acquaintances from International House had also moved into the Sylvan Arms. Edward Erickson, the native Chicagoan, occupied an apartment just down the hall from Jack. Joseph, the Israeli student was living below on the second floor, and Aladdin, an economics student from Yemen was residing a few doors down from Joseph.

Aladdin was a rather extraordinary person. He was small and frail, and his hair was black and very curly. Often he wore dark spectacles perhaps because his eyes were sensitive to light. He would speak very eloquently and forcefully and had an excellent command of the English language. When he was very young, he studied English in a school in Africa run by Catholic nuns. He had a close personal relationship with the Crown Prince of Yemen, and every month he received a check from the Yemen Royal Treasury to help defray his educational expenses. As a graduate student in the Economics Department, he was frequently in contact with a number of Israeli students in the same department. On one occasion he told

Jack, "The Arab Student Union wanted to make me their president, but I turned them down."

"How come?" Jack asked.

"They insisted that I stop associating with Israeli students, and I told them to go to hell."

"Good for you!"

Jack made a new friend in the Sylvan Arms who was completing his doctorate in Political Science: a very interesting fellow named Mohammed who was from Syria. He and Jack had some profound and extensive discussions about Middle East issues. Mohammed had received an offer to teach at Columbia University and said he would never return to Syria. He described it as an oppressive country ruled by a butcher. And he was sympathetic toward Israel, pointing out that it was the only democracy in the Middle East, and that Arab dictators used Israel as a scapegoat in order to consolidate their internal power. Mohammed was tall, slender, and very good looking. Occasionally he and Jack went out to Jimmy's, a bar and popular student hangout, for a few beers. While they were there, it didn't take long before an attractive woman would cast Mohammed a flirtatious glance. Then he was gone. Late that night or the following day, Jack would ask:

"Hey, Mohammed what happened to you last night? You disappeared."

Smiling, he replied: "Well, Jack. You see, this woman picked me up."

Jack spent time with Edward Erickson. Occasionally they would visit Jimmy's for a few beers or go out to eat in the evenings.

A popular restaurant was the Tropical Hut: great ribs, barbecued chicken, and sandwiches. But most of the time Jack prepared his own meals. Fried chicken and a spaghetti sauce with pasta were his favorite dishes. Once in a while he broiled a steak. During the week Edward would return from work later in the evening. He worked part time in an administrative job at the downtown University of Chicago campus. He disdained cooking. If he and Jack didn't go out to the Tropical Hut, he heated up some frozen processed food. Later they would talk and reflect on current events.

Some years had passed. It was November, 1960, and John F. Kennedy was elected President of the United States. Jack had completed his course requirements and began to prepare for PhD comprehensive written exams. For nearly four months he studied intensively, reviewing notes and readings. Sometimes he fell asleep on the couch fully dressed with papers or a book having fallen on his lap. Bright daylight pouring in through the windows or Edward's heavy knocking on the door would awaken him. After passing a sequence of PhD core examinations, he passed another in an area of specialization Following that, he satisfied a language requirement entailing a written exam and the English translation of a work by a Latin American sociologist. Now he was ready to prepare a proposal for his PhD dissertation. For a number of reasons this would be the greatest hurdle in earning the doctorate degree. To begin with, the submission process of a proposal was especially difficult because of certain political ramifications. Once a student had prepared a proposal, he or she was expected to round up a committee of at least three faculty members. Once this was done, a hearing would be held; and if the proposal were accepted, the student was advanced to candidacy for the PhD. However, faculty members were not required to serve on any particular committee and might refuse for a variety of reasons. Perhaps most important to them was whether a student was "known" or performed well in their courses, that the research proposal be workable or "viable", constitute a potential contribution to sociology, and that it lie within a faculty's scope of interest. These could be difficult criteria to meet.

Jack drafted a proposal. Its main thrust was the study of social conflict among managers or administrators in a large scale work organization. He eschewed explicitly referring to "social conflict" as he felt that doing so would risk arousing apprehensions and reduce his chances of gaining entry into a work organization and implementing the research. He believed that social conflict could be inferred from certain kinds of interaction or absence of interaction as well as responses expressed in the course of interviewing and observation. The proposal was submitted to three members of the faculty: Everett Hughes, Peter Blau, and Harrison White. Two members of his committee, Hughes and Blau had very distinguished records in the areas of organizational theory and research and were quite enthusiastic over Jack's proposal. A hearing was held, but Jack could not be advanced to candidacy until he found an organization allowing him to conduct his research. But progress on his dissertation came to a standstill. Although he had a number of interviews, including one at Sears, Roebuck and Company, he was unable to gain entry into an organization.

Meanwhile, Jack decided to do some part time teaching and had his résumé prepared and filed at the University Office of Career Counseling and Placement. He called the Department of Sociology at Northwestern University, but nothing was available. However, there was an opening at Indiana University extension in Gary, Indiana.

It was an evening class in Introductory Sociology with about twenty or twenty five students. Jack was somewhat nervous and delivered his first lecture rather rapidly. At the end, he asked if there were any questions. There were no questions, and he thought the students had been strangely quiet. A few days later he again met the class.

"Before I begin, are there any questions?" He inquired.

One student slowly raised his hand and hesitatingly said, "I'm sorry, but I was completely lost on your last lecture. You talked so fast."

"How many of you were lost?" Jack asked

All hands went up. Jack shook his head and smiled. "Forgive me this is my first time teaching. I'll slow down and repeat the lecture." After that he lectured at a slower pace, and students seemed to follow him without any difficulties.

About halfway through the semester, Jack gave the class an exam. When he graded and returned their tests, one of the students approached him appearing a little upset. "May I see you after class?" she requested. "It's about my test grade." After class he and the student walked to the cafeteria and sat at a table. Jack sipped a cold drink as the student asked: "Is there anything more I can do to raise my grade?" At the same time, she was pressing her leg against Jack's thigh. He moved away slightly; and looked at her sternly.

"Perhaps you need to spend more time studying."

Jack taught at Gary for two semesters. It was only a one year appointment, but it was an exalting experience. He felt teaching would be his career, but he needed to earn his "union card", the

PhD. Another year passed, and no progress was made with respect to his dissertation. He was still having difficulty gaining the cooperation of an organization, and his committee was not providing him with much help. The head of the committee Everett Hughes had left Chicago, and the remaining members were disagreeing over some methodological aspects of Jack's proposed research. But Jack continued to do some part time teaching. He was hired to teach a course at the University of Illinois in Chicago which was located at Navy Pier in a collection of buildings near the shoreline of Lake Michigan across from the Loop. The location was temporary, as a more permanent and massive campus was being constructed west of the Loop. Shortly after he started teaching, one of the Illinois faculty read Jack's dissertation proposal and agreed to show it to the President of Bell and Howell Company who was an alumnus of the University of Chicago. The president expressed some interest but the final decision as to whether Jack could conduct his research in the company had to be decided by the Company's Director of Research. An interview was arranged, and Jack was confronted with a barrage of questions from the director who was a University of Chicago PhD in Economics. During the course of the interview, he asked a critical and fair question:

"Jack, if we let you come in here and do your research, can you guarantee us that it will have no adverse effect on the morale and productivity level of our management staff? They may feel intimidated."

Jack knew he had to be candid in his response: "No, I can't give you any such guarantee."

The interview ended, and the door to Bell and Howell closed. Jack made one last attempt to gain entry into a work organization. He contacted a relative who was the chief executive officer of a large company in Boston. But the response was the same as it had been at Bell and Howell. His faculty committee could not offer him any further help. They had difficulties themselves in accessing organizations. An added problem was that the head of his committee had left to teach elsewhere, and it was rumored that one of the remaining two members of his committee was also planning to leave the university. Hughes recommended a new faculty member, Morris Janowitz to replace him as head of Jack's dissertation committee. And in a phone conversation, Peter Blau urged,

"You've spent nearly a year on this. Don't go on wasting your life. Give it up."

As a last resort Jack appealed to Morris Janowitz for possible help. But Janowitz offered only a tongue lashing.

"You will never get into an organization to do this research!" he exclaimed. "You don't measure up to University of Chicago standards! Go down state to Champagne to the University of Illinois for your PhD!"

Jack was stunned, humiliated, and angry. He could have openly cursed Janowitz or slammed the office door as he quickly departed.. But what would that accomplish? Instead he said nothing; he simply walked away, returned to his apartment and reflected. He knew he had no other alternative except to abandon the proposed research and begin again. He approached James Davis, the Assistant Director of the National Opinion Research Center and requested access to a data set in order to design a a dissertation proposal involving secondary analysis where the researcher makes use of data collected by others. Davis encouraged Jack responding, "We certainly like to have students working on our data."

As the semester was nearing an end at the University of Illinois, Jack had a rather disturbing experience making him first aware of the lack of integrity and corruption in higher education. There was a foreign student in his class from Iran who was performing very poorly. Not only was the student failing all exams, but he also rarely attended class. Shortly after Jack had given his students their final examination and preparing to submit final grades, the Iranian student confronted him in the university parking lot asking if he were going to receive a failing grade. Jack answered affirmatively, and the student threatened him.

Jack countered angrily. "Listen, carefully! I'm going back into the building and report what you have said to security! If anything happens to me, you can be held responsible! Just remember that!"

A few days later Jack received a memorandum from the Director of the Social Sciences Division stating that he would not be retained to teach the following September if he insisted on failing the Iranian student. He shuddered and shook his head in disbelief.

"This is unbelievable", he murmured to himself. Immediately he took the memorandum, copies of the student's tests, and attendance record and went to the office of the Chairman of the Sociology Department. Paul, the chairman was in the office with another faculty member. Jack showed them both the memorandum as well the student's tests and attendance record. Paul and the other faculty member agreed with Jack. Clearly, the student deserved to fail. But the chairman pointed out:

"Jack, I can't help you. If you don't pass this student, you won't be able to teach here again; and it won't look good if a Jewish instructor fails an Arab student. What do you want to do?"

The fact that an Iranian was not an Arab was beside the point. But Jack wondered how does this guy know I'm Jewish? I never told him. Maybe Jack did mention it to one of the faculty. Once it's known, it can spread like wildfire. He was outraged, bit his lip, and snapped back angrily at the chairman: "What the hell does my religion have to do with this? The student will fail, and you know what you can do with the teaching appointment!"

A few days later, Jack submitted his grades and felt a wave of relief as he departed the University of Illinois. Subsequently, he made an appointment to meet with the head of the Sociology Department at DePaul University concerning part time teaching beginning in the fall. On the day of the appointment, he took the Illinois Central down to the Loop and walked a couple of blocks to DePaul University. He waited in the Sociology Department office while the secretary announced his arrival. Shortly, she came out of the chairman's office, saying:

"Father Moroney will see you now."

The chairman rose from behind his desk to greet Jack. They shook hands and Jack handed the priest his résumé. Father Moroney looked it over and smiled. He was a short and stocky man with reddened cheeks. He sat down again at his desk and motioned Jack to sit.

"I see that you taught this past year at the University of Illinois. Will you be teaching there again this fall?"

"No," Jack replied

The chairman looked again at Jack's résumê. He appeared a little puzzled, his brow wrinkled.

"Do you mind if I ask you, why not?" the chairman asked.

"No. I don't mind at all," Jack answered. He then related in detail what had transpired at Illinois.

Father Moroney rubbed his chin and frowned. "I've heard similar incidents like that happening there. You certainly won't have problems like that here. You've come at an opportune time. We have an instructor who's going on a sabbatical this year. Could you teach two courses in September and continue for the academic year?"

Jack responded enthusiastically. "Yes! Of course!" adding, "What courses would I be teaching Father?"

"Introductory Sociology and Industrial Sociology, "he replied.

"Sounds great!"

"Very nice meeting you, Jack. See you in September."

They shook hands again and parted. Jack returned back to his apartment. He had much to do, as he was working on another dissertation proposal based on a data set from the National Opinion Research Center (NORC). He tried to work quickly and diligently. But after some time had passed, Davis informed Jack that he was leaving to teach at Yale and that Jack should submit his dissertation proposal to Peter Rossi, the Director of NORC.

Jack was pondering some research materials when suddenly he heard someone knocking at his apartment door. As he opened the door, he was startled by the sight of Lydia, Aladdin's girlfriend.

"You're back!" Jack said. She was a tall young woman about eighteen or nineteen years old with large blue eyes and long blonde hair falling down over her shoulders. For the past year she had been away attending Bryn Mawr college in Philadelphia and had just returned to Chicago for the summer. "Come in, come in Lydia," he continued. "It's great to see you again. How did it go at Bryn Mawr?"

"I had a good year there. I loved it," she replied.

"So what will you be doing for the summer?"

"Oh, I've been working at a broker's office in the Loop just for the summer." She paused briefly before continuing. "Listen, Jack I want to fix you up with this girl in my office. She's from Sweden, and I believe she's the one for you."

Jack groaned and shook his head. "No, no!" He said emphatically. "Not another blind date!"

But Lydia was persistent. "Look, Jack have I ever tried to fix you up before?"

"No." Jack replied.

"Well," she continued. "I've been waiting for the right one for you, and this is it."

"But maybe you should fix Edward up with the Swedish girl. He's a Swede, too."

"No, no!" Lydia insisted. "The Swedish girl is for you. She's a real beauty!"

"Okay, Lydia. Suppose I meet the girl for lunch? What's her name?"

"Hilda. I'll talk to her, make the arrangements, and then get back to you."

A few days later Lydia contacted Jack telling him she had spoken to Hilda. The arrangements had been made. Jack was to meet Hilda at noon on a certain day in the downstairs lobby of the building where Hilda worked. Jack arrived in the lobby about ten minutes early and waited. It was surreal: a mixture of fact and fantasy, as Hilda came down some stairs and looked back smiling at Jack. Wow! He thought. She is beautiful! She was tall and slender; her long auburn hair fell down over her shoulders. She had arched eye brows, blue eyes, a fair complexion, and very attractive facial features. He noticed, too that her cheeks were slightly flushed. They walked to a nearby restaurant where they sat and ordered lunch. Hilda ate only a small sandwich. She was quiet and spoke in very soft voice. There was little conversation, but Jack felt very much at ease with her. Before he left her at work, he asked her to go out with him again; and she said: "Yes." He was jubilant! In the weeks that followed, they were together frequently and their relationship gradually became more intimate.

Hilda and her sister had immigrated to America in 1960 and joined relatives in Detroit, Michigan. A few years later she migrated to Chicago, rented a room, and found work at a brokerage firm. Although Jack and Hilda came from very different backgrounds, they had certain commonalties. From the time that they first met, they felt a mutual attraction and were at ease with each other. Without even speaking, they could anticipate and comprehend each other's thoughts and feelings. Both had experienced tragedies in their lives. When Hilda was about six years old, her mother died of tuberculosis; and her father became dysfunctional from traumas suffered in a terrible war. He was one of the Swedish volunteers who fought with the Finnish Army in the Winter War against Russian aggressors. In the face of overwhelming odds and firepower, Hilda's father and other defenders were forced to retreat. It was at that time that Hilda's father met her mother and helped her to escape from the Russians who seized her estate in the Karelian Isthmus Now Jack remembered when he was growing up in Boston and had witnessed vivid accounts of the war. After her mother passed away and her father was incapacitated, Hilda was forced to spend a number of years in an orphanage until she was later cared for by an aunt. Jack, of course, never knew his father who died of dysentery due to unsanitary conditions of the trenches in World War One. But he did recall his sister who died from cancer at a very young age. Also, he had an uncle who joined the American Expeditionary Force in World War One who returned suffering from shell shock and later died from schizophrenia. Jack and Hilda had grown up in different cultures separated by a great ocean. He was a Jew and she a Lutheran, but neither of them was really religious. But their values were very similar, and past tragedies drew them even closer together.

The summer months passed quickly. Jack had completed a research proposal and began to seek out a dissertation committee. He first submitted the proposal to Professor Peter Rossi, the Director of the National Opinion Research Center (NORC). The director read it and responded positively:

"I'm surprised. I didn't think you had it in you, Jack. It's very good. I'll work with you." He said decisively.

Jack found another faculty willing to serve on the committee. He needed only one more faculty member. At this time Professor James Davis returned to the University of Chicago and to his former position as Assistant Director of NORC. Subsequently, Jack submitted his proposal to Professor Davis. A week later Jack was informed by the department chairman that the proposal had been dropped at a departmental meeting. Professor Rossi gave Jack a note from

Professor Davis stating that he felt that the research proposal was not "viable," due to "no solid connection between your concepts and measures". Following this, Jack attempted to contact Davis to discuss his criticisms. When he finally reached him by phone and expressed a wish to talk further about his proposal the response was:

"Did you get my note?"

"Yes, but-"

"There's nothing more to discuss," Davis insisted.

There was a clicking sound, and the conversation abruptly ended.

Then in November Jack received a letter from the acting head of the department, Professor Morris Janowitz. The regular chairman, Professor Hauser was temporarily in the Far East. The letter stated that the Department of Sociology recommended that Jack abandon his efforts to earn a PhD at the University of Chicago, and that the recommendation was based on "your inability to prepare an acceptable thesis proposal coupled with your previous minimum pass on the core examination". Jack was infuriated. Clearly, there were certain inaccuracies. To begin with, Jack had received an official letter stating that he had passed the core examination at the PhD level. Also, he had defended his first dissertation proposal successfully although his candidacy depended upon him gaining access to an organization to do his research. Enraged Jack showed his Israeli friend, Joseph the letter.

I'm mad as hell!" Jack cried out. "It's time to fight back!"

At the time, Joseph was completing his PhD in economics and was working as a teaching assistant in the Economics Department.

"Calm down, Jack!" He shouted. "Get a pencil and some paper! You're going to a write a reply and send it to all members of your department, even the visiting faculty. You have to point out the kind of treatment you got from Janowitz and Davis. Be clear, logical, concise. Provide all the details", and added, "Don't give them an inch!"

Jack sat alone and began to write. As he worked on the rejoinder to Morris Janowitz, he weighed every word, sentence, and paragraph making sure that he commented on Janowitz's inaccuracies as well as Davis' assertion that his proposal was not "viable, due to no solid connections between your concepts and measurements." Jack felt that Davis' criticism was the kind that could be directed at much respectable sociological research. Of course, the question that Davis raised was certainly a legitimate one. Jack was familiar with Logical Positivism and the Vienna Circle comprised of scientists and philosophers concerned with problems of the measurement of concepts. If Davis had at least given Jack the opportunity, he would have argued that not all concepts can be measured directly but many only indirectly in both the natural and social sciences. But Davis had shut the door to any further discussion. In closing his rejoinder to Janowitz, Jack requested that any reevaluation of his record occur under the guidance of Professor Hauser, the Department Chairman. When he completed the letter, he visited Alice an old friend from International House and her husband, Kent who was a visiting faculty member and demographer in the department. Alice had once advised Jack to specialize in population studies and work on a dissertation with faculty demographers rather than main line sociologists. She was aware of the instability and turmoil among the latter. Jack showed them both the letter saying that he was sending it to the entire faculty. Kent expressed some apprehension.

"It's well written Jack; but it may create a worse situation".

"Kent, I have to send it. I don't think my situation could be any worse."

The next day Jack sent the letter. After that, there was a departmental meeting. Kent was present and told Jack later that faculty reaction to his letter was very positive. "You won their respect," he noted. At the same time, Jack received some encouraging and supportive responses. One came from Philip Hauser who was away temporarily in the Far East. The message was written on a sheet of hotel stationary and essentially read, "Hold on. I will help you." There was also a response from Jack's former mentor, James Coleman who was now at Johns Hopkins University. Urging Jack to take a stand, he wrote, "I know someone in Chicago will help you."

Phillip Hauser had a forceful personality and was very direct and succinct in dealing with students. When you stepped into his office, he would typically say: "What can I do for you?" tapping his fingers on his desk; and it behooved you to answer clearly and briefly. Now Hauser had returned from the Far East ;and Jack stood before the chairman, his voice quaking with emotion.

"I had to write that letter! I felt that I was fighting for my life!"

"It's okay, Jack. I understand." Hauser replied in a sympathetic tone. "You're a Johnny Come Lately. I'll work with you. But you need to pick a dissertation topic that I'm interested in."

"Something related to the labor force?" Jack knew that this was an area of special interest for Hauser. "But how or where do I start?"

" Read *Theory of Wages* by Paul Douglas. That'll help you get started. And it might be a good idea for you to take the two

Population Workshop courses. See Donald Bogue about that; and remember this, even though you lose a battle you can still win the war."

Jack thanked Professor Hauser and departed. Leaving the Social Science building, he walked across the campus and turned right on East 57th Street. He felt exhilarated! This would be a new beginning! He remembered Professor Hauser's last words: "You're a Johnny Come Lately. And you can lose a battle but still win the war." It seemed to evoke certain lines of a poem by British Nobel laureate Rudyard Kipling, titled *If* which had hung on his bedroom wall when he was just a boy:

If you can make one heap of all your winnings

And risk it on one turn of pitch-and-toss'

And lose, and start again at your beginnings

And never breathe a word about your loss:

If you can force your heart and nerve and sinew

To serve your turn long after they are gone

And so hold on when there is nothing in you

Except the Will which says to them: 'Hold on!'

Jack turned left on to S. Kenwood Avenue; and reaching the Sylvan Arms he entered his apartment.

CHAPTER FIVE:
A NEW BEGINNING

Another academic quarter was about to begin as Jack knocked on the door of Donald Bogue's office.

"Come in." the professor responded.

Professor Bogue was rummaging through some papers and looked up from his desk as Jack entered. He was a short stocky man with a round pasty face, and strands of light brown hair hung over his forehead. He was a very prominent demographer with a number of outstanding scholarly publications In addition, he was one of the founders of the University of Chicago Population Research Center and at one time President of the Population Association of America and Editor of "Demography," the official journal of the Population Association of America. Jack had already taken a course with him in Human Migration in which he had earned an A grade.

"What can I do for you?" Bogue asked.

"I would like your permission to enroll in your Population Workshop courses."

"Well, I don't know if you would be able to make it in those courses. They're very quantitative, and I believe you didn't exactly excel in your statistics courses."

Jack hesitated before continuing. He remembered what Alice had told him about Bogue. She had taken both of his Population

Workshop courses and had forewarned Jack: "When you see Bogue," she said, "He'll try to feed you a bunch of nonsense about how difficult and quantitative his courses are. Don't buy it. He likes to exaggerate."

Then Professor Bogue unexpectedly interjected: "You know, I don't think you were very fair to Professor Janowitz with that letter you sent to the faculty."

He's entitled to his opinion, Jack thought. But what was I supposed to do: roll over and die? The important thing is that I'm still here. He may be trying to bait me. But I'm not going to let him succeed..

Jack ignored Bogue's comment, replying firmly, "Professor Hauser has strongly recommended that I take your workshop courses."

"Oh, he did!" Bogue exclaimed. "That's different. Certainly you can take them." Clearly Bogue would not counter a recommendation from the department chairman and Director of the Population Research Center who was widely respected and held in high esteem by the faculty.

Jack enrolled in the Population Workshop courses; and, at the same time, worked as a research assistant to Professor Nathan Keyfitz at the Population Research Center located in an old wooden building along East 60th Street.

One afternoon he stopped at Gordon's Restaurant for a late lunch. Inside he saw a friend, Dave Simon another sociology student sitting alone at a table. Dave had been sipping coffee and was gazing down at a half empty cup. He appeared somewhat depressed. He and

Jack had known each other for a few years and had become close friends. When Jack was frustrated over the fate of his first dissertation proposal, Dave had tried to console him:

"Hang in there, Jack!" He had said. "Come along with me; the best is yet to come!"

Dave looked up as Jack approached.

"Okay if I join you Dave?" Jack asked.

"Sure, sit down."

A waitress came hurrying to the table, and Jack ordered a sandwich and a cold drink.

"Are you going to have anything else, Dave?" Jack asked.

"No, nothing."

"What is it, Dave? Something is bothering you."

"Well, Jack," he began. "I feel I've been used and tossed overboard. I worked on Professor Bogues's research project on homeless people. I thought he would support me in getting started on a dissertation. But he's reneged."

According to the student grapevine, Bogue was not especially popular with the sociology students. Generally he was a pleasant fellow often wearing a smile, but students were wary of him. "Stay out of his way, and don't rely too much on him" was the caveat circulated by the student grapevine.

"I'm sorry, Dave. Anything I can do?"

"No. I'll just have to try something else."

At that moment, they were distracted by another sociology graduate student entering the restaurant. It was Jane Bolten looking rather distressed and sobbing as tears filled her eyes. Jack and Dave beckoned to her.

"Please, sit down Jane. What is it?" Jack asked.

Wiping away the tears, she tried regaining her composure and spoke in a shaky voice:

"It's my dissertation committee. My major professor is leaving the university, and the two other committee members disagree on a number of issues. I'm caught in the middle!"

Jack and Dave attempted to console her, but it didn't help much. There had been a lot of turnover and disagreement among the sociology faculty making it more difficult for students to complete their PhD degrees. By this time, Jack had finished his food and gulped down the rest of his drink. He glanced at his watch. It was getting late, and he was supposed to call Hilda. As he walked back to his apartment, he was relieved that he had changed his area of specialization to population or demography. Years ago, Alice had given him good advice when she encouraged him to switch over to population. Perhaps he should have done it then. But it's okay, he mused. So I'll be a "Johnny come lately".

Returning to his apartment, he called Hilda. She was preparing to take the bus to Detroit where her aunt and uncle would meet her and drive back to their home on the fringe of the Detroit Metropolitan Area. Hilda's sister, living in Detroit, was getting married within several days. Jack was invited to the wedding, and planned to follow Hilda after his next Population Workshop class.

He spoke briefly with her, left the apartment, picked her up, and drove her to the bus station where they kissed and parted.

It was a clear Sunday morning when Jack drove out of Chicago on Interstate 94 which cut across the State of Michigan to Detroit and beyond to Mount Clements. The wedding wasn't scheduled until the afternoon, so Jack shouldn't have had any problem arriving on time. But mistakenly, he drove south and then east and later discovered that he was on the Ohio Turnpike. By that time he was close to Toledo, and he began looking for an exit that would enable him to turn north toward Detroit and reconnect with Interstate 94. It was already nightfall when he passed the Detroit city limits and exited at Mount Clements. He tried following the directions Hilda had provided, but it was becoming difficult. He was on a country road without street lights. He passed homes that were lighted, but the houses were far between and located considerable distances from the road. He had been able to read street signs, so he knew he was in the right neighborhood. But it was a problem trying to read numbers on nearby mailboxes A flashlight would've been very helpful. Growing more anxious, Jack stopped at one of the houses and asked for directions to the Olsen home. Luckily, he was only a few houses away. Lights were on in the Olsen home, as Jack drove up a long, narrow driveway. Hilda was waiting for him on the front porch.

"Where have you been? My uncle has gone to bed. He thought you had gone to Saint Louis."

"Just a slight detour to Toledo." Jack replied.

Jack had missed the wedding, but he did have an opportunity to spend some time getting acquainted with Hilda's sister, three cousins, and her aunt and uncle. After Jack and Hilda returned to

Chicago, they quarreled over a trivial matter and didn't see or talk to each other for a few weeks. Then one day it hit him! He was in love with this woman and decided on a strategy! Near the end of the day, he drove down to the Loop and waited outside of the building where Hilda worked. She came out of the building; and seeing Jack, she cried out in surprise:

"What are you doing here!"

He took her arm and walked with her along State Street. It was rush hour, and the street was crowded.

"I love you! I want to marry you!" Jack shouted.

She shook her head, saying emphatically: "No, no!"

People in the crowd stopped and smiled. Then somebody kept shouting:

"Kiss her! Kiss her!"

He pulled her close and kissed her.

And in the days and weeks that followed, she finally said, "Yes"

Jack had been very persistent. He had chased Hilda until she had finally caught him. They were married in June and honeymooned on the Maine coast. Later in the summer, Hilda became pregnant. She had to quit her job in the Loop and, with Edward's help, she was employed at the reception desk of the University of Chicago Hospital. Jack was still working as a research assistant at the Population Research Center. He thought he had better share the news of Hilda's pregnancy with the department chairman. In about nine months he would be a father, and some changes might be needed. When Jack informed Professor Hauser, he looked at Jack quietly as if to say:

"My, this happened quickly. Maybe you should've taken better precautions. But it's happened."

"Okay, Jack,"Hauser responded," I'm sending you to work at the Population Division, Bureau of the Census in Washington. I spent some years there myself. You'll get hands on experience working with Census data and then get back to you dissertation. When you feel you're ready, send me your proposal. Here's a form to fill out. You'll be contacted, but it will take some time."

It was November 22, 1963. Leaves were turning a mixture of colors, as they fell from trees. Temperatures were dropping, and chilly winds whipped across the lake. There was a loud knocking at the apartment door. It was Edward who was the first to tell Jack the terrible news. Jack was stunned, shaking his head in disbelief. A great tragedy had struck the nation. President John F. Kennedy had been assassinated in Dallas. Texas, and Vice President Lyndon Johnson was sworn in immediately as the new president. The body of President Kennedy was flown back to Washington and placed in the White House for twenty four hours. On a rainy Sunday President Kennedy's flag covered coffin was carried on a horse drawn caisson to the Capitol Rotunda. Thousands of people lined Pennsylvania Avenue from the White House to the Capitol. They watched and listened to the sounds of drums and horses' hooves. Many onlookers wept.The entire nation mourned not only for the death of a president but a war hero as well. He had led the nation through some difficult times during the years of the Cold War: the Bay of Pigs debacle, the Cuban missile crisis, and the Berlin Blockade. Perhaps most memorable was President Kennedy's message to the people of America:

"Ask not what your country can do for you. Ask what you can do for your country."

The academic year drew to an end, and the spring of 1964 approached with warmer and gentler winds blowing across the lake and the level terrain of Chicago. Jack was just returning home from his last class in the Population Workshop Course. As he opened the door to his small apartment, the phone was ringing. Hilda was still at work. He quickly picked up the receiver. It was the long awaited call from the Population Division of the U.S. Census Bureau. He had been accepted for a position in the Demographic Statistics Branch of the Population Division. The caller provided him with all the details such as salary and when and where to report for employment. When Hilda returned, he told her the news. They were heading to Washington, D.C., and they were both relieved and elated. Jack would leave within a few weeks, and Hilda would follow. Subsequently, they invited Edward to their apartment for a farewell dinner. Edward had agreed to move from the Sylvan Arms to the Dorchester Avenue apartment that Jack and Hilda rented and take over the apartment lease; therefore helping to facilitate their departure.

It was a very early Sunday morning when Jack was prepared to leave Chicago. He had already packed basic necessities in a couple of suitcases, and was planning to drive to Washington, D.C. without stopping. Once there, he would stay overnight with a friend working for the government. He hugged and kissed Hilda and promised he would call her when he arrived at his friend's Washington apartment. She would join him in a few days. In the meantime he would search for an apartment to rent close to the U.S. Census Bureau in Suitland, Maryland. It was a long drive, but weather and road conditions were favorable. By evening he had reached the capital, his friend's apartment, and telephoned Hilda to let her know that all was well. The next day he rented an unfurnished two bedroom apartment in Suitland, Maryland. A few days later he picked up Hilda at the airport, and they stayed overnight at a motel.

The following day they went shopping for furniture, so they could move into the apartment as soon as possible. Jack had already started to work at the Demographic Statistics Branch of the Population Division, and it was only a five minute walk to work. Not long after Jack and Hilda were settled in their apartment, Jack took his wife on an early Sunday morning to George Washington University Hospital where she gave birth to a baby girl, and they named her Ellen. His responsibilities were indeed growing.

For about a month, Jack's principal task was to review past Current Population Survey Reports (CPS) particularly those relating to population mobility and migration. Subsequently he became more involved in data analysis and the preparation of CPS annual reports related to population mobility and migration. They were initially written by the Head of the Demographic Statistics Branch, and Jack did much of the editing. Also, heeding Professor Hauser's advice, he began reading Paul Douglas' *Theory of Wages*, looking for some clue which would help him prepare an acceptable dissertation proposal. Douglas' work had been published back in 1934, and at times he had taught in the Economics Department of the University of Chicago and served as a United States Senator from the State of Illinois. Jack found Douglas' work somewhat complex, as his training in economic was somewhat limited. Much of it involved discussions of production functions, especially relationships between land, capital, and labor on the one hand and wages on the other. But ultimately he found the clue. What was most germane was

Douglas' analysis of relationships between wages and the gainfully employed for cities using data for manufacturing industries from the 1920 Census of Population; and later Douglas had examined relationships between earnings and the labor supply for U.S. cities in 1930. Although he did try to partial out the influence of women and children in the earnings data, he only considered the extraneous effects of a single independent variable. He was constrained by the limited scope of U.S. Census data. In the early 1960's a more extensive analysis of aggregate labor market participation rates for males in different age groups and in different Standard Metropolitan Areas (SMSA's) was done by two economists at Princeton University, Bowen and Finegan. Their study incorporated several independent variables. Jack perused other research as well and then conjured up a strategy. Before developing a dissertation proposal and submitting it, he would first conduct a pilot study utilizing 1960 Census of Population data for SMSA's or labor markets. These were generally spatial areas where people lived and worked. Relevant and detailed aggregate data on social, economic, and demographic characteristics of total and nonwhite populations were available in published U.S. Census of Population reports. Jack would develop a theoretical model hypothesizing relationships between an extensive number of independent variables and age specific labor force participation rates of nonwhite males for a sample size of 64 SMSA's. The data had to be coded, measures of the variable calculated, and finally multiple regressions computed to evaluate the hypothesized relationships. All this was done manually with the assistance of a desk calculator. There were main frame computers in use at the U.S. Census Bureau. However, Jack never had access to them. A considerable amount of the coding and computations were done at work but not at the neglect of regular duties. During evenings, he spent time working out differential and integral calculus problems seeking to to master the basics of differential and integral calculus in order to strengthen his statistical skills.

The 1960's were the years of the Great Society. It was an ambitious program with the main goals of eliminating poverty and racial injustice. It had been initiated during Kennedy's New Frontier and gained full momentum with the advent of the Johnson administration. Some of the major programs included the Civil Rights Act of 1964 which prohibited job discrimination and segregation in public places, the Voting Rights of 1965 which eliminated discriminatory voter procedure requirements for minorities,, and the Civil Rights Act of 1968 which forbid housing discrimination. Perhaps most controversial were the War on Poverty programs which included significant federal aid to education, job training, and community development. When the War on Poverty was in full swing, Jack was moved over to the Economic Statistics Branch of the Population Division to work on poverty statistics data for individuals, families, and census area units. He was involved in analyzing much of these data. A longitudinal study was contemplated focusing on how do people fall into poverty, and how do they work their way out. But as far as Jack knew, the study was never launched. These were exciting years for him, and he felt that a good deal was being accomplished. Throughout the 1960's poverty rates were cut in half. However, the War on Poverty had its critics claiming that the federal government had no business dealing with social problems, that the Great Society programs were contributing to the disintegration of families, and that the massive efforts of the War on Poverty yielded only modest results.

While Jack was working in the Economic Statistics Branch, the Chief of the Population Division called him into his office. Jack had just finished and submitted an analysis on the misreporting of income in the 1960 Census of Population. The Division Head was at his desk and rose with a copy of Jack's report in his hand.

"Jack, this is an excellent piece of work," he said, waving the report in the air. "You can have a great future here. In fact, I'm going to promote you."

"Well, thanks Doctor Allen. I really appreciate it." The Division Chief had earned a PhD in Economics from New York University and had a number of academic publications.

"There's something else, Jack," Allen continued his brow wrinkling slightly. "I understand you have been trying to develop a dissertation proposal for the PhD at the University of Chicago. Look, you don't need that degree here. Why don't you give it up?"

Jack shrugged his shoulders replying, "Maybe so." But then he thought, I can't do that. I've come too far. I'm too committed.

Some time ago Jack had applied for a position with the U.S. Bureau of Labor Statistics. He realized that he needed to leave the Census Bureau if he were to complete his pilot study and develop a dissertation proposal. The Bureau of Labor Statistics had stipulated that they would allow him time on the job to pursue his research interests.. Consequently when they offered him a position, he immediately accepted. In view of the circumstances, he was convinced this was an appropriate decision even though the Population Division Chief, and some others were somewhat upset about his unexpected departure. He felt it was a great opportunity. The Bureau of Labor Statistics was interested in his research and appeared willing to grant him time at work to complete his pilot study and prepare a dissertation proposal. In making the job change, there was another unanticipated and important benefit. His division head came to his office one day with a suggestion:

"Jack, there's a guy here from RCA offering a crash course in writing Fortran programs. Maybe you would be interested? We have an IBM 360 main frame just down the hall."

Jack was nearly overwhelmed with excitement:

"You bet I would! When does the course start?"

"Tomorrow morning, ten o' clock, Room 22."

"Great, thanks Susan!"

The following morning Jack sat in a room with about twenty other employees. A representative from RCA stood in front of a blackboard and began to instruct the group in the basics of the Fortran language. It only took a few hours before Jack and others were told to write a simple Fortran program which involved computing an arithmetic mean, a variance, and standard deviation for some numerical data. Although it was a minor exercise, it was a big step forward for Jack. Later he obtained a Fortran manual so as to expand his knowledge of the language. He had already completed all of his computations for his pilot study. It had been an arduous and time consuming process with the use of a desk calculator. Writing Fortran programs, he replicated measures of all his independent and dependent variables. He also repeated his multiple regression analysis using an IBM multiple regression program. What had taken months to do manually was done in a matter of days. The main frame computer yielded research results closely corresponding to those he had obtained with a desk calculator. Also, the empirical findings were generally consistent with his theoretical model. The final task was to write up the research results.

When Jack was still preparing and running programs related to his study, Hilda had become pregnant again. The months passed and eventually it was drawing very close to the delivery date. It was an early Monday morning; and he thought it might be a good idea to stay home just in case, but Hilda persuaded him to leave for work. They were now living in a house in a northwest suburb; and as usual, Jack drove to a nearby shopping center, parked his car, and took a bus to work. After arriving at the Bureau of Labor Statistics he stopped in the cafeteria for a brief cup of coffee; but when he reached his office he was told that his wife had called. It was urgent, she had gone into labor. He dashed out of the Government Accounting Office (GAO) building, and caught a cab that rushed him to his car at the shopping mall. When he drove up his driveway, his daughter was in front waving hysterically. Hilda came out of the house. They all entered the car, and off they went. His daughter, Ellen was sobbing, and Hilda was experiencing quite a bit of discomfort. Jack pressed down on the accelerator and the car horn. He sped through all red lights and stop signs heading for George Washington University Hospital. Other traffic came to a standstill. He hoped he would draw the attention of the police to provide an escort. But he failed to see an officer until he was a block away from the hospital.

"My wife is having a baby!" Jack screamed

The policeman waved and shouted back, "Go!"

He drove into the emergency entrance. About thirty minutes later, the baby was born. It was a boy; and Jack and Hilda named him, William who seemed to be in a hurry to be born.

Over a year passed. It was the early spring of 1968. By this time, Jack's pilot study was complete; and he sent a copy of the study with a dissertation proposal to Philip Hauser at the University of Chicago. The proposal suggested that the pilot study be expanded to include white as well as nonwhite male groups in SMSA's. Professor Hauser responded enthusiastically, setting a date for a formal hearing and assigning two other demographers to serve on Jack's dissertation committee.

The 1960's had been turbulent years for America. It began with the Cuban missile crisis, followed by the assassination of a president, and a growing involvement in an increasingly unpopular war. Originally Vietnam had been part of the French Empire, and its people had fought against Japanese aggression during World War Two. Later the Vietnamese fought against the French to achieve national independence and successfully defeated the French at Dien Bien Phu. Subsequently, the country was split between a communist North Vietnam and a noncommunist South Vietnam, and a general election was to be held throughout the nation in order to achieve unification, But the United States refused to participate, fearing a Communist takeover and supported separate elections in South Vietnam. But the new president in South Vietnam ruled so abusively that he alienated many South Vietnamese which led to an increase in communist sympathizers and guerrillas who fought against the South Vietnamese government and became known as the Viet Cong. When the North Vietnamese fired on U.S. warships in international waters in the Gulf of Tonkin 1965, the first U.S. ground troops were sent to Vietnam. As the war escalated, protests and strife swept America. Much blood and treasure were spent. Our goals were unclear. Some supporters of our participation advocated what was known as the "domino theory": a belief that if South Vietnam fell to the Communists then the rest of Southeast Asia would capitulate to Communism as well. It was unclear who the enemy was. By daytime the Viet Cong were peasants toiling in the fields, but at night they became guerrilla fighters setting ambushes and booby traps. The morale of American troops deteriorated as the war dragged on, and they further suffered either from drug addiction or the effects of Agent Orange.

In 1967 and in another part of the world, war broke out in the Middle East. Israeli forces launched a preemptive strike against Egypt in response to an illegal blockade of Israeli shipping in the Gulf of Aqaba. At the same time, Syria increased its border clashes with Israel and mobilized its troops. Arab leaders were calling for the annihilation of Israel. When the war ended, Israel had gained control of East Jerusalem and the West Bank from Jordan, the Golan Heights from Syria, and captured the Sinai Peninsula and Gaza from Egypt. Jack wondered: Would there ever be peace in the Middle East? He didn't think so. Not as long as the world needed scapegoats and pariahs.

Then in the spring of 1968, America was struck by two horrific tragedies. On April 4, Martin Luther King, Jr. a prominent leader of the African-American civil rights movement was assassinated. About the same time Robert F. Kennedy was campaigning for the 1968 Democratic presidential nomination. On April 4, while preparing to leave Indianapolis, he learned of King's death and spoke to a crowd in a black neighborhood informing them of the death of

Martin Luther King. People screamed, cried, and shouted angrily, but Kennedy quieted them speaking only for a few minutes:

For those of you who are black and are tempted to fill with – be filled with hatred and mistrust of the injustice of such an act, against all white people, I would only say that I can also feel in my heart the same kind of feeling. I had a member of my family killed, but he was killed by a white man.

He continued to speak for a short time, pleading for unity between blacks and whites. Two months later Robert F. Kennedy was also killed by an assassin's bullet. In the weeks that followed Martin Luther King's assassination, riots spread throughout major U. S. cities including the nation's capital. Government workers were sent home in the early afternoon as billows of smoke rose above the city. Jack joined his car pool in the underground parking area of the GAO building. They rode through predominantly black neighborhoods where crowds of rioters filled the streets, and shops and stores were being looted and sometimes set afire. Jack was dropped off at the shopping center where his car was parked, and reached home safely. Throughout that night, the capital was like a combat zone. The National Guard was mobilized to assist the police. Personal injuries were minimal, but property damage was extensive.

The date for Jack's hearing on his dissertation proposal was nearing. His plan was to drive to Chicago. Hilda and the children would accompany him as far as Mount Clements, Michigan where they would visit Hilda's aunt and uncle. Then Jack would continue on alone to Chicago arriving there a day before the hearing. Throughout the time had been working in Washington, Jack had stayed in touch with Joseph who had received his PhD in Economics and was currently teaching at Northwestern University in Evanston, Illinois. He related his plan to Joseph who suggested that Jack stay at his home in Evanston when arriving in Chicago. Jack was granted a week's leave from work, and he and the family departed for Michigan. The night before he was to drive to Chicago from Mount Clements, Jack could not sleep. He tossed from side to side. So much filled his mind and he was overwrought. By three in the morning, he turned to Hilda:

"It's no use. I can't sleep. I want to leave now and make Chicago by seven or eight o' clock."

"I understand," Hilda replied, "But please be careful driving."

The expressway was nearly deserted. Jack drove across Michigan in a few hours and passed Gary Indiana just as the sun was rising. As he drove along the South Shore and Lake Shore Drive, he could see the Chicago skyline gleaming in the sunlight; and a feeling of elation swept over him. It's good to back! He mused. Within a short time, he arrived at his friend's home in Evanston.

"You're here early!" Joseph exclaimed as he opened the door.

"I know. I had trouble sleeping, so I hit the road about three this morning".

"Come on in. Have some breakfast. You'll have to stay up until tonight. No napping," Joseph insisted. "You'll need to be fresh and rested for the hearing tomorrow."

That night Jack slept soundly. In the morning, he drove down to the university. Joseph accompanied him. They entered the social science building along East 59th Street and walked up a flight of stairs to the Department of Sociology office. They were a little early and waited outside the office door. Shortly, the chairman and two other faculty members came down the hallway. Professor Hauser was smiling.

"Hello, Jack. Good to see you again!"

"It's good to be back, Professor Hauser."

Jack shook hands with the chairman and other members of his committee: Evelyn Kitagawa a prominent demographer and Robert W. Hodge also a demographer who possessed considerable expertise in statistical methodology. As Jack introduced Joseph, Professor Hauser suggested:

"Why don't you join us, Joseph. You can serve on the committee, too."

They all stepped into the chairman's office. After they were all seated, Professor Hauser began to speak; and as he spoke, he waved some paperwork in the air.

"This is a copy of a pilot study that Jack sent me. The empirical results are impressive. It's the basis for his dissertation proposal. Jack, will you give us a summary of your proposal."

"Sure," Jack replied. And he began to describe his proposal or research design in detail. Especially helpful in developing the proposal was the research paradigm that he had obtained in his first research methods course taken so many years ago at New York University with Matilda White Riley. Members of the committee grilled him for about forty five minutes. It seemed like an eternity. One question was somewhat complicated pertaining to the multiple regression method which was to be Jack's primary method of analysis. It was the chairman who raised the question.

"Tell me Jack, how you would test for any evidence of heteroscedasticity?"

Jack responded quickly. "You can't really test for that. You would need to replicate your analysis for fixed values of your independent variables to determine if there is really any evidence of heteroscedasticity."

Professor Hauser was taken aback by Jack's reply. Finally, the hearing ended; and Jack was asked to step outside in the hallway while the committee deliberated. It took was only several minutes, but it seemed much longer. The door swung open, the committee emerged, and Professor Hauser gripped Jack's hand:

"Congratulations," he said emphatically. "You are now a PhD candidate!"

Jack took a deep breath and exhaled. The chairman continued:

"The first thing we need from you is a complete outline of your dissertation. You can submit it at your leisure."

Jack readily understood the professor's last comment. What he really meant was: "Do it as quickly as you can!" For if you dragged your feet or lingered, the committee could forget you. After the hearing, Joseph urged Jack to move swiftly on the dissertation advising him stay in touch with the committee frequently.

By the end of a week, Jack and his family returned home. Drastic changes were taking place in the capital and throughout the country. Resistance against the nation's involvement in the Vietnam War had been mounting, and the Johnson administration had become increasingly unpopular. A national election was impending, and President Johnson had already decided not to run for reelection.

It seemed likely that the country would have a new Republican president in November which would probably spell the beginning of the end for the War on Poverty. Indeed after Nixon was elected the Office of Economic Opportunity, which had been the spearhead in the War on Poverty programs, was eliminated. Later, the War on Poverty was completely terminated during President Reagan's administration. Many talented and able people were beginning to leave the federal government and more would follow. Jack had been working with two labor economists, one trained at Massachusetts Institute of Technology and the other at Harvard University who both left the U.S. Bureau of Labor Statistics for positions in academia. Even Jack's immediate supervisor, a PhD in sociology with considerable research skills, was departing. Many positions were being vacated at the Bureau of Labor Statistics, and there were few if any replacements. More importantly, Jack was informed by his new supervisor that he would not be allowed time on the job to work on his dissertation. Consequently, Jack contacted Joseph regarding his circumstances. Joseph had taught in the Business School of Roosevelt University in Chicago, and he knew the president of Roosevelt quite well. He offered to make inquiries to help Jack get a faculty position at Roosevelt. There was an opening at the Business School of Roosevelt University, and Joseph called Jack suggesting that he phone the dean of the business school about the vacancy. Subsequently, the dean invited Jack to fly into Chicago for an interview after which he was quickly offered the position. It was an ideal situation. Relocated in Chicago, Jack could better communicate with his dissertation committee; and he was granted a reduced teaching load giving him ample time to work on his dissertation. Fortunately, Jack and Hilda were able to sell their Maryland home quickly, and the family moved into a town house on the north side of Chicago just off Western Avenue close to an elementary school and a park with a children's playground.

As expected, it took a while to get resettled. Their daughter, Ellen had to be enrolled in the nearby public elementary school, and Jack had to prepare for his teaching at Roosevelt University. There was a small parking space behind their house which was part of a larger housing development. In addition, they were living only several blocks away from Lake Shore Drive. Roosevelt University was on Michigan Avenue in the Loop area a short distance off the Drive; and conveniently a faculty parking area was situated close to the university. All this facilitated Jack's trip to work.

Jack had been hired as an assistant professor in the Management Department of the Business School which comprised only four faculty members including himself. His first week at the university involved getting acquainted with departmental faculty and attending faculty orientation sessions. He sat in at a number of meetings with the dean of the business school, Robert Smith, a tall and heavyset man with an ambitious agenda for the business school. His major objectives were to promote research, teaching quality, and improve computer facilities which favorably impressed Jack. Although the Management Department was quite small, there were plans to hire additional faculty. During his first week at the university Jack met Kim who had also just joined the department and who was a graduate student at the University of Wisconsin, Madison working on a PhD dissertation in Industrial Relations. He was tall and muscular. His black hair was very short, and his face was smooth and oval shaped with features that were unmistakably Oriental. Originally he was from South Korea and had studied in Japan before immigrating to America. Jack and Kim soon became very close friends.

Dean Smith was very supportive in helping Jack and Kim complete their respective dissertations. Both men were assigned reduced teaching loads of only nine semester hours per week. In addition, they were allowed almost unlimited secretarial assistance. The dean's help, however, aroused resentment and envy among other business faculty. Another problem was that the university lacked adequate computer facilities. There was a computer, but it was outdated and essentially dysfunctional. Jack wished to introduce a new course into the curriculum entailing Fortran programming and analysis of U.S. Census of Population Data. The dean was very enthusiastic about the suggested course and provided Jack a budget so computer facilities would be available by students at a nearby corporation. This further aroused the ire of business faculty who appeared envious and resistant to such an innovation. But, more importantly, Jack needed access to a main frame computer in order to move ahead on his dissertation research. Although he was a registered student at the University of Chicago, he was denied free access to their computer systems. Again, Dean Smith was helpful. He contacted the vice president of Joseph T. Ryerson & Son, Inc. located on the Chicago West Side and set up an appointment for Jack to visit Ryerson's computer facilities. The company had, at one time, donated a building to the University of Chicago; and they granted Jack unlimited access to their facilities from after eight o' clock at night until six o' clock the following morning. Jack would often spend entire nights running his programs. The company kept their computers operating day and night, since shutting them down would have been more costly.

About a year after Jack had been teaching at Roosevelt, a problem arose in his computer course. A large number of students were uncooperative in learning Fortran, applying it to the analysis of population data, and preparing research reports. Jack felt he had no choice except to fail the students. After he submitted their failing grades, the students angrily assembled outside the dean's office. At the same time, a senior faculty member called on Jack. He was a fat man with a ruddy complexion. He stood in the doorway of Jack's office shaking his forefinger and uttering a reprimand:

"Jack!" he shouted, "You go upstairs to the registrar's office and change those grades! You can't fail all those students. We can't afford to lose them. That's money for the university."

Jack looked back at the fat man in disgust and replied defiantly, "You want them changed! Then you change them!"

Shortly, Dean Smith entered Jack's office.

"Jack, what's going on? I have a lot of students complaining about their grades. But if they deserve to fail, then I'll back you up all the way."

"They deserve to fail. They simply refused to complete their major course assignments, a research project."

"Okay, you're doing the right thing. Fail them."

It was gratifying that the dean supported Jack, and the incident was closed. But in trying to maintain academic integrity, Jack had placed himself in a precarious position regarding his future at Roosevelt University.

The Management Department faculty grew even more with the addition of Yasser, a PhD candidate at the Illinois Institute of Technology in Chicago. He was originally from Turkey, and in earlier years had taught at the University of Istanbul. Like Jack and Kim, he was granted a reduced teaching load to facilitate completion of his PhD dissertation. Yasser's specialties were Operations Research and Management Science which were critical teaching areas needing to be staffed.

It was the fall of 1969, and Jack's work on his dissertation was nearing completion. He had only the last chapter to write; and he learned that one member of his committee, Robert Hodge was leaving shortly to spend a year at Cambridge University in England. He immediately called his major professor, Philip Hauser for confirmation. The departing faculty member was a methodologist, as well as a demographer, and had considerable expertise in Jack's major statistical method of analysis. Professor Hauser encouragingly responded.

"Jack, can you submit the last chapter in another week? If you can, we can schedule your final hearing on Friday of next week."

"Yes," Jack replied.

It was Friday morning of the following week. Jack parked along East 60th Street near the Population Research Center. This was it: the final defense of his dissertation! He was ready! He entered the Center and walked up the stairs to Director Hauser's office. Inside the director and other members of the committee were waiting for him. They all sat down around a small table. Professor Hodge, the methodologist had a suitcase next to him, as he was on his way to the airport. There was a pot of coffee and cups on a table.

"Anybody like coffee?" asked the director as he filled his cup. Then he looked at his watch and added: "We'll wait a few more minutes. Maybe some faculty from the Economics Department will join us."

Oh, my God! Jack thought to himself. He was apprehensive, but then felt relieved when Professor Hauser addressed the group again: "Okay, let's get started."

It was surprising. The procedure was very informal. A few questions were asked and suggestions made. One suggestion was that Jack exclude a section of his dissertation dealing with the labor force participation rates of total males which the committee felt didn't add anything to Jack's research. After about twenty minutes they all rose. Each faculty congratulated Jack and shook his hand.

"Graduation will be in March, and before that there'll be some paper work for you to fill out at the department office," noted Hauser.

A few months later, Jack received some heartening news. A British academic journal had accepted his pilot study for publication. The editorial advisory board included prominent sociologists such as Professor Robert Merton of Columbia University, Talcott Parsons of Harvard University, and economist, Professor Boulding of the University of Michigan as well as affiliated faculty of the London School of Economics, London University. When he returned to Roosevelt, the dean and other faculty members congratulated him on finally earning his PhD. Jack's graduate date March 20, 1970 was nearing; and a few weeks earlier, he stopped at the Department of Sociology office to fill out forms required for his graduation. As he sat at a table perusing some paper work, he heard a voice from behind saying,

"What are you doing here?"

He looked up at a man who had just entered the office. It was Morris Janowitz currently Chairman of the Department of Sociology.

"I'm graduating. I've earned my degree," he replied staring back at the chairman. Janowitz said nothing. He simply scowled, turned, and walked away.

Jack didn't really want to attend the graduation ceremony. The awarding of the degree was bitter fruit. It had all been a grueling process. But Hilda kept on insisting that he attend. His mother and stepfather were flying in from Boston, and Hilda's aunt was arriving for the occasion. On graduation day they all squeezed into Jack's small Volkswagen Beetle, even the children. Jack's stepfather sat in front, three adults were in the back, William sat in Hilda's lap, and Ellen curled up in a small space behind the back seat. They were a spectacle as they rode along Lake Shore Drive. People in other cars shook their heads in disbelief. The graduation ceremony was held in Rockefeller Chapel. One by one the candidates walked across the stage to receive their degrees from the University President, Edward Levi. When it was Jack's turn, little William jumped to his feet and excitedly shouted:

"That's my dad!"

CHAPTER SIX:
CHICAGO DEPARTURE

The academic year was nearing an end when Dean Robert Smith called Jack, Kim, and Yasser to his office. His demeanor was somber, as he began to speak:

"You guys better sit down." He paused briefly shaking his head. "I'm going to leave Roosevelt this coming fall. I've been offered a dean's position at the business school at the University of Connecticut."

"Gosh!" Jack exclaimed. "We're going to miss you, Bob!"

Kim and Yasser were also surprised and looked doleful.

"I don't know what we're going to do without you." Kim responded sadly.

"Yes," Yasser spoke with a sigh.

"It's simply no use," the dean continued. "I've tried to promote changes here like encouraging research, getting new computer facilities, improving the library, but the faculty and the president have resisted. There's just too much dead wood here. I've had it." He stopped for a moment, cleared his throat and added a caveat: "You guys better get out of here as soon as you can. You'll never get promoted or get tenure. And be careful. Don't accept temporary appointments or become a utility man. There's a lot of that going on."

Jack and his colleagues looked bewildered. All three had finally earned their degrees, and Jack had even published. However, that wouldn't make any difference. With Dean Smith gone, the rest of the faculty would come after them. Slowly they walked out of the dean's office and along the hallway. Jack turned to Kim and Yasser:

"Let's go next door, have some coffee, and talk awhile," suggested Jack.

Outside on Michigan Avenue, they entered a restaurant which they frequented either for lunch or just coffee. Seated at a table, they ordered a pot of coffee and began to mull over their predicament.

"We'll be in for a fight next year." Kim asserted clenching his fist, his eyes narrowing.

"Coffee anyone?" asked Jack as he picked up the pot. Kim and Yasser nodded affirmatively and Jack filled the cups. Sipping his coffee, Jack said:

"We better take the dean's advice about finding a teaching position elsewhere."

"Yeah," Kim agreed, "I've already started applying to other places. The job market is very bad, but we have no other choice."

"In the meantime there are things that we can do," suggested Jack.

"Like what?" Yasser inquired, gulping his coffee.

"I've been in situations like this before: conflict situations in the army in Germany, trying to finish my PhD. When somebody pushes you, then it's time to push back and if needed hit hard!" Jack slammed his fist on the table. He had never believed in turning the other cheek. "We can sew discord, use a divide and conquer strategy. We'll keep the faculty busy going after each other so they stay off our backs. Maybe even involve the administration."

Kim broke into a broad smile and enthusiastically responded, "Yes, yes! We'll build fires! Pour gasoline here and there!" Of course, he didn't mean that literally.

During the summer months, the three men met, usually at Jack's home, discussing a strategy for the impending academic year. Jack did much of the talking and advising. The process of social conflict was very familiar to him through his experiences and studies in sociology. The conflict writings of Georg Simmel, Rolf Dahrendorf, and Lewis Coser fascinated him. When he lectured to his sociology students, he emphasized the applicability of conflict theory to real life situations. "Sociology is a living discipline!" he would tell his students: "Learn it, use it! Someday your welfare, even your life may depend on it!"

It was about this time that Jack learned a lot more about Kim, his background, aspirations, and apprehensions. It was Kim who introduced Jack to Korean food most of which Jack enjoyed eating except for the raw meat and raw egg. That he could not eat. He would offer the dish to Kim and say almost apologetically:

"You have to eat this, Kim. I can't." And Kim was accommodating.

Kim had an interesting background. His father had been a professor at Soul University in South Korea. During the Korean War he spent some time hiding in the basement of an apartment building when North Korean troops entered Soul. He could see them through a small window. Tanks would roll by and enemy infantry followed with assault weapons. Many of the soldiers looked like young teenagers, and they were firing at everyone in sight. When he was older, Kim attended a University of Tokyo and subsequently immigrated to America where he met his future wife at a small college in Illinois. He was very candid in expressing his feelings. On one occasion, he said to Jack:

"You know, sometimes I feel uncomfortable in America. I didn't know what it felt like being a minority until I came here."

Jack, of course, could readily empathize with him.

Jack also had a close relationship with Yasser. It involved not only Yasser but also Yasser's wife and their two children, a boy and a girl. The families visited each other often. Yasser's wife was a wonderful cook and introduced Jack and Hilda to some very tasty Turkish dishes. Although Jack and Yasser were very good friends, Yasser tended to be more reserved than Kim.

It was somewhat extraordinary. They were three men each from distant parts of the world: an American, a Korean, and a Turk and of different faiths: a Jew, a Christian, and a Muslim.

When the fall semester began at Roosevelt, there was an incident which literally drew Jack and Yasser closer together. Jack shared an office with another faculty, Fred who was much older than he and who had been at Roosevelt quite a few years. Jack had just returned to his office and could hear Fred swearing and appearing very irritated.

"What's your problem?" asked Jack.

"It's those damn Jew boys in Marketing!" He exclaimed.

"Well, Fred I happen to be one of those Jew boys!" Jack retorted loudly.

Fred was flabbergasted and began to stammer.

"But- but –I had no idea that you were-"

"Never mind!" Jack interrupted him. "I'm checking out! You can have this office to yourself!"

Jack picked up some notes and books on his desk; and placing them in a small flat case, he walked down the hallway to Yasser's office.

"Do you mind if I move in with you?" he asked Yasser who looked up from his desk in surprise. Jack explained what had happened, and Yasser readily understood and was sympathetic.

"It's okay, Jack. We've only the one desk, but we'll manage."

The fall semester was just starting. Dean Smith had departed from Roosevelt; and the chairman of the Marketing Department, Joe Silverman replaced Dean Smith as the acting dean. After Jack had moved in with Yasser, he explained the circumstances to the acting dean and asked if another desk could be placed in Yasser's office. But Joe felt it really wasn't necessary, as the business school faculty would be moving soon into new offices. The university business school had received a generous donation of millions of dollars from a wealthy alumnus, and the money was used to create lavish changes in the business school. The new offices were spacious, luxuriously carpeted, and filled with an assortment of expensive furniture. All this was considered essential in creating a more favorable impression on the Chicago business community. None of the donation was applied to securing viable computer facilities or improving the university library which remained in deplorable condition.

Course registration was nearing an end, and classes were about to start when Kim accosted Jack, as he had just completed a lecture and was leaving the classroom. Kim was wearing a mischievous smile.

"Hey, Jack. I just came from registration and poured some gasoline around."

"What did you do, Kim?"

"Oh, I just told some of the faculty working registration that certain other faculty were discouraging students from enrolling in their courses."

"Good work! That ought to light some fires," Jack chuckled.

Early in the fall semester, Dean Silverman requested that the Management Department faculty meet in his office to discuss the appointment of a new chairman for their department. Faculty members were seated around a large table, as the dean began to speak:

"Listen guys, I thought I should let you know that we're hiring a new faculty member to act as your departmental chair until you hold an election in the spring."

"Who is he?" Jack asked.

"His name is Herbert Kraus. From South Africa originally. He's had some administrative experience at one of the Illinois State Colleges."

"So you're bringing him in. Just like that. We don't get to interview him or provide any input." Kim spoke in a disapproving tone. It was customary for potential faculty hires to be questioned by a faculty selection committee which would then make binding recommendations.

"There's no time for that. In the past, Dean Smith ran your department. I don't want that responsibility," Dean Silverman replied, and looking directly at Kim he spoke in a deprecating tone:

"Kim, there have been some complaints about your teaching. You seem to have some communication problems. Maybe it has something to do with you being different, being from Korea."

At this point, Jack pushed his chair back, rose from the table, shook his forefinger at the dean and shouted: "Kim is an excellent teacher! I've even attended some of his classes! How can you begin to criticize him because of his background? You say he's different! You're a Jew, Joe! You know what it is to be different, and so do I! That's what this country is all about! Shame on you!"

The dean was speechless, his face reddened with embarrassment. Jack felt disgusted, turned, and left the office. Yasser and Kim followed him into the hallway. Kim drew close to Jack saying:

"I'll never forget what you just did. You're a real friend." And he added: "We need to get the hell out of here. But it's so difficult. I get one reject letter after another. At the end of the letters, they wish you good luck in your job hunt. It's very funny. I even get form letters with apologies because schools have had so many applicants for a single opening."

"I know", Jack replied. "But look, things are about as bad as they'll ever be. I think we've hit the bottom here. When we do move, the only direction we can go is up. That should be some consolation."

Kim grinned and laughed softly, responding, "I think you're right about that."

For over a year Jack has been receiving teacher opening position notices from the Office of Career Counseling and Placement Office of the University of Chicago; and, almost without exception, the notices expressed preferences for minorities particularly blacks, women, and Latinos. And many schools were constrained from hiring new faculty because of budget reductions, or in some cases only temporary appointments and one year appointments were offered. These circumstances made it more difficult for Jack to relocate.

Returning home one day, Jack found Hilda bursting with excitement:

"You had a call this afternoon from a Professor Lane at Wayne State University in Detroit! He wants you to call him back right away!" Hilda was almost breathless. Perhaps she was already envisaging a move to Detroit where her sister and other members of her family lived.

Jack immediately returned the call:

"Hello, Professor Lane. This is Jack Rubin."

"Oh, hello Dr. Rubin. Good to hear from you so quickly. Listen, we're in need of a demographer. You have a very impressive résumé."

"You have my résumé?" Jack replied surprised.

"Well, yes. Philip Hauser sent it to us. He recommended you very highly. Can you come here next week for an interview? Also can you present a research paper to the faculty?"

"Of course," answered Jack.

"Great. Let's see. How about booking a flight here on April 12, and we'll take care of your ticket."

"That sounds fine."

There were a few moments of silence before Professor Lane spoke again.

"By the way, do you happen to be black?"

What the hell difference does that make! Jack thought to himself. Almost reflexively, he answered in a resentful tone:

"No, I'm not. But I wish I were. In this job market black is beautiful."

Professor Lane's voice quivered, sounding somewhat nervous and apologetic.

"We're under a lot of pressure from the federal government to hire a black. This sheds a new light on things. Maybe I'll call you back tomorrow."

"Sure, I understand." Jack noted.

The conversation ended, and Jack reflected: What do I really understand? Perhaps this kind of thing is becoming widespread in education signaling the beginning of the end of the so called American Dream? Levels of competence and meritorious performance are to be displaced by background characteristics: race, gender, religion ethnicity reinforced by government's expanding role in higher education.

Another disquieting incident occurred when Jack unexpectedly received a phone call from the chairman of the Sociology

Department at Illinois State University in Decatur, Illinois. He didn't even remember applying for a position at the school. During the past year, he had sent out over forty applications.

The ensuing conversation was brief. The chairman was interested in having Jack visit the department for an interview.

"We can't pay for your traveling expenses. We're strapped financially. Maybe you could drive down here. It's not far from Chicago," he suggested. " Oh, one other thing. You have a very impressive résumé, but our department members might feel intimidated."

As far as Jack was concerned, the chairman's caveat was a red flag. He didn't want to encounter the potentiality of a conflict situation.

"In that case," he replied. " I don't think it's a good idea for me to come for an interview."

Then there were two other calls related to position openings. One came from Jersey State College in New Jersey and the other from Saint Cloud State University in Saint Cloud, Minnesota. They happened almost simultaneously. The one from New Jersey was from the head of a selection committee. He requested that Jack come for an interview for a "generalist" position, whatever that meant. Of course, Jack had a broad background in main stream sociology as well as demography. But the caller told Jack that he would have to pay for his own airline ticket, as the college had financial constraints. Despite this, Jack paid for his ticket and flew into Newark for the interview. He arrived a little early at the college in order to investigate the school's computer facilities and library. There were no computer facilities whatsoever, and the library was in deplorable condition. However, the beginning of the interview seemed favorable. He met two members of the committee: one with a PhD in anthropology from Columbia University, the other was finishing up his dissertation at Rutgers University. In addition, he briefly met the department chairman. But then the interview hit some snags when Jack spoke with the head of the selection committee. First, Jack indicated that the salary offered was unacceptable. It was less than what he was paid at Roosevelt.

"I can't bring my family here on the salary you're offering. We would have to live in a slum. I need at least a salary equivalent to my present one," Jack insisted.

"The salary is negotiable," the head replied and continued: "What courses would want to teach?"

"Statistics,population, research methods," Jack responded quickly.

"You can't teach statistics. I teach that course, and we already have someone teaching population."

When do faculty own the courses they teach? Jack thought

After returning home, he received a call from the head of the selection committee telling him that he would be paid a higher salary, but the offer would have to be made in person by the dean; and again Jack would have to pay for his airline ticket. All things considered, he declined the offer and continued negotiations with Saint Cloud State University. It was about this time, that he received a call from the editor of *Demography*, a publication of the Population Association of America first published at the University of Chicago. He was informed that a manuscript he had submitted several months ago had been accepted for publication. Oddly, the paper was based on research material which his dissertation committee wanted excluded from the final draft of his PhD dissertation.

Nick Angelo, Chairman of the Sociology, Anthropology, and Social Work Department at Saint Cloud State University telephoned Jack and offered him a position as assistant professor of sociology. But, for the first year it would be only a temporary appointment. Jack considered the salary acceptable, and he would be teaching desirable courses namely statistics, population, and research methods. However, he was not pleased with the other stipulations. He mentioned that he had a paper just accepted for publication in a leading academic journal which he felt should help qualify him for an associate professor appointment. Also, under no circumstances, would he move his family to Minnesota for a temporary teaching position. He felt it was too risky and insisted that the offer had to be a tenure track position.

"Okay, Jack," the chairman responded, "I sympathize with your concerns. Let me talk to our dean, and then I'll get back to you."

Within the hour, Nick Angelo called back:

"Jack, the dean agrees on a tenure track appointment. But he wants you to teach here at least one year before you're considered for a higher appointment. That's the best I could do."

"That'll be acceptable," Jack replied

"Good. I'll send out the contract and other information. By the way, when traveling up here look out for any Indians."

"Wooden Indians?"

The chairman chuckled.

It was only a few days before the contract with supplemental materials arrived. Jack signed the contract and mailed it forward. In the meantime, he had received a contract from Roosevelt University for the coming academic year. Despite the fact that he had completed his PhD and published, there was no salary increase. After a few weeks had passed, he received a phone call from the secretary in the university president's office.

"Jack, you haven't returned your contract. You better send it in right away or it will be void." Her tone was threatening.

"I've torched it," Jack replied.

"You what!"

"You heard me." Then he hung up.

In an almost ceremonial fashion, he had burned the contract in the backyard of his home.

Jack and Hilda put their town house up for sale, and the whole family drove up to Saint Cloud to find a new home. They purchased a house just a few blocks from the Mississippi River and only a mile from the university campus situated on the opposite banks of the river. Returning to Chicago, they were able to sell to sell their town house in the short time left before Jack was to begin teaching. They did attend Edward's wedding performed in the backyard of his home on the north side of the city. Edward had been teaching in the Chicago City College system and was marrying one of his former students. Edward told Jack: "Marriage seemed to work for you, so I thought I would give it a try." Before departing the city, Jack paid farewell to both Kim and Yasser:

"I'll miss you guys. Take care, and let's try to stay in touch with each other."

It was not easy for Jack to leave Chicago. He loved the city which was like a second home to him. It was here that he met his future wife. He believed his teachers at the University of Chicago were the greatest he had ever known. Although they were pressured to conduct research and publish, they were always diligent in fulfilling their teaching responsibilities and sharing their wisdom and knowledge with students. It had been a long and difficult road to the PhD, but he had managed to make it. Others, perhaps more gifted than he, had relented. But Jack had been indefatigable and had no misgivings. Throughout the years of his Chicago experience, he met many interesting people. With a few he forged friendships; some short- lived others more enduring. Regrettably his relationship with Joseph ended. He had been a good friend and helped Jack in times of need. Jack could never fully understand why their friendship ended. Perhaps a contributing factor was Joseph's pompous and controlling personality, which Jack sometimes found intolerable.

It was a clear sunny day when Jack and his family headed north on the expressway toward Wisconsin. Within a few hours they were traveling westward nearing Madison about halfway to the Minnesota state line. For a few hours more they drove through hilly and thickly forested country and to the Saint Croix River and into the Land of Ten Thousand Lakes. Then crossing the Mississippi River, separating Saint Paul and Minneapolis and bypassing the Twin Cities, they were on a highway leading to Saint Cloud. A light breeze caressed the many trees, bushes, and lakes visible along the highway It took slightly more than an hour to reach Saint Cloud where they registered at a motel for the night. The next day, their belongings were delivered to their new home. Moving in was hectic, and it was nearly two weeks before they were resettled. By then, Jack's classes were about to begin. It was only about a mile from Jack's home, across the bridge spanning the Mississippi, to Stewart Hall where the Sociology Anthropology, and Social work Department, and most other social science departments, were located. At the first department meeting, Jack met most of the faculty comprising ten sociologists including himself, three anthropologists, and four social workers. His classes, except for an Introductory Sociology course, were small usually averaging fifteen to twenty students.

One morning, after several weeks of teaching, Jack found a note scrawled on a sheet of paper taped to his office door. It read: "Dr. Rubin demands University of Chicago standards of performance from his students." Jack smiled and removed the note thinking it probably came from some student in his statistics classes suffering anxieties which he had once experienced himself when a graduate student in Chicago. A few days later, as Jack sat at his desk with his office door open, a short, plump, and dark skinned man stopped and stood in the doorway gazing at Jack.

"I saw the note on your door, and really wanted to meet you," the man said smiling and added: "I thought somebody is doing things right here. I'm Hashim, a professor in the History Department."

"Come in, come in," Jack responded, waving Hashim into his office. The two men shook hands, sat, and talked for some time. Hashim was originally from Iraq and had a PhD in history from the University of Wisconsin at Madison with a specialty in the history of the Middle East. In the days that followed he and Jack spent many hours together conversing while eating their lunches, usually consisting of sandwiches and fruit, which they had brought in brown bags from home. At lunchtime Jack would stroll down the hall to Hashim's office; and they would invariably discuss issues related to the Middle East, especially the ongoing conflict between the Israelis and Palestinians. Although they differed in their opinions concerning the conflict, they often agreed to disagree and both hoped that someday there be a better understanding and peace between Israelis and Palestinians. Hashim was very well informed. His knowledge of the history and different cultures of the Middle East and his scholarly publications were impressive. Despite his training and achievements, he was treated shabbily by the History Department. They even frustrated him from teaching his specialty. In fact the department even hired another faculty, much less qualified than Hashim, to teach courses in Middle East history. Hashim disclosed that his department chairman fraudulently claimed a scholarly publication. Although he informed the dean and the university vice president of the deception and even presented supporting evidence, the matter was ignored by the administration. Hashim customarily left his office door open whenever he and Jack were together. Other history faculty members would sometimes pass by and curiously peer in at the two men eating their lunches and conversing. One day, an odd and surprising incident occurred. Jack was at his desk studying some lecture notes when a member of the History Department faculty stopped in front of his office doorway:

"Hi, Jack. How are things going?" she asked.

It was Marianne. Jack didn't know her too well. He had encountered her a few times at faculty gourmet meetings.

He looked up from his notes.

"I'm okay. How about you?"

"All right. But there's something I don't understand."

"What is it?"

"Well," she continued, "how can you spend so much time with Hashim? He's an Arab, sympathetic to Palestinians. You're Jewish, and he dislikes Jews."

Jack rose from his desk and gaped at her. Is this woman for real and an educator? he wondered.

"Listen, Hashim has nothing against Jews. He knows more about their history and Judaism than I'll ever know. We do have some disagreements but only on political issues."

Marianne simply shrugged her shoulders, looked puzzled, and walked away.

Jack's department met about every few weeks. Sometimes the meetings lasted as long as two hours, and much of the discourse was simply rhetoric. The faculty sat around a large square table; and Nick, being the chairman, guided the discussions that dwelt more on cosmetic rather than real substantive matters. Generally there was a preoccupation with the size of class enrollments, and suggestions would be made as to what gimmicks could be implemented to attract larger numbers of students. At one point, Jack became so irked that he suggested that the faculty exhume bodies from the local cemeteries and prop them up in the classrooms to increase enrollments. A few of the faculty laughed; but nobody, of course, took his suggestion seriously. As far as Jack knew, very few of the faculty were engaged in any research. References to any ongoing research were almost never brought up at the departmental meetings. It was as if it were a taboo subject. Jack thought it strange; and on one or more occasions, he mentioned his concern to Nick who brushed it off, saying:

"Jack, we're a teaching institution. Research is for the bigger universities not for us. We're not Harvard on the Mississippi."

But this made no sense to Jack. After all, didn't teaching and research complement each other? How do you separate them? Periodically, teaching materials need to be revised in view of new information arising in one's discipline. But Jack's opining fell on deaf ears, At least Nick never interfered with Jack's research interests and activities.

During that first semester, Jack had another visitor to his office: a tall, slender fellow with sharp features who suddenly appeared in the hallway outside his office doorway and spoke in a friendly manner:

"Hi, I heard you just came here from Chicago. I just arrived from there, too. The name is Mike, Mike Lusky. I'm in the Economics Department, next door in Lawrence Hall. But we'll be moving over here soon to Stewart Hall."

Mike spent a while seated in Jack's office. They chatted for some time about Chicago. Mike had grown up in the city and earned his PhD at Loyola University on the far north side close to Evanston. After their meeting, Jack visited Mike occasionally at his office in Lawrence Hall; and later after the Economics Department moved over to Stewart Hall and relocated up a flight of stairs from Jack's office. Subsequently, he visited the Economics Department more frequently and met a number of their faculty busily engaged in quantitative research. If he had questions of an analytical or statistical nature, he could easily consult with them. This was not possible with the sociologists who either lacked interest in research matters or had little, if any, training in statistical methods and population or demography. Jack and Mike even collaborated on research entailing a multiple regression analysis of crime rates in U.S. metropolitan areas and presented results of their research at meetings of the Iowa Academy of Science at Iowa State University. Later Jack presented a revised version of their study at meetings of the Criminal Justice Statistics Association in Boston.

During Jack's early years at Saint Cloud State University, certain events transpired which were of either national or international significance. First there was the Watergate scandal which rocked the nation and led to the threat of an impeachment of the U.S. President. It began with five men burglarizing the Democratic National Committee headquarters at the Watergate complex on June 17, 1972. About a year later the evidence grew implicating top advisors to the president as well as the president himself. Facing almost certain impeachment and a strong possibility of conviction, President Nixon resigned the presidency on August 9, 1974. By April 1975 the war in Vietnam came to an end. North Vietnam and South Vietnam became one nation. Groupthink had been the norm guiding America's growing intervention in the Vietnamese war. Our policies and participation had been based upon the false premises of the so called "domino theory". Although these two events had an impact nationally they did not seem to create much of a stir on the Saint Cloud State University campus. But the Roe versus Wade decision by the United States Supreme Court seemed to arouse considerable interest especially among the social workers in Jack's department. In brief the Roe versus Wade decision challenged many state and federal restrictions on abortion in the United States.

Jack was seated in his office working on his personal computer when there was a knock on the door.

"Come in," he said.

The door slowly opened. It was one of his students, a heavyset woman probably in her late twenties or thirties. Jack recognized her. She was a social work major in his Social Science Research Methods class, and appeared very distressed. Her eyes were slightly bloodshot, and her face was moist with tears.

Jack rose quickly and motioned to the student:"Sit down. What is it? You've been crying."

"Dr. Rubin," she spoke in a halting voice, "I'm a devout Catholic and have strong feelings against abortion."

"I understand," Jack responded." You certainly have a right to feel that way. So what is the problem?"

By this time she had completely regained her composure and resumed talking."Well, you know I'm a Social Work major. The Social Work faculty strongly advocate a pro-choice position on abortion, and they've warned me that I will not be able to complete my major unless I change my views on abortion."

Jack squinted and shook his head: "This is outrageous!" he exclaimed. "If there's anything I can do to help you, please let me know!"

"Thank you, Dr. Rubin. I've already turned the matter over to an attorney, so maybe they'll back off."

"Sounds like the right way to go. Let me know how it works out."

Unfortunately this was not an isolated incident where faculty members were attempting to indoctrinate rather than teach. A number of students visited Jack's office with similar grievances. One student, attending a class in Introductory Sociology, angrily declared that he would never take another sociology course again. He said that the instructor was constantly expressing admiration for Castro and the Communist regime in Cuba. Another complained that he was in a Human Relations class where the instructor was promoting practices of homosexuality. These were just a few examples of indoctrination displacing teaching.

Toward the end of 1975, Jack was informed that a research paper he had submitted to present at the 1976 annual meetings of the Population Association of America had been accepted. The meetings were to be held in Montreal, Canada. It was an achievement, but his department refused to allocate him any travel money despite the fact that every year each department was allowed a budget for faculty to attend or participate in professional meetings. Nick claimed that the budget was depleted but did suggest that Jack ask the dean for funds. When Jack showed the dean the program of the meetings with the inclusion of a research paper from Saint Cloud State University, he was very pleased

"This is great Jack! We'll take care of your expenses."

At one department meeting, Jack was convinced that educational standards were further reduced when a motion was introduced to eliminate the advanced statistics course as a requirement for sociology majors. He was teaching the course and vehemently opposed the motion, contending that the move was in the direction of lowering academic standards and reducing skill levels students needed in future employment or career advancement. Those supporting the motion argued that students felt that a requirement of two statistics courses was unreasonable or too demanding, and that in many other undergraduate sociology programs only one statistic course was required. When the faculty finally voted on the motion, the course was eliminated as a requirement. Increasingly students were beginning to exercise control over the curriculum. Jack's two population courses, Introduction to Population and World Population Problems were offered much less often because of their low enrollments. Someone suggested if the word "Population" could be changed to "Copulation" then enrollments would skyrocket. Then there was a course, the Sociology of the Occult which drew huge numbers of students. Additional chairs were brought into the classroom or more sections were added to accommodate the overflow of students. When the instructor entered her classroom she dressed in black and puffed away on cigarillos. A wide brim black hat and broomstick would have made her appearance more complete. After a few years, she left the department and accepted a position at one of the California State Universities reputed to be on the cutting edge of changes occurring in higher education. Nick asked if anyone would teach her course, but no one volunteered. It was about this time that Jack received a call from Kim who had joined the Management Department at Fullerton State University in Fullerton, California. They had a lengthy conversation, and Kim mentioned a higher education innovation becoming increasingly popular in California. There was a proliferation of training programs for teachers emphasizing facilitation in the classroom rather than instruction. The goal was to highlight student experiences, exchanges, and self-gratification. Form rather than substance and impression management were being stressed. Above all, teachers were expected to learn to ingratiate themselves to their students. One effective gimmick, of course, was a good sense of humor.

Grade inflation was rampant not only in Jack's department but in other university departments as well. He had sometimes seen some of the final grading sheets of faculty where all students were assigned grades of A or B. It was also rumored that a professor in the History Department, referred to as "Professor AB", routinely gave only final grades of A and B. According to the grapevine, he graded a student an A if he or she simply attended classes and took all required tests; otherwise a student would automatically receive a B. Grade inflation was also reflected in the form of social passes in the public schools of Saint Cloud. At times Jack and Hilda attended gourmet groups held at the homes of faculty members who would act as a host or hostess. These were potluck affairs where participants would bring various dishes to share, and it afforded opportunities for faculty and wives to socialize with one another. Many of the wives were teaching in the Saint Cloud public school system, and Jack got into impassioned arguments with some of them who ardently supported the practice of social passes. They adamantly believed that prohibiting failing children from being promoted to a higher grade stigmatized them and seriously damaged their sense of self-esteem. The teachers were strongly opposed to academic competitiveness or extending special recognition to outstanding performing students. Their rationale or justification was that such practices would be demeaning to other students. Jack was dismayed by their comments but calmly expressed contrary views.

"Ladies, we live in a competitive society. If you pass your students to a higher grade when they are failing, they'll be ill prepared and disadvantaged in later endeavors. You are sending the same message when you don't encourage and reward achievement. In either case you help to promote incompetence and a dysfunctional society."

But the teachers were impervious to Jack's words and persisted to disagree with him. On one occasion, he and Hilda visited one of their daughter's teachers regarding the paucity of assigned homework. which they felt reflected low academic standards. The teacher responded, saying:

"It's a matter of policies in the public schools. We're pressured not to overburden the students. But I wish more parents would complain then maybe something would be done about it."

It seemed to Jack that such policies facilitated serious repercussions in higher education. Surely one does not build a house from the roof down; you begin with the foundation. Colleges and universities have sometimes tried remedial education programs to cope with deficiencies in basic writing and reading skills of students, but these skills needed to be developed at the lower levels of education institutions with parents playing constructive and influential roles.

Winters were extremely cold in Saint Cloud. By December Arctic air masses were moving south with temperatures falling far below the freezing point. Howling winds, contributing to lower wind chills, made the cold even more intolerable. Ice steadily formed on the many nearby lakes and the narrow stretches of the Mississippi River behind the university campus. Heavy snow began falling with layers accumulating several feet or higher. One winter the snow was so deep that Jack was able to climb up banks of snow that sloped down from the roof of his house, and both Ellen and William enjoyed sledding down from the roof of the garage and on to the driveway.

Jack shunned the bitter cold and had no affinity for outside winter activities such as cross country skiing or ice fishing: popular winter pastimes among Minnesota residents. But he felt a growing need to engage in some kind of exercise.

He started to thumb through the yellow pages of the local phone directory and under the martial arts heading he found a listing for "Shotokan Karate": traditional Japanese karate. He recalled that during his boyhood years he had a friend who took lessons in jujitsu. It had fascinated him, and he desired to pursue some form of martial arts, but an overprotective mother restrained him. He visited the karate dojo or training hall, in the downtown area. to observe a class and subsequently enrolled and began training. The word, karate translates as "empty hands", and its origins are somewhat obscure. However, it is believed that Japanese karate may have evolved from Chinese martial arts such as kick boxing, first engaged in by Buddhist monks for physical exercise and self-spiritual development. At the time of the reign of Napoleon, an art of defense known as karate became popular among the people of the Ryukyu Islands later referred to as Okinawa. Prohibited by law from bearing arms, they engaged in a form of self-defense with their hands and legs as their only weapons. For many years in Japan it was generally practiced only behind Buddhist temple walls and later by the samurai. Gichin Funakoshi was known as the father of modern day Japanese karate especially Shotokan which was the name given to the first karate dojo ever erected in Japan. It was also the pen name that Funakoshi used when writing Chinese poems in his youth. Later karate would have a deeper meaning for Jack. He would come to know the karate way as a faith and way of life.

It was midwinter in the 1970's when Jack received a phone call from Kim telling him that there was a position opening in the Management Department of California State University at Fullerton. If Jack were interested in applying for the position, Kim could make the necessary arrangements for an interview, and travel costs would be taken care of by Kim's department. Jack reacted positively and took a flight into Los Angeles and joined Kim and his wife Helga at their home near Fullerton. They spent an enjoyable evening reminiscing, and the following morning the interviewing began with a meeting with the dean of the business school with whom Jack had excellent rapport. But during the day he clashed with a few of the faculty. That evening at a dinner, one of the management department faculty had drank wine rather freely and spoke to Jack in a hushed voice:

"Jack, I really like you. Your credentials are impressive. It's not fair. The department turned you down because of your background."

Jack knew what that meant, and he responded:

"I understand, and it's okay. I have a position back in Minnesota."

Later Kim told Jack that he had inadvertently mentioned to a faculty member that Jack was Jewish, and it was only afterwards that he learned there was some feeling in the department against Jews.

"Perhaps it's good you mentioned it," Helga remarked. "If Jack had been hired, it would've been learned sooner or later. Then he and his family might have become castaways on the beaches of California."

Jack smiled and nodded in agreement.

"Thanks for everything. Let's stay in touch."

He said farewell and returned to Minnesota. Sometime later Kim informed Jack that a new faculty member had been hired in his department: a fresh PhD out of the University of Michigan and someone with a number of academic publications. But when it was discovered that he was Jewish, the faculty planned to terminate him.

"I was outraged," Kim told Jack. "I went to see a business school dean at a nearby university, and fortunately the school hired him."

"That was very kind of you, Kim. By the way, I compliment your wife for her insight. Your letting people know I was Jewish was a good idea. If I had been hired, your faculty would have eventually found out, and I probably would have been terminated, too."

For some time Jack and Hilda had been considering leaving Saint Cloud and moving to one of the western suburbs of Minneapolis. Neither of them were content living in a small and rather parochial community like Saint Cloud. They felt the style of life was somewhat stifling; moving from Chicago they experienced what might be called "culture shock". And there were other issues or problems. A drug culture appeared to be prevalent in Saint Cloud which the community seemed to either deny or ignore. Also, the academic quality of the public school system seemed to be steadily declining. Several faculty members were already living in the Twin Cities and commuting to Saint Cloud, and Jack found he could easily join their car pool. All these circumstances disposed them to sell their Saint Cloud home and build a new one in the Minneapolis suburb of Minnetonka.

Shortly before moving from Saint Cloud, Jack received an unexpected phone call from Yasser his Turkish friend who was leaving Roosevelt University and Chicago. Yasser was already on the road with his family and planning to visit Jack and Hilda. Jack was pleased to see an old friend but regretted his unhappy circumstances. Roosevelt University had refused Yasser tenure and had terminated him.

"How did it happen?" Jack asked him.

"It was a setup. The Chairman of the Management Department, Ralph encouraged me to apply for a sabbatical; but I really wasn't eligible for the leave and didn't realize it. Anyway it was grounds for my termination."

"Where do you go from here, Yasser?"

"We're returning to Istanbul. I can get my old teaching job back."

Yasser and his family remained in Saint Cloud a few days before departing. That was the last time Jack saw his friend. Years later when Jack visited his daughter and her husband on the island of Crete, he tried to contact Yasser but was unsuccessful.

A number of sociologists had left Jack's department. One had retired and three others had found teaching positions elsewhere. There was a need to hire at least one replacement, and Nick asked Jack if he would serve on a selection committee. He reluctantly agreed for he had tried to limit his participation on committees feeling that it might lead to disagreements or controversies with other faculty and detract from his teaching responsibilities and research activities. The selection committee was composed of four faculty including Jack, another sociologist, one anthropologist, and a social worker. The department chairperson supposedly functioned independently and sat in at the committee meetings. At the first meeting Nick pointed out that the faculty needed to elect a committee head who would have quite a bit of discretion in the choice made of candidates invited to departmental interviews. Although Jack was elected, he declined; and the other sociologist, Wendy also refused to serve as committee head. Lena, the social worker leaped into the breach eagerly agreeing to act as the committee head. Jack's refusal to accept the position was a mistake that he would later regret. Lena was incompetent, and she and Jack were destined to clash. The committee examined the résumés of several applicants. Jack was most impressed with the credentials of one applicant who had a PhD from Southern Illinois University and several professional publications. But Nick had some apprehensions concerning the candidate since there were already two other recently hired sociologists who had earned doctorates at the Southern Illinois, and all three had known each other as graduate students. However, he was willing to consider the applicant, George Romano especially since he was an Italian American. As Wendy, the other sociologist, remarked:

"How could Nick Angelo turn down a good Italian boy?"

Throughout the committee's discussion of applicants, Lena strongly favored a very mediocre candidate and resorted to some disingenuous tactics to prevent Romano from being invited to an interview. But Jack exposed her tactics; and consequently the committee and the chairperson overruled her. She was quite upset with Jack and would inflict her revenge years later. Lena's choice was the first candidate to be interviewed, and he was questioned by the entire department. His answers to questions were clearly inadequate. Also, he claimed his dissertation as his sole publication; and when asked who published it, he stated, "I published it myself."

"This is ridiculous!" one of the sociologists scoffed.

Lena squirmed in her seat appearing uneasy.

In contrast, George Romano's performance at the interview was impressive. Nick spent some time talking with him privately, and Jack was pleased when he was subsequently hired. Both were to become very good friends and supportive of one another.

Far away momentous events were developing in the Middle East. In 1970 Anwar Sadat succeeded Nasser as president of Egypt; and in 1973 Sadat launched a surprise attack, with the assistance of Syria, against Israel in an effort to recover Sinai and the Golan Heights seized by Israel during the 1967 six day war. The war became known as the Yom Kippur or Ramadan War. Initially Egyptian forces were successful in being able to penetrate several miles into the Sinai Peninsula. But the Israelis counter attacked, crossed the Suez Canal, and advanced toward Damascus. At that point, the United Nations Security Council called for an immediate cease fire, and the war ended shortly thereafter. In 1977 Sadat was the first Arab leader to visit Israel officially where he met with the Israeli Prime Minister Menachem Begin and addressed the Knesset, the Israeli Parliament, expressing his hopes for peace. With the assistance of U.S. President Jimmy Carter, a peace treaty was finally signed between Anwar Sadat and Menachem Begin in March 26, 1979. Both leaders were awarded the Nobel Peace Prize. Sadat's acceptance speech was memorable:

Let us put an end to wars, let us reshape life on the solid basis of equity and truth. And it is this call, which reflected the will of the Egyptian people, of the great majority of the Arab and Israeli peoples, and indeed of millions of men, women, and children around the world that you are honoring. And these hundreds of millions will judge to what extent every responsible leader in the Middle East has responded to the hopes of mankind.

Both sides made concessions. Israel agreed to withdraw from the Sinai Peninsula and was granted free passage through the Suez Canal. In addition, the Strait of Tiran and the Gulf of Aqaba were recognized as international waterways. Perhaps most important was the mutual recognition of each country by the other. Sometimes a good fight is needed to clear the air and for adversaries to achieve respect for one another. Tragically, Anwar Sadat was assassinated on October 6, 1981.

When Jack had been much younger and more naïve, he questioned the need of a Jewish national state. He thought that Judaism was just a religion not a nationality and believed that Jews and Arabs or Muslims could live peacefully together in a secular state. After all, they sprang from the same tree, the sons of Abraham. However, later he realized that historical circumstances dictated otherwise. For thousands of years the Jews had been pariahs driven from one nation to another, yearning for freedom, and a return to their ancient homeland Israel. Finally came the horror of the Holocaust, the birth of the state of Israel, and the resounding cry: "Never again!" And Jack realized how can there really be peace as long as there are those who insist Israel does not have the right to exist? Isn't this the nub of the problem? Let there be a mutual recognition of two states: Israel and Palestine as mandated by the United Nations in 1948, and then perhaps there will eventually be peace between the sons of Abraham.

During the 1980's the faculty at Saint Cloud became part of the Minnesota Education Association. Many educators felt that collective bargaining was essential in dealing with either the university administration or politicians in Saint Paul. The principal function of university administrators was supposed to "to help or assist", but too often their actions obstructed and frustrated the efforts of faculty. This may have been largely due to a lack of understanding or misunderstandings on the part of both parties and to systemic factors contributing to divergent and conflicting agendas and goals. Similar circumstances may have contributed to the hiatus between faculty and state legislators. It was felt that only through a union and collective action could the faculty clear the air and effectively present its case to university administrators and state legislators. Each year or every few years a new contract was drawn up binding all parties: faculty, administrators, and the state to specific regulations and conditions. One stipulation of the contract was that the tenure of department chairpersons was to be limited to two terms or a total of six years. This meant that Nick had to step down as head of the Department of Sociology, Anthropology, and Social Work and return to full time teaching. He had been the chairperson for nearly twenty years and had done a pretty good job; but relinquishing the role proved to be a traumatic experience for him. Somehow he was unable to reconcile himself to the realties of the situation. He had just been too immersed in his position as chairman. It appeared to be a case of what sociologists might call: "role engulfment". Jack recalled a similar situation where one of his cousins had divorced her husband, a neurosurgeon. When he questioned her regarding the divorce, she complained that her husband had constantly treated her like one of his nurses. Also, this phenomenon was perhaps depicted vividly well in a play titled: *The Death of a Salesman*. At various times, Nick was observed by other faculty wandering aimlessly about the hallways muttering to himself. There would be an election soon for a new chairperson, and Nick was favoring a particular faculty member, Jenny who had been in the department about as long as Nick. However, Jack was supporting a younger and newer faculty member, John Kearney who appeared to be more enthusiastic about encouraging greater emphasis on research and the development of a graduate program in sociology. This put Jack on a collision course with Nick. The first indication of a conflict came one day when Nick called Jack into his office. Their private offices were practically next door to each other separated only by the regular department office where the secretary, Josephine performed her chores.

"Sit down, Jack. I want to talk to you."

"Okay, what's going on Nick?"

"Listen, I'm backing Jenny to take over the department and run things. Why aren't you cooperating?"

"Nick, I like Jenny. She's competent enough. I just feel that Kearney would do a better job. I 'd like to see change, growth in the department."

"I know, Jack. But we're not a big university."

Jack smiled and shook his head. "I know that, Nick."

Nick paused for a few moments before continuing. "There's another thing."

"What's that?" Jack asked.

"There have been certain reports about your teaching, that you may be sexually harassing students. There's been some talk coming from the dean. Better watch yourself, Jack. The jury is still out."

Jack grew angry, shot up from his chair, and pointed his forefinger at Nick. "What are you talking about? What reports? Are you making this stuff up?" He turned and walked out of the chairman's office slamming the door behind him. Leaving Stewart Hall he walked briskly to Dean Walker's office where he related Nick's accusations. At first the dean was nonplussed, but then responded firmly and unhesitatingly:

"Jack, I have no idea what Nick is talking about. There's been no complaints about your teaching or behavior in relation to students. As far as I'm concerned, you've been doing a great job."

Something is going on, Jack mused. He needed to become more guarded.

It was spring 1985, and the semester was nearing an end. Jack had been teaching a course in Urban Sociology, and the text book he was using had been written by a very prominent sociologist and human ecologist. During one of his lectures, a student raised her hand to ask a question. "Doctor Rubin, why do you constantly refer to cities and land as she or her? Land is exploited or used. I'm from the Human Relations Department. You know you could get into trouble talking like that."

It's here, Jack reflected we're into the era of Political Correctness. The Human Relations Department was a big advocate of this ideology which was becoming more widespread. Responding Jack smiled saying: "You may have a point. But let me get back to you on this at our next class meeting." A few days later, Jack started his lecture by addressing the student's question:

"Sally," he began, "I've given your comment some thought. First of all, the author of our textbook continually refers to land and cities in the feminine gender. But more importantly, let me point out that land can be viewed from a very positive perspective. Doesn't the term Mother Nature have positive connotations? Doesn't land use yield bountiful harvests?"

The student was flabbergasted. She could only say, "Yes, Doctor Rubin. You're right. I hadn't thought of it that way."

There was another student in this class who seemed to be especially preoccupied with her final grade. "Am I going to get a B grade in your course?" she would often ask Jack.

He simply replied: "Certainly, if you earn it."

The semester had ended, and Jack submitted all of his grades. His office door was wide open, as he pondered some written materials. The faculty had been advised to leave their office doors open, especially when students were present. There were a number of cases being processed by the affirmative action officer involving student charges of sexual harassment. Faculty had to be wary. George Romano had already told Jack about a female student visiting his office dressed in a very low cut blouse. Sitting close to him she would recurrently lean over toward George providing an almost full exposure of her breasts. Outside of Jack's office the secretary, Josephine was chatting with a few social work students. Suddenly, a student confronted Jack. It was Connie who had been so concerned about her grade in Urban Sociology. She had wanted a "B" but had received a "C" grade. Her face was red with anger, and she began shouting at Jack.

"You promised me a B in Urban Sociology!"

"I never promised any such thing," Jack retorted. "Listen, if you wish I'll review your final exam."

"No! Never mind!" she growled. "I don't like the way you grade!"

"Grading is my responsibility, not yours," Jack replied.

Connie grimaced and stormed out of Jack's office in full view of the secretary and the few social work students standing nearby. As far as Jack knew, the incident was closed. But some weeks later, he received a telephone call from Lenore, the university's affirmative action officer.

"Jack, this is Lenore."

"Yes, Lenore. What is it?"

"Well, there's a student who's filing a sexual harassment charge against you. Do you know anyone who might hold a grudge against you?"

Jack was quiet, thinking for a few moments. "I can't think of any one, Lenore. This sounds crazy. What are the details?"

"I'll send the written charges over to you, and the State of Minnesota guidelines for this sort of thing. Of course there will have to be a hearing."

"I understand."

Within a few days Jack received the materials in the campus mail. It was incredible! The student accusing Jack of sexual harassment was Connie, the social work major who had been so disgruntled about her grade in Urban Sociology. She charged that he had made comments about her appearance such as: "What a nice tan you have," and "that he made a point of standing outside his classroom before class so as to accost her." Jack remembered he had once made a remark about the student spending a lot of time in the sun and that he hoped she spent as much time preparing for her exams. Moreover, it was habitual for him to stand outside his classrooms and greet incoming students. His accuser had taken these incidents out of context and distorted the facts. It was clearly a case of character assassination. Also disturbing were the State of Minnesota guidelines for processing sexual harassment cases. Charges of sexual harassment were made in "the eyes of the beholder" or accuser. Jack recalled his earlier encounter with Nick and suspected that he was involved and that there was a great deal more to this than just the student's anger concerning her grade. It was just the start of summer, and the sexual harassment hearings would not begin until September. In the meantime, there was news that Nick had collapsed and died from a massive stroke attack while on vacation in Italy. Funeral services were held in Saint Cloud which Jack did not attend. He had lost all respect for Nick and was preoccupied preparing for the impending hearings. He even questioned the secretary, Josephine and the students who had been present when Connie had burst into his office in a tirade. They all shook their heads and denied hearing or witnessing anything. But they had sat or stood only a few feet away from the open door to Jack 's office when the student was shouting at Jack. This was going to be a long fight, but he had fought battles many years before as a boy against lies and bigotry and engaged in conflicts later in the military in Germany and in Chicago. He would be ready in September. But now he would leave all this behind and visit his daughter, Ellen and her husband, George on the island of Crete. She had been married for over a year. George was an officer in U.S. Air Force Intelligence and expected to be stationed on Crete for another year or two. Ellen was attending classes at a University of Maryland extension on the island and made arrangements with her instructor for Jack to deliver a lecture in her class. This enabled Jack to receive compensation from Saint Cloud State for the cost of his airline ticket. He was looking forward to this interlude, a trip to an ancient civilization and away from the stress and turmoil of Saint Cloud.

CHAPTER SEVEN:
CONFLICT AND RESOLUTION

Throughout the 1970's and 1980's, there had been numerous hijackings of airline flights. Ronald Reagan, serving his second term as President of the United States, had recurrently issued caveats to American travelers especially those flying abroad and in the Middle East. Jack was somewhat apprehensive, as he hugged and kissed Hilda and William farewell at the Minneapolis- Saint Paul International airport. It was early evening, and the plane took off as scheduled, nonstop to London, England. Nearly twelve hours later, the plane alighted at Heathrow Airport. Jack hurried to a waiting bus which would take him to Gatwick Airport and his connecting flight to Athens, Greece. The ride to Gatwick was about an hour. It was relaxing, and he dozed intermittently. As he stepped off the bus, an English lady waved her arm in the air clasping something and shouting,

"Sir! I say, you left your wallet behind!"

"Oh! Thank you! Thank you so much!" Jack shouted, retrieving his wallet. It had probably slipped out of his back pocket while he was dozing. That was careless of him. Carefully he placed the wallet more securely in one of his front pockets and hurried on to his waiting flight to Athens. The plane's engines roared; and shortly the aircraft accelerated and was airborne. After a while, a hot lunch was served. Jack was hungry. He had not eaten since leaving Minneapolis. A few hours had passed when the pilot announced that they were approaching Athens and requested that all passengers fasten their seat belts. Jack had been chatting with a father and daughter from Canada who were planning to visit family in Athens. As the plane began its descent, the father of the girl sensed that Jack was becoming apprehensive.

"Listen," he said to Jack. "My daughter speaks Greek. She can help you through customs."

Jack felt some relief. "Thanks, I really appreciate that."

All passengers filed off the plane. Soldiers with assault weapons were patrolling throughout the airport, and didn't appear too friendly. The country had been vulnerable to terrorist attacks and had become increasingly concerned about its effects on tourism, one of the nation's major industries. Outside the airport, Jack hailed a cab to take him to Olympic Airlines where he would embark on a short flight to Iraklion. Inside, crowds of people were waiting to be processed. There were a number of lines. He went to an information booth and was told to join any line. After waiting some time, an attendant told him he was in the wrong line. He was exasperated; but then, finally he found the right line. The flight attendant looked at his ticket, shook her head, appearing puzzled.

"This is not the right ticket," she asserted.

"What do you mean?" Jack responded.

"It's the color. It should be blue and white." These, of course, were Greece's national colors.

Jack was about to lose his patience, becoming more vexed. His ticket had been issued by Northwest Airlines and was colored red and white. He pointed at the ticket with his forefinger and shouted. "Lady, never mind the colors! Read the ticket! The origin is Athens, the destination is Iraklion, Crete! For heaven's sake, process this before I miss my flight!"

Immediately the attendant acquiesced and stamped Jack's ticket. He dashed to the appropriate gate and boarded his flight. He found an empty seat next to another passenger and shoved his suitcases into an overhanging storage compartment. All seats were filled, but the plane remained motionless. For some reason, the pilot was running back and forth to the terminal. Finally he settled into the cockpit, and all entry doors were closed and locked. The engines reverberated, growing progressively louder. Then the plane accelerated along the runways, rose, and flew across the sunlit waters of the Mediterranean. It would be a short flight of thirty or forty minutes. The passenger next to Jack mumbled something to him in Greek. Jack responded in English. Since neither could understand the other, that was the end of the conversation.

It was a smooth landing at Iraklion. Jack's daughter and her husband, George were at the airport to greet him. Jack gave Ellen a hug and shook hands with George who helped Jack with his luggage to a waiting car. They then drove to a rented house several miles outside of Iraklion.

"How was the trip over here?" George asked.

"Not bad." Jack replied. "I am very tired. Haven't slept since leaving Minneapolis."

"Are you hungry? I can fix you a sandwich, dad," offered Ellen.

"No, no thanks. I had a big lunch on the flight from London to Athens."

"I think I'll just sit out here on your veranda. You have quite a view."

Jack was exhausted from the trip but felt too excited to sleep. He sank into a soft chair and gazed out from the veranda overlooking the Mediterranean. The sun was just beginning to set slipping slowly beyond the far horizon. Soon the island and the sea became cloaked in darkness. He must have drifted off to sleep for quite a few hours because when he awoke he saw the sun rising in the east. Bright rays broke through the darkness and sparkled as they danced on the still waters of the sea. Behind the house, high and rugged mountains were visible in the spreading sunlight like some great protective shield. What a magnificent and unforgettable spectacle! Quietly he stepped inside the house, undressed and fell asleep again on his bed.

He slept soundly until late morning. When he rose and looked about the house, it was empty. Ellen had left a note behind on the kitchen table. She had gone shopping for groceries, George had reported for duty at the air force base, and a house key was lying next to the note. There was coffee already made and an open bag of muffins on the table. He chewed on a muffin and gulped down a few cups of coffee and quickly dressed into a bathing suit, shirt, and a pair of moccasins. It was a hot sunny day, perfect for the beach, and he was eager to swim in the Mediterranean. He found a towel in the bathroom and stepped outside, locking up the house. Then he sauntered down a sloping, winding path to a small beach passing a few homes and a cafe along the way. The sea was so calm like some massive sheet of glass. He waded slowly into the still waters which were warm, very different from the cooler midsummer shoreline waters of New England. He continued wading and swam out some distance before he could no longer touch the sea bottom. The waters were so clear that he could see all the way to the bottom. After splashing about for a while, he returned to the beach, dried off in the sun and started to walk back toward the house. He was a little hungry; and as it was about lunch time, he decided to stop at the nearby cafe. Inside he perused a menu and motioned to a waiter:

"What is this on the menu?" He pointed at a selection: "calamari."

"It's squid," the waiter responded. "I think you'll like it. It's breaded and fried in olive oil."

"And what about some cheese?"

"We have saganaki. It's a flaming cheese."

"Sounds good. Oh, yes and a glass of red wine."

The waiter first served the saganaki and some bread. Ouzo, a rather strong liquor was poured on the cheese making it inflammable. As it burst into flames, the waiter exclaimed, "Oopah!" and later returned with the calamari and wine. The calamari was tasty and the wine extraordinarily good. Wines were produced on the island, and grapevines could be seen almost everywhere.

In the weeks following, Jack made almost daily trips down to the beach and frequently ate lunch at the nearby cafe. He had hoped to do some fishing but heard that it would probably be frustrating and impracticable. There were very few fish in the surrounding waters. For many years fisherman had used dynamite which was clearly illegal; but the law was frequently ignored, and whatever fish survived were driven away.

He was fascinated with the history of Crete and its culture, and avidly read pertinent literature he found in local bookstores. The island had an advanced civilization, Minoan dating back as early as 2700 BC. Its culture was suffused with mythology: tales of the god Zeus whose birthplace was believed to be a cave in the mountains of Crete, legends of King Minos, Theseus, and the Minotaur half man and half bull which was confined in a labyrinth in Crete and fed on human flesh. There were evidence of influences of the Ottoman Empire, Greece, and Turkey; and the Cretan State was born about 1898. During World War II there was a famous battle on the island when German paratroopers encountered fierce resistance from the natives and the British but finally subdued the defenders after sustaining very heavy casualties. Jack could read about the history of Crete and its culture, but it all became more meaningful when he paid a visit to the Palace of Knossos which had been the center of the Minoan civilization. The layout of the palace was quite unusual. There were over a thousand rooms connected with corridors, water management systems where water was directed through pipes to fountains and spigots, a Throne Room which served as a bathroom for the Queen Ariadne and contained gypsum benches and what looked like a tub. On the palace walls were brightly colored murals, one of a leaping bull. According to legend, the Minotaur with the body of a man and a head of a bull was slain by Theseus in the labyrinth of the palace of Knossos. Theseus was described as the mythical founder king of Athens, the unifier of the Attica peninsula of Greece.

It was the middle of July when George unexpectedly heard from his father who wrote that he would visit Athens soon and asked if his son and Ellen could join him. There was a burst of excitement; and all, including Jack planned an overnight voyage to Athens. They left on an early evening from Iraklion. It would be an overnight voyage on a small ship but certainly adequate for a trip of a few hundred miles. After the ship set sail, an interesting and dramatic incident occurred on board. Suddenly, there was a great deal of commotion. Passengers were crowding on a stairway just below the main deck where there was much noise and shouting. A passenger and the ship's captain or purser were having a heated argument. Of course Jack couldn't understand a word, as it was all in Greek.

"What's going on?" Jack asked one of the onlookers.

"Oh, the passenger doesn't have a ticket. He claims he lost it."

"But there's so much shouting. They're so worked up about it."

"Well, this is Greece. People love to debate. It happens all the time."

Finally it grew quiet with the crowd dispersing, and the matter seemed to have been resolved.

It was a hot, humid night. Jack had sleeping quarters and a private bath but no air conditioning; he was extremely uncomfortable and unable to sleep. Grabbing a pillow and a blanket, he headed up a stairway to the main deck. There he found a cushioned spot cooled by a sea breeze and spent a restless night sleeping under the stars. When daylight broke through the curtain of darkness, the ship was approaching the port of Piraeus. Many small boats were moored in the harbor, and rows of homes, shops, and cafes could be seen ascending a concave shoreline. The ship slowly moved into a dock, and the passengers disembarked. Pirraeus was located within the Athens urban area, and a train took Jack and his family to the center of Athens. From there, it was a short walk to a hotel where they had made reservations. Jack gazed out of the window of his hotel room. Few cars were moving on the street below; and in the distance was the Acropolis high on a rocky hill overlooking the city. I have to climb that hill, Jack thought.

A day later, George's father arrived in Athens joining his son, daughter-in-law, and Jack at the hotel. He discovered that he had left a rather expensive camera in the cab which brought him from the airport. Fortunately, the cab driver came back to the hotel and returned the camera. In the days that followed, they all wandered about the narrow winding streets of the ancient city, visiting historical sites, museums, shops, and cafes. Especially impressive was the daily changing of the Guards in front of the Parliament Buildings in Syntagma Square. The soldiers on duty would stand very straight with their heads held high for hours. They dressed in traditional uniforms, once worn by mountain fighters in the War of Independence, consisting of kilts, shirts with baggy sleeves, woolen leggings, shoes with pompoms on the toes, and fezzes with long tassels topping their heads. When a relief column arrived, the guards who had stood motionless for so long began moving about swinging their arms and stomping their feet. The climax of Jack's visit to Athens came when he and George climbed to the Acropolis. It was a very hot day, over 100 degrees Fahrenheit, as they ascended the rocky slopes which rose hundreds of feet above the city. On their way up they encountered a vendor selling bronze statuettes. One was an ancient Greek warrior arched back in a chariot drawn by a pair of horses which was mounted on a marble base. With one arm he held a spear; and with the other, a protective shield and the reins of two rearing horses.

"I must have that." Jack said to George, pointing at the statuette.

The vendor quoted a price.

"She wants too much Jack. Offer her less, You have to negotiate," George asserted.

They haggled over the price until George approved, and Jack carried it the rest of the way to the top of the hill. The archeological remains of the Acropolis were a spectacular sight. Most conspicuous was the Parthenon surrounded by temples, sanctuaries, and statues. Marble and limestone had been used in much of the construction of buildings, and statues of goddesses were made of wood and bronze. Entrances to temples were lined with Ionic columns. There was a bronze statue of the goddess, Athena towering about thirty feet and holding a lance and shield. The public was barred from some buildings undergoing restoration. Ruins were evident due to centuries of decay, pollution, and warfare. As Jack gazed about in awe, he felt almost transported back to the Age of Pericles or fifth century BC. Then he and George began their descent from the Acropolis. It was midday; the sun was very strong and the heat was becoming more oppressive. Although it was much easier going down the rocky slopes, they had become quite thirsty and stopped at a cafe where they quenched their thirst drinking a pitcher of beer.

Another time, Jack visited the ancient agora of Athens. Agoras had been centers of political and public gatherings in many cities throughout Greece. However, the one in Athens was of special significance. It was here where Socrates tutored his pupils and delivered his philosophical views described by his disciple, Plato. It was Socrates who laid the foundation for the modern scientific method and Western philosophy. The Socratic or dialectic method of inquiry involved a thesis, antithesis, and synthesis: an attempt to arrive at a truth. It is a negative method of hypothesis testing where false assumptions or hypotheses are rejected mainly because of contradictions. It is a procedure compelling one to confront the validity of one's beliefs. And Jack recalled how as a young and inquisitive student he had been stirred by Socrates' saying: "I only know that I know nothing" and the importance that Socrates placed on "the love of wisdom". Aristotle had been another important figure of this time: a protégé of Plato, the father of modern logic, and tutor of Alexander the Great. They had all been here in this "gathering place".

About a week had passed, and it was time to return to Crete. Back in the island Jack began packing, as he had only a few more days before he was to begin the journey home. His relationship with his daughter was strained, as it had been for a number of years. Also, he sensed that her marriage was not going well even though she was pregnant. The baby was due in the fall. A number of times during Jack's visit Ellen and George had quarreled bitterly. It didn't appear that this marriage would last. But Jack had enjoyed his sojourn in Crete and Athens. He said farewell to his daughter and son-in-law and thanked them for their hospitality, as they dropped him off at the airport in Iraklion. His trip back to Minnesota was uneventful except for a delay in Athens which nearly caused him to miss his plane out of London. But he arrived in Minneapolis on schedule, and Hilda and William greeted him at the airport. From there it was a short drive home.

Another semester was about to begin at the University; and the sexual harassment hearing, mandated by the State of Minnesota, was to start shortly. Jack quickly consulted with his attorney in Hopkins. The lawyer read the student's charges and shook his head in disbelief: "It's ridiculous, a travesty! She has no case. But if you need me, I'll be available."

There was trouble even before the start of the hearings. Jack received a memorandum in the campus mail from the vice president claiming that there had been a flurry of complaints about the quality of his teaching and that many of the complaints were originating in Dean Walker's office. Here we go again, Jack thought. There's a pattern here. It started with Nick Angelo's sexual harassment accusations months earlier. He was angry and immediately headed over to Dean Walker's office. The office door was open, and Jack entered. "Charlie!" he began. Seated at his desk, the dean had been studying some papers and looked up.

"What is it, Jack? You look upset. Sit down."

"Yes, very upset." Jack replied, slipping into a nearby chair and handing the dean a copy of the vice president's memorandum.

Charlie glanced at it and quickly reacted. "This is utter nonsense! You know I've had my problems with this vice president, too!" He exclaimed.

"I know," Jack agreed. "But maybe you can set him straight about this."

"I'll do what I can."

Within the week, Jack received a call from Lenore, the university affirmative action officer. "Jack, I need to send you a notice of our first meeting regarding the sexual harassment charges. Should I send it to your home or would you prefer that it be sent to your office, in the campus mail?"

"It doesn't matter, Lenore. My wife knows all about this. It's your call."

The meetings were to be held in the vice president's office. All participants were seated at a large rectangular table. The vice president, Sheldon was seated at the head of the table. Jack was flanked by the affirmative action officer and the Minnesota Education Association (MEA) grievance officer. Jack was a member of MEA and had requested that the grievance officer, Warren be present in the event of any irregularities or violations related to the union contract. Seated across from him was Connie, the disgruntled student and his accuser. Sitting next to her was an aggressive looking woman with a pasty complexion and wearing a jacket and trousers. Jack didn't recognize the woman.

"Who is she?" he inquired

"I'm Kathleen Howard from the Human Relations department." The woman responded. "I'm an attorney representing the student."

"Okay, let's get on with this meeting," urged Sheldon. It seemed that he would be directing or guiding the discussion. He turned to the student, saying, "Connie, can you summarize the nature of your complaints filed against Professor Rubin?"

The student quickly obliged stating that she had felt very intimidated by Professor Rubin, that he stood outside in the hall before class waiting for her to appear and that he made remarks about the way she was dressed and what a nice tan she had. She felt he was flirting with her. He even promised her a good grade. It all made her feel uncomfortable. Then she complained to one of her social work instructors, Lena Rose who encouraged her to file sexual harassment charges against Doctor Rubin

Sheldon turned to Jack, asking, "Is this all true?"

"Of course not. The student is distorting the facts. I make a practice of standing in the hallways just before my classes. I never made remarks about the way she dressed or promise her a good grade. My remark about her tan was lifted out of context. I had said to her that I hoped she spent as much time studying as she spent in the sun, so that she would do well in my course. When she finally received her grade, she came to my office in an uproar and very angry. My office door was open, and there were witnesses."

"But where are your witnesses, Jack? We don't know what you are saying is true? Maybe you are guilty of sexual harassment," asserted Kathleen.

"The witnesses probably fear to testify because of possible retaliation, and I don't have to prove my innocence, Kathleen. Don't you know how our system works? There is a presumption of innocence until one is proven guilty. Where did you study law?"

She didn't answer but only stared back at him haughtily.

"Okay," Sheldon interjected. "We'll continue this next week."

Jack was not surprised to hear the student's account of Lena's involvement in this murky affair. She was probably getting back at him because of a conflict years ago when they served together on a faculty selection committee. Also, Nick had been in on it probably because Jack had supported an opposition candidate as a future chairperson. A few days later Jack passed Lena on his way to a class. They said nothing to each other. She smirked at him, and he glared back at her. He had been warned about this woman by Patricia, one of the other social workers.

"Jack, don't mess with Lena", Patricia cautioned. "She's a destroyer. If she decides to do it, she could tear a whole organization apart."

It was late September, and Hilda had left for Germany where her first grandchild was due to be born at a U.S. military base, in Frankfurt. George had arranged for his wife to deliver the baby there because of the questionable quality of hospital facilities in Crete. Following the birth, Hilda planned to spend some time in Crete with George, Ellen, and the baby.

During the following weeks there were more sexual harassment hearings. In one of the later meetings, Jack felt his rights were being violated. The affirmative action officer presented what she identified as evidence from interviews with other students and faculty: "I talked with a number of students and faculty regarding the charges against Professor Rubin and his behavior with other students. The chairperson of the Human Relations department said that a student would never lie about such charges. Also, one student claims that she saw Professor Rubin embrace a female student in front of her class."

"Oh! My goodness! Did you do that?" exclaimed Sheldon.

"No!" Jack replied emphatically and added: "The student is lying! I want to cross examine her and the chairperson of Human Relations."

"You cannot do that. This hearing is closed to other participants", Sheldon insisted.

Jack rose from his seat and declared: "I believe I'm being denied due process. I have nothing more to say until I've consulted with my attorney."

The affirmative action officer gasped in surprise and started to speak: "Jack, you can't___."

"Yes he can," the vice president interrupted. "This meeting is adjourned until further notice."

Later that same day Jack called his attorney, Arthur Wright and related the details of the meeting.

"Where do I go from here?" Jack asked. "I think they're out of line."

"Yes, they are. I'll have them in court if they're not careful. But Jack you have to continue attending the hearings. In the meantime the university attorney will get a call from me."

For a few weeks there were no sexual harassment meetings scheduled for Jack. His attorney did contact the Saint Cloud State lawyer cautioning him regarding irregularities in the hearings. During the interim an information meeting for faculty was called by the affirmative action officer. It was held in a large auditorium. Lenore was at the podium and spoke some time describing guidelines followed in sexual harassment cases. One of her remarks was clearly an absurdity:

"Ninety nine percent of the time when students charge sexual harassment by a faculty, the charges are true," she claimed.

Jack was stunned. What evidence did she have to support her claim? There was a brief silence before Lenore continued. Jack looked about the room. No one dared to challenge her statement. They were intimidated. Perhaps Jack should've said something, but it was widely known that he was in the eye of this storm. Why doesn't someone speak up, he thought. No one did; and in that silence, he lost respect for the faculty. But this was no isolated incident. Generally, the faculty were cowed when it came to matters of political correctness and affirmative action. The university was becoming steeped in an atmosphere of suppression. On a related occasion, Hugh Goodman one of the department sociologists stopped into Jack's office.

"Hi, Jack. How are things going with the hearings?"

"Nothing is going on right now, Hugh."

"Do you mind if I say something?"

"No. Go ahead."

Hugh picked up a pencil on Jack's desk; and on a blank sheet of paper, he drew a line. "You see that line, Jack?"

"Of course, Hugh. What is your point?"

"Well, Jack," Hugh said, striking the pencil repeatedly at the line. "You're having problems now because you crossed that line."

"Okay, I get your point Hugh. This is an old cliché. But Hugh I don't like what's going on at this university. As far as crossing that line, I've crossed it many times in my life. And I'll continue to cross it."

Jack also approached Richard, a social worker concerning Lena's involvement in the sexual harassment case, but Richard balked, saying: "I don't want to talk with you about one of my colleagues."

Soon the time came for another sexual harassment hearing. All participants were seated, and Sheldon opened the discussion. "Let's not drag out this discussion any further. I want to suggest a compromise," he said turning to Jack. "I have a memorandum here that I am going to place in your personnel file. It summarizes the results of these hearings. Will you accept it?" He handed Jack a copy of the memorandum and then read it aloud.

"I don't think I can accept this," Jack responded. " It's a letter of reprimand and violates the union contract."

"It's not a reprimand," the vice president insisted

"Sheldon, let me read aloud what you've written". Jack began reading from the memorandum: "Although we could not find sufficient evidence to prove the sexual harassment charges brought against Professor Rubin, we caution him to be more discreet and careful in his future dealings with students. This is definitely a reprimand!" Jack repeated.

"No, it isn't!" the vice president argued.

The grievance officer, a faculty member turned to Jack saying: "Accept it. It's a good deal. You can't do any better."

Jack addressed the vice president. "I'll think about this, and let you know my decision at the next meeting."

For the next few weeks, Jack mulled over Sheldon's suggested "compromise". He wrote a detailed letter, stating his case and claiming unjust treatment, to the Saint Cloud State University President. But the president failed even to answer the letter. He also pleaded his case in a letter to the Minnesota Civil Liberties Union. But they too turned him away simply recommending that he hire an attorney. He tried discussing his circumstances with the head of the local union on campus who similarly shunned him

"Jack, I'm sorry", he said. "The affirmative action officer is my wife. I can't talk to you about this. It involves a conflict of interest."

What was his recourse? As a last resort he could go to the Star Tribune newspaper and give them a story with all its documentation. This might violate state or even federal law. But what did he have to lose. If that letter remained in his file, he was finished, dead professionally. One way or another, he was going to fight back. The State of Minnesota might prosecute him; but if he went down, he would try to take Saint Cloud State University with him. But perhaps there was another way to go. He arranged an appointment to consult with Steve Conway, Director of the Minnesota Education Association in Saint Paul.

It was a very cold day in the middle of January. The sky was overcast and a light snow was falling. But the roads were clear as Jack parked his car in Saint Paul close to the state capitol. He crossed a few streets and entered the building of the Minnesota Education Association. Walking down one of the hallways, he found the director's office. Steve Conway, seated at his desk, was waiting for Jack; He rose and the two men shook hands

"Sit down, Jack." Steve waved his arm at a nearby chair. "Now," he said, "I want to hear the whole story." When arranging an appointment, Jack had provided Steve with only fragmentary information.

Jack described the sequence of events leading up to the student's accusation, what had transpired at the sexual harassment hearings, and showed Steve documentation: a copy of the formal charges, the letters that he had sent to the President of Saint Cloud State University and the Minnesota Civil Liberties Union, and a copy of the letter that Sheldon, the vice president had placed in his file.

The director listened intently to Jack's account and scanned the documents. Steve shook his head, bit his lips, and became increasingly angry. "There's no question about it, Jack! This letter in your file is a reprimand which shouldn't be there without justification. This is a violation of our contract with Saint Cloud State."

"What can we do about it, Steve? I can't get any help on campus."

"We can file a grievance. What do you want to do, Jack?"

"Let's do it!" Jack replied emphatically.

"I'll be coming up to your campus to set the grievance procedure in motion." Steve continued. " In the meantime, stay in touch. Oh, let me make copies of these documents. They could prove useful."

"You don't need to. I have my own copies." They shook hands again, and Jack departed.

A few days later, another sexual harassment hearing was scheduled. As usual, the vice president opened the meeting. He turned to Jack.

"We heard from your attorney. He was really heated. But I hope we can wrap things up today. Will you accept my letter or compromise as a resolution?"

"No, I can't" Jack retorted. "It's clearly a letter of reprimand unjustly placed in my personnel file. Let me read you my response. As a matter of record, I 'll have it typed up and sent to you in the campus mail." Jack drew a sheet of rumpled paper from his pocket and began reading its contents:

"Your compromise regarding the sexual harassment charges made against me is unacceptable. The letter you have unjustly placed in my personnel file inflicts injury on me and my family. It's a letter of reprimand and in violation of our union contract. There is no compromise with lies; and were I to accept any such compromise, it could set a precedent endangering the welfare of other faculty."

An expression of frustration flashed across Sheldon's face. He squirmed in his seat and breathed deeply in exasperation: "For heaven's sake, accept a compromise!" he exclaimed.

"Remove your letter from my file!" insisted Jack

"No!" Sheldon replied firmly.

"Okay. I will be a filing a grievance." Then Jack turned toward the student, his accuser seated across the table from him. He shook his forefinger at her, and raised his voice: "You are a liar! You have taken facts and twisted them to feed your anger! And your lies will follow you for the rest of your life!"

This was the last meeting of what Jack labeled the "Star Chamber" which referred to an oppressive and unjust court established in the late 15th century by the British Crown. In Jack's case, he felt the affirmative action officer had acted as prosecutor and the vice president as judge and jury.

It wasn't long before Steve Conway visited the Saint Cloud State campus. As he sat in Jack's office, he began explaining the grievance procedure.

"It will start next week. You'll meet again with the vice president. If he refuses to remove the letter of reprimand, then you'll meet with the president of the university. If he refuses to remove the letter, then an appeal will be made to the Chancellor of the State University System. That's it Jack."

"What about the grievance officer?"

"You don't need him. He's useless. But one thing else is very important. When you meet with the vice president and then with the president, stay calm. Don't lose your temper."

"I'll remember that," Jack replied. "How long will the process take?" He inquired.

"I don't know. Sometimes these things drag on for months."

So now the conflict that had already gone on for months was moving toward a resolution. But it had taken its toll on Jack. His office had been like a war room. There had been wasted appeals to the Saint Cloud State University president and the Minnesota Civil Liberties Union, repeated consultations with his attorney and the director of the Minnesota Education Association, and finally a rebuttal to the vice president's so called "compromise". Anger and stress nearly overwhelmed him. His karate training helped to alleviate the strain, and Hilda had been very understanding and supportive. He had initiated a research project before the sexual harassment hearings had begun but found he had to abandon it. All of his energy was devoted to the hearings and fulfillment of his teaching responsibilities. He remembered Conway's caveats to practice restraint during the grievance procedures and some lines from the poem by British Nobel laureate Rudyard Kipling:

If you can keep your head when all about are losing theirs and blaming it on you. If you can trust yourself when all men doubt you. But make allowance for their doubting, too. If you can wait and not be tired by waiting, or being lied about, don't deal in lies, or being hated, don't give way to hating. And yet don't look too good, nor talk too wise.

The grievance procedure began with a meeting with Sheldon, the vice president. He and Jack were the only participants. It was held in Sheldon's office and was uneventful. Jack again requested that the vice president remove the letter of reprimand from his file. But again, he balked. The process then moved to the next step: a meeting with the president of the university, Bryant McCarren. Jack arrived punctually at Bryant's office. The secretary looked up from her desk.

"You may go in," she said, motioning to the open door to the president's office. "They're waiting for you."

Two men were seated inside. The one at the desk was obviously Bryant whom Jack had never seen before. Who's the other man? he wondered.

"You must be Jack Rubin," said Bryant.

"Yes, I am," he replied settling into a nearby chair directly facing the president. "And the other man next to you, who's he?"

"Oh, he's Marvin, the university attorney."

Why in the devil does this guy need an attorney present? Never mind, I'm not going to ask. Why risk any more confrontation, Jack thought.

Bryant started the discussion: "Jack, why do we have to go through this grievance procedure? What is it that you want?"

"Your vice president placed a letter of reprimand in my file. I want it removed. I want justice," he insisted.

"Why don't you give me a detailed account as to what this is all about."

"I appealed to you in a memorandum some time ago and described all the details. But you never sent me a reply. But I can go through the details again."

At this point Bryant lost his composure. His face became twisted and colored with anger. "I don't recall any such letter from you!" he shouted.

Marvin, the university attorney grimaced and patted the president on the shoulder: "Calm down, Bryant!"

Jack handed the president a copy of the letter containing his appeal and asked, "Do you want me to continue?"

"Yes." Bryant replied.

Jack related in some detail the events leading up to the grievance procedure. When he was finished, Bryant responded with a firm and unequivocal statement: "The letter will remain in your file, Jack. I will support the vice president's decision."

Jack sprang from his chair: "That's it then. We have nothing more to discuss." He turned and quickly departed.

The grievance procedure progressed into its final phase. Any day now a decision would be rendered by the office of the Chancellor of the Minnesota State University System. Jack was sitting in his office, looking over some lecture notes when his phone rang. He picked up the receiver:

"Jack, Steve Conway here. I've just heard from the chancellor's office. It's good news! You've won the grievance!"

"That's great, Steve!"

"I'll fax you over a copy of the chancellor's memorandum."

The memorandum, addressed to the President of Saint Cloud State University, was brief but very clear: "The placement of a letter of reprimand in Professor Rubin's file was an inappropriate and unjust act and must be removed immediately."

Within the next few days, Jack verified that the letter was removed. But was this the end of the conflict? He had spent nearly a year defending himself against false accusations and innuendos. Wasn't this a kind of character assassination? There are a variety of conflicts where one party attempts to inflict injury upon another. They can arise from differences in ideology, struggles over scarce resources such as money, power, prestige, or grudges or resentment of a personal nature. Compromises are then practicable; but in Jack's circumstances, members of the university administration and some faculty and students were intent upon discrediting him and possibly destroying him and his family. In this type of conflict there is no compromise, and perhaps one needs to strike back hard; otherwise your adversaries may be more likely to attack again. Also, he had felt forced to abandon research which could have contributed to his career and to the university as well. What a waste! And even though the evidence did not support the charges made against him, his attorney had said,

"When one is accused of something like this, it can stigmatize you and follow you through the rest of your career."

"So let's investigate," Jack reflected. "Would it be feasible to pursue the conflict further and file a law suit against Saint Cloud State?" He consulted another attorney specializing in labor relations.

But after some research, on the details of Jack's case, the lawyer concluded:

"A law suit would not be worth it. They can be very expensive, time consuming, and have unexpected or unanticipated consequences. Look, you won your grievance. Let that be the resolution," and added, "Discretion is the better part of valor," a line recorded in poetic form by Charles Churchill in 1477.

As Jack left the lawyer's office, he thought: "He's right. I've won this battle. It's time to move on to other things."

CHAPTER EIGHT:
HEADING WEST AGAIN

Jack had become increasingly disillusioned with academia and even felt like resigning his position at Saint Cloud State. But that was not feasible. Now he was a full professor with tenure which granted security for him and his family. And where would he go? He had grown older; and age discrimination was commonplace in academia as well as elsewhere. At the same time, he still enjoyed teaching and did so with zeal and dedication. It was discouraging that many of his students were mediocre or lacked basic reading, writing and mathematical skills. But there were always a few who excelled and others who yearned to learn. Perhaps Jack's most difficult course for students was Introductory Statistics. He recalls that for one student it was an anathema and a struggle. But the student came to Jack for additional help and eventually turned completely around. By the end of the semester, he earned an A grade in the class. It was an achievement for the student as well as a rewarding experience for Jack. Then there were two other students who excelled in his courses and distinguished themselves academically. One had been accepted at the George Washington University Law School, and the other had earned a graduate studies scholarship at Washington State University. The latter visited Jack before she left to commence graduate studies and thank him for his encouragement and support.

"I felt I was sailing against the wind here," she said. "I studied very hard to get good grades and was able to do so even though other students ridiculed me, calling me a book worm."

The social climate at Saint Cloud State University, especially in sociology, was not conducive to academic endeavors or achievements which was probably true in many other schools and disciplines as well. A dumbing down of standards in American education was well underway. The comments of the student departing for graduate studies made Jack reflect on his own situation. He had been principally trained for doing research and teaching in a graduate program but was prevented from doing the latter. And, in fact, he believed he had experienced a more academically oriented environment years ago when working at the Population Division of the U.S. Bureau of the Census. At Saint Cloud he had been largely isolated in his research efforts. He had even tried to participate in counseling students on their dissertations in interdisciplinary graduate programs; but controlling faculty had thwarted him possibly because they felt intimidated. But at least his faculty position was secure. These had been difficult times when many PhD's were underemployed: even forced to work at pumping gas or driving taxis. Also, after Jack was hired at Saint Cloud he was informed by a member of the department selection committee that he been chosen out of fifty applicants to fill the one open position. Despite all this, he had a number of uplifting moments throughout his teaching career. One occurred when a student in a Social Research Methods class handed him a farewell card as the semester was nearing an end. The card read: "Your loving Sociology 379 class" with all the students' signatures. On the cover was a picture of students seated in a classroom with one raising his hand to address the instructor, saying: "Doctor Rubin, may I be excused? My brain is so full". Then there was that overload class at North Hennepin Community College with Minneapolis police officers as students in the Juvenile Delinquency course. Jack's research activities included sociological analyses of crime; and Jim

Crain, one of the sociology instructors, asked Jack if he would be interested in teaching an additional course in Juvenile Delinquency at North Hennepin Community College.

"I have been teaching the course, "Jim said. "But the students are police officers, and they make it very difficult for me. They're constantly giving me a hard time and show me no respect. I would really appreciate it if you would take over the class for me Jack, at least for this semester."

Jack agreed, and one night a week he would be driving about fifty miles to meet his new class. It was to become an interesting and gratifying experience. He had a plan he believed would ingratiate himself to the students. Taking a page from Erving Goffman's, *Presentation of Self in Everyday Life*, he would play a role involving impression management. At the first meeting he strode into the classroom exuding an aura of confidence. Some officers were already seated in the room. Carefully he placed his attaché case on a small table, opened it, drew out the course textbook, a collection of lecture notes, and copies of a syllabus describing the content and requirements of the course. Gazing about he smiled as other police officers, impeccably dressed in their uniforms, slowly entered the room. Shortly a bell rang signaling the beginning of classes. Jack cleared his throat and began to speak.

"Good evening, gentlemen. Make sure you're in the right class. This is Sociology 305, Juvenile Delinquency. First, let me introduce myself. I'm Professor or Doctor Rubin. I earned my PhD at the University of Chicago. It was difficult and took some time. Also, I worked at the Population Division of the U.S. Bureau of the Census and the Department of Labor as a statistician demographer. I've been active in the Population Association of America, done research in the area of crime, and have a few publications."

For a few moments, Jack stopped speaking. He had really "poured it on", and the officers appeared impressed. Then in a more humble tone he continued.

"I'm here to teach you about juvenile delinquency, and I'll try to do a good job and hopefully you will learn from me. But, at the same time, I should learn from you. You guys are out on the streets dealing directly with juvenile delinquents. You're on the front line, and we should have some meaningful exchanges. And, by the way, here are copies of a description of the course content and requirements." He then began to distribute the syllabi.

The officers responded enthusiastically. There was much discussion throughout the course, and everything ran very smoothly. When the course was over, Jack received compliments from Bob Prow, the chairman of the Criminal Justice Department. Bob had received some feedback from students taking the course.

"Jack, I hear you did a great job teaching those police officers. They felt the class was really informative and stimulating."

As a teacher Jack would never win a "beauty contest", but he certainly won the respect of his students.

Since Nick Angelo's passing, one of the social workers had acted as temporary chairperson of the department. It was now time for the election of a regular chairperson. The two candidates were both sociologists: John Kearney and Jenny Carter. Jack supported John believing that he would more likely advocate research and encourage the development of a sociology graduate program. Jenny had been Nick Angelo's favored candidate, and Jack had always had a good relationship with her. But she was part of an old boys' network which was more resistant to change. John won the election overwhelmingly; and in the aftermath, the affirmative action officer insisted on interviewing each faculty regarding the nature of his or her vote. The question raised: "Had there been any evidence of gender discrimination?" The faculty complied; no one protested the inquiry. When Jack entered Lenore's office, she asked:

"Did you vote for Jenny?"

"No, I voted for John," Jack responded thinking that maybe he should have told her that it was none of her business.

"Why didn't you vote for Jenny? Was it because of her gender?"

"No. That had nothing to do with it. I just felt that John would do a better job as chairperson".

As the 1980's were nearing an end, colleges and universities throughout the country were increasingly engaged in abusive and illegitimate practices linked with affirmative action or political correctness. Many of these practices were eventually challenged in the courts frequently involving questions of violations of due process and the First Amendment to the Constitution. Schools were applying very nebulous and ambiguous sexual harassment guidelines as well as speech codes infringing on freedom of expression. Clearly, Jack Rubin's encounter with affirmative action was not a unique or isolated incident. At the same time, there were certainly genuine acts of sexual harassment and violations of civil rights. But more care needed to be exercised in determining the authenticity of such acts.

It was not long after Jack's conflict and its resolution that he received a phone call from Kim who was still teaching at California State University at Fullerton. Kim seemed very distressed.

"What's going on?" Jack inquired. "You sound pretty upset."

"I am! There are two students who are filing complaints against me. They're unhappy about their grades and insisting I'm discriminating against them because of religion and gender. One is a woman. The other is male and Jewish. He's claiming I'm anti-Semitic."

"This is ridiculous!"

"I know. My dean is giving me a hard time about this. She's siding with the students. I've gone to an attorney and threatening a law suit. Listen, Jack will you send a letter to my attorney defending me on any charge of anti-Semitism?"

"I'll be happy to do it, Kim. This is terrible! I'll get a letter out right away!"

Another issue of growing concern was "teaching versus indoctrination". Jack studiously avoided the latter. Nearly every semester he taught Introductory Sociology in conjunction with other assigned courses. The class was quite large comprising about forty or fifty students. During one meeting the lecture addressed the propriety of the "Don't Ask. Don't Tell Policy" related to homosexual members of the armed forces. Jack suggested that the class discuss this question and that students express opposing views. They quickly responded. Some students favored the policy, some didn't; and Jack encouraged them all to provide some rationale or arguments to support their views. There was quite a lively discussion and considerable controversy. A few students asked Jack to state his position, but he declined saying:

"No, I don't wish to risk influencing you. I want you to feel free to express your own feelings and opinions about this issue."

The social work component of the department continued to endorse certain political agendas in their inclination for indoctrination. Complaining students reported that social work faculty and members of the Human Relations Department were ardently promoting a speech code of political correctness and a biased perspective with respect to sensitive issues such as sexual orientation and sexual harassment. One specific example arose later during the early 1990's when Clarence Thomas, a United States Supreme Court nominee, was interrogated by members of the U.S. Congress regarding accusations of sexual harassment made by one of his former work associates, Anita Hill. The social workers responded by proclaiming "Anita Hill day", claiming that Thomas was surely guilty of the charges. Their students were instructed to demonstrate in support of Anita Hill; and if any students refused, they were told they would be penalized. Jack could only feel disgust and revulsion for these and other such practices. But he was pleased when both the social workers and sociologists agreed to separate with the social workers "picking up their marbles" and establishing their own department.

Throughout America and in other parts of the world momentous political, economic, and social changes were occurring at the end of the 1970's and during the 1980 decade. Jimmy Carter served only one term as U.S. president. His domestic and foreign policies generally resulted in dire consequences. Economic conditions were characterized by stagflation, high inflation coupled with high unemployment. In addition, the U.S embassy in Teheran was overrun by Islamic extremists and diplomatic personnel were seized as hostages. An attempt was made to rescue the hostages but failed rather miserably, and the hostage situation was followed by an Islamic Revolution commencing in 1979. The Shah Mohammed Reza Pahlavi, who had been supported by the United States and the United Kingdom, was forced to abdicate; and an Islamic Republic was established. The Carter administration, as well as earlier administrations, had meddled a great deal in Iran's internal affairs and had aroused considerable resentment against the United States, secularism, and other Western influences. Throughout his reign the Shah had attempted to modernize Iran and promote aspects of Western culture. But his actions provoked strong reactions by members of the clergy, traditionalists, and Islamic extremists. His position became even more precarious when he resorted to repressive measures which stifled criticism from not only conservative but liberal and democratically oriented groups as well. Another issue, increasing resentment and hostility, was the fact that the Shah and his Queen indulged themselves lavishly and accumulated fortunes amounting to billions of dollars. Moreover, growing poverty among the Iranian people contributed to greater instability and insurrection. Finally, Ruhollah Khomeini returned from exile and spearheaded the imposition of a repressive theocracy. The Revolutionary Guard was established by Khomeini to consolidate his power and wipe out all opposition. There were revolts by various parties and factions; but in the end, they were either executed or cast into prisons. Following this, the Iranian Islamic revolutionaries sought to impose Islamic republics on their Sunni Arab neighbors which facilitated the lengthy Iran-Iraq war. The regime also helped to set up and support Hezbollah, a terrorist organization operating in Lebanon and launching indiscriminate attacks against Israel. The revolution did have some positive effects in bringing about a broadening of education and improved health care for the poor. Illiteracy rates as well as maternal and infant mortality rates were reduced significantly.

Some progress was made in promoting peace in the Middle East during the years of the Carter Administration. President Carter worked tirelessly to forge a peaceful settlement between Egypt and Israel which resulted in the Camp David Accords. Unfortunately, other Arab nations and the Palestinians rejected the agreements which involved Israel giving up occupied territories to Egypt in exchange for recognition of the legitimacy of the state of Israel and other concessions. Essentially conflict continued in the Middle East, and the seizure of the American embassy in Teheran, and the holding of hostages by Islamic extremists was an ongoing embarrassment to the Carter administration.

However, by 1980 change appeared to be on its way. Ronald Reagan defeated President Carter overwhelmingly in a presidential election. In campaign speeches Reagan had warned Iran that they would face dire consequences if they did not release American diplomatic personnel. Like Theodore Roosevelt, he would walk softly but carry a big stick. Almost immediately following his inauguration, the Iranians released the hostages. In his early political career he had strongly supported President Franklin Roosevelt and President Harry Truman. He was president of the Screen Actors Guild and played leading roles in many Hollywood films. Although he opposed the blacklisting of actors by the Un-American Activities Committee, he did inform on actors suspected of Communist or pro Communist activities. He also served as governor of the state of California. During his first term as president, he took steps to revive the economy by endorsing tax cuts to encourage business investment and a tight money policy. He reduced government spending on social programs but increased spending on national defense. The inflation rate, which had been in the double digits, dropped dramatically; and both poverty and unemployment rates declined. Reagan engaged in an aggressive foreign policy. He was strongly anti-communist and labeled the Soviet Union the "evil empire", and gave support to insurgents fighting the Soviets in Afghanistan and to Poland's Solidarity Movement. Perhaps his closest ally abroad was Margaret Thatcher, the "Iron Lady," and the United Kingdom's first female prime minister. Ronald Reagan served two terms as U.S. President extending over the years 1980 to 1988. During that time the United States became involved in a war between Israel and Lebanon as well in the lengthy war between Iran and Iraq. The Reagan administration was disposed to provide military and financial assistance to Iraq partly due to threat of Islamic fundamentalism emanating from Iran. Shortly after his term as president, the Berlin wall finally came down and the Soviet empire crumbled. There were those who credited Reagan for this demise of Communism. But that was disputed, as it was a complicated phenomenon. In any event, Ronald Reagan possessed a lot of personnel charm and was exceptionally congenial even among adversaries and critics. He was dubbed by many as the "Great Communicator".

Except for the election of John Kearney as chairperson; and the departure of the social workers together with their political agenda, there were no further changes in the Sociology and Anthropology Department. But there were more departmental meetings which Nick had predicted if John were elected as chairperson. Jack almost dozed off at the meetings amid a torrent of rhetoric with much attention focusing on cosmetic rather than any meaningful substantive issues. As usual, there was an avoidance of discussion related to research, and considerable attention was devoted to "massaging" the curriculum. Faculty speculated as to what new courses or programs could be initiated to draw more bodies into the classrooms. However, one sign of impending change was the setting up of a committee to develop a graduate program in sociology. Jack, with considerable assistance from George Romano, headed the committee which in the beginning was quite successful in drafting a tentative program. But the committee was destined to fail in later endeavors, and the program was eventually scuttled and largely co-opted by the Department of Human Relations. As one might expect, the title and content of the new graduate program were radically altered. A graduate degree in Social Responsibility was offered, and the new curriculum provided knowledge and skills on an extensive number of issues such as animal rights, racism, sexism, xenophobia, lesbian, gay, bisexual, and transgender matters, lookism, and other issues of so called "social responsibility".

It was time again to fill another vacant sociology position in the department, and preference was given to an applicant whose specialty was in the area of organizational theory and behavior. It was hoped, too that the new sociologist would better enable the department to attract students from the Business School of the university. The selection committee was composed of five faculty, four sociologists and one anthropologist. Scores of applications were submitted, and the committee was permitted to select three finalists who would be invited for interviews and to lecture before the faculty and a class of sociology students. Jack was again serving as a member of the selection committee and favored a fresh PhD from the University of California, Berkeley as a finalist. The applicant had already published a research paper in the American Sociological Review and had presented a paper at meetings of the American Sociological Association. But his choice was not supported by other members of the committee or by the chairman who was supposed to function independently in the selection of the finalists. Unfortunately John was inclined to meddle in department affairs, not only in this instance, but at other times as well. Jack argued vociferously with John emphasizing the Berkeley applicant's outstanding credentials.

"Sure, he's a star," John retorted. "But he'll be too much for us and make too many waves."

Jack shook his head, turned, and walked away. He knew what "making waves" meant. There would be no real changes in the department. Perhaps he had made a mistake in supporting John as chairperson. Consequently, the Berkeley candidate was excluded as a finalist. The most favored applicant was a recent PhD who had done some teaching at Indiana University but had no other professional accomplishments. Included in his credentials was a glowing recommendation from a former President of the American Sociological Association as well as a very poorly written manuscript which was based on his dissertation and which he planned to submit to a professional journal for evaluation for publication. His oral presentation to faculty and students was almost completely incomprehensible. Jack and another sociologist simply walked out of the room in disgust during the presentation. But the selection committee and the chairman were enthralled by him. Jack tried to influence other members of the selection committee, pointing out that the candidate's credentials were unimpressive and his writing and oral presentation were largely incoherent. Committee members argued that all that didn't matter. Some faculty made comments such as:

"The students loved him!"

"He'll be a great addition to the department. He's an Arab and a Muslim and will promote more diversity in the department!"

"And he's such a handsome and charming fellow!"

"The women will be falling all over him! His class enrollments will skyrocket!"

Jack finally relented, saying:

"Okay, guys. You want him then you can have him. Maybe it will work out. I'll just abstain on the vote."

After the committee voted to hire Abdullah, Jack stepped into the chairman's office. John, of course, was elated with the committee's choice.

"He'll be our connection to the Business School!" John exclaimed. Then he added: "Abdullah will do anything I ask him to do."

Jack could hardly believe what he was hearing.

"Fine, John. Have it your way. But don't ask me to ever serve on another faculty selection committee. I've had it."

There was no question that Abdullah was quite attractive and possessed a certain charisma. He was tall and slender and well groomed His complexion was smooth and slightly dark. He had a full head of wavy black hair, bushy eyebrows, and handsome features. He was very glib and spoke in a soothing tone. Jack found him to be quite congenial and spent some time conversing with him. For a while they even commuted together to Saint Cloud, as Abdullah had rented an apartment not far from Jack's home. But his knowledge of sociology seemed limited and shallow. Furthermore he didn't seem to be taking his teaching responsibilities very seriously. Often Jack had evening classes which would meet a few hours once a week, and Abdullah would also have classes scheduled at about the same time. After about an hour of lecturing, Jack would take a break and stroll down the hallway passing Abdullah's darkened classroom. Frequently Abdullah dismissed his classes following only an hour of lecturing. Jack felt that this kind of action, especially by a newly hired and junior faculty, was irresponsible. He referred the matter to Kearney who simply shrugged his shoulders, replying:

"It really isn't that important Jack. The students still love him; they give him great course evaluations. Maybe I'll say something to him about it."

But the matter was ignored. In the long run the students would suffer. There was nothing more that Jack could do, except become more disgusted with academia. Nevertheless he fulfilled his teaching duties and pursued his research interests, writing, trying to publish, and presenting papers at professional meetings. Often he would visit the Economics Department and consult with his friend and colleague, Mike Lusky. On a number of occasions, Mike talked about Abdullah.

"We were sending our majors to his class on Organizational Theory and Behavior but then discontinued doing it. Now we send them over to the Business School instead."

"How come?" Jack asked.

"Our students have complained about him. He's incompetent, a bad teacher."

"What is the problem? I know that he dismisses his classes early."

"It's not just that," Mike continued. "The guy assigns readings from his textbook for each class meeting. Then he has the students break up into small groups and discuss what they were assigned to read. That's pretty much it. I don't think he does any real teaching or lecturing."

"That's too bad, Mike. I'm afraid there's nothing we can do about it. A few more years and I think I'm going to get the hell out of here."

Despite all this, Abdullah became a "star" in the department. The student sociology club honored him with a "teacher of the year award" and proudly presented him with an engraved plaque. Ultimately, he was promoted to the rank of full professor and granted tenure.

There was some progress in the development of a graduate program in sociology. Jack, with a good deal of help from George Romano, filled in many of the details of the program, and it received approval from the Dean of the School of Social Sciences. Specification of required graduate statistic courses, however did encounter resistance from the Mathematics Department; but in a series of meetings their objections were overcome. But, in the end, the program was abandoned mainly due to a lack of support from the department and the chairman. Sometimes the committee would meet in a clandestine fashion and modify or reduce aspects of the program until nothing remained except an empty shell. Even George Romano, who had been enthusiastically involved, began to withdraw his support of the graduate program and eventually it was co-opted largely by

Human Relations and other departments. Jack was also disturbed with the increased pervasiveness of political correctness and affirmative action abuses. He felt many of the new words or expressions mandated in the university speech codes were misleading or simply didn't make sense. For example, the meaning of terms such as "persons of color" and even "Afro American" or "African American" seemed confusing. Just who do you include as "persons of color"? Isn't white a color? And what about Latinos or Hispanics? Aren't they a heterogeneous group coming in all colors? What about people in New Orleans? Walk along the streets of New Orleans and you'll see whites, blacks, French, Spanish, Latinos, Indians. How do you differentiate? One time, Jack's department hired a new faculty who was considered a "person of color" or a preferred minority according to affirmative action guidelines. The new hire was a woman from Argentina whose parents had immigrated to Argentina from a north European country. Nevertheless she was considered a Latino, a preferred minority.. Also, he had a debate with one of the faculty who was a Caucasian from South Africa who insisted he was an African American. But amusingly Jack pointed out that the fellow really couldn't be an African American because he wasn't the "right color". Of course, you can be almost any race, color, or nationality and have come originally from the continent of Africa. Then there was a matter of Saint Cloud State capitulating to threats and failing to enforce contractual stipulations. In one of the university departments an African American or black instructor failed to complete his PhD degree which, according to his contract, should have resulted in his termination. But he succeeded in retaining his faculty position and even gaining tenure by threatening to sue the university for racial discrimination. Increasingly, Jack was losing respect for his department and the university and tended to reduce his participation in university and departmental concerns. As the 1990 decade approached, he began to contemplate retirement.

It was about this time that Kim, who was still teaching at Fullerton State University in California, contacted Jack encouraging him to submit a research paper to present at meetings of the Western Social Science Association to be held in Albuquerque, New Mexico. Kim would be serving as a chairman or moderator of one the panels dealing with the labor force participation rates of Asian Americans. Jack was completing a related research paper and agreed to attend the meetings and present his research findings. He and Hilda flew into Albuquerque and registered at the hotel where the meetings being held. Jack and Kim had not seen each other for more than ten years and spent much time reminiscing. It was a very short but pleasant reunion. The day following Jack's presentation, Jack and Hilda boarded a tour bus to Santa Fe. Then something quite unexpected happened when they stopped temporarily at an Indian reservation. Suddenly Jack experienced a sharp pain spreading across his shoulders and upper arms together with a shortness of breath. He became very anxious: perhaps he was having a heart attack. When they reached Santa Fe, he continued to have breathing difficulties and could walk only short distances. After returning to Minneapolis and consulting his primary physician, he was quickly referred to a cardiologist and given a stress test. It was clear that he had suffered an angina: a prelude to a heart attack and after further diagnosis he underwent triple bypass heart surgery during which he suffered a mild heart attack. The aftermath of heart surgery was excruciating, but gradually he recovered and resumed teaching

Sometime later Jack and Hilda received a phone call from their daughter,Ellen. She and her husband, George had returned from Crete and were living in California where George had attended an army intelligence school. Her marriage was breaking up, and she wished to rejoin her parents in Minnesota. Jack was not surprised, as he had observed a great deal of tension and conflict between Ellen and her husband during his sojourn in Crete. He pleaded with her to work harder to save their marriage, but it was to no avail. She insisted it was over and that she needed to return to her parental home with her new born son. Jack and Hilda agreed helping her care for their grandson and complete her baccalaureate at the University of Minnesota. After that she set up a household with an old friend and later remarried. Later a rift developed between Ellen and her brother and parents, and she eventually became completely estranged from the family.

Over the years William had grown a great deal, and in a few months he would turn twenty one. Also, he had been working diligently in the area of sales. One day in early spring, he spoke to Jack in a very serious tone.

"Dad, there's something I need to talk to you about."

"Sure, William," Jack replied looking at his watch. "Hey, it's almost time for lunch. Why don't we go out for a bite and talk it over." The father and son had a very close relationship, something that Jack never had when he was growing up.

They entered a nearby restaurant and sat at a table facing each other. The waitress approached quickly, and they ordered some food and beverages.

"Okay, son." Jack began. "What's going on? You sound pretty serious."

"Well, dad I'm thinking of getting married."

"Wow!" Jack exclaimed. "That is serious! Who is she? Have I already met her? You have been dating so many different girls."

"Her name is Marie, Marie Walensky."

"Oh, yes. I have met her. So when do you plan to marry?"

"Sometime in the fall, dad. But we're having a problem."

"What is it?"

"Marie was brought up Catholic; but like me, she's not serious about her religion. I called Temple Israel and asked if a rabbi would perform the wedding ceremony. They got upset with me and said it couldn't be done unless Marie converted to Judaism. But I don't want to make that an issue. It could be difficult for her. After all, she went to Catholic schools and was taught by nuns."

Jack smiled. "I don't think it's really a problem, William. You and Marie will work it out. Your mother, of course, converted to Judaism. I didn't insist. I even suggested that we get married by a justice of the peace. But she converted to keep peace in the family, to placate my stepfather. Your situation is much different. Son, whatever you decide will be okay."

However, this certainly came as a surprise to Jack. William was growing up so fast. When he was only thirteen William worked part time at a gas station recording sales on a computer. Somehow there were discrepancies in the recordings. William was blamed, and his wages were withheld. But it was unclear as to why the discrepancies had occurred.

Jack had spoken to his son firmly, saying: "We're going to go to court on this one. You're going to plea your case." He coached William, they went to court, and William pleaded his case. It was an impressive presentation, and the judge ruled that William was entitled to half of his withheld wages.

When William was a few years older, Jack purchased a boat, about eighteen feet long with an enclosed engine in the stern. Pulling the boat up to a resort at Leech Lake, they spent a few days fishing; but when they were preparing to leave for home, they had difficulty in mounting the boat back on to the trailer. William made a suggestion:

"Dad, why don't you take the car and trailer to Walker. I'll take the boat and meet you there."

Jack felt very apprehensive. It was about twenty miles to Walker, but they really had no choice. He drove to Walker and waited anxiously at the marina. He became more worried as the sky grew darker and winds blew stronger across the lake creating a cascade of whitecaps. But then he felt relieved, as he saw William appear on the horizon.

His son looked a little shaken. "Dad it was scary. I thought a storm was coming up."

Jack was always careful not to compare William with himself. He would have never been ready to marry so young. The times and circumstances were so different. He had so much else to do; and he did not meet his love and future bride until many years later. He was sure his son would successfully find his own way. In September William and Marie were married by a priest. It was a simple ceremony with few religious overtones, and a small band played and sang a popular song.

From 1989 to 1993 George H. W. Bush served as President of the United States. He was a flyer in the U.S. Navy during World War II, engaged in combat in the Pacific, and attended Yale University following the war. Early in his presidency, both the Berlin Wall and the Soviet Union collapsed. Initially he was a very popular president, but the onset of an economic recession resulted in a decline in his approval rating. He was quite active in foreign policy. Shortly after the fall of the Berlin Wall, he met with Premier Gorbachev; and they signed the Strategic Arms Reduction Treaty. In 1990 Iraq invaded Kuwait, Bush condemned the attack; and in 1991 the United States led a coalition of forces which repelled the invasion and pushed Iraqi forces back into Iraq. Critics contended that Bush should have continued on to Baghdad and toppled Hussein from power. But he felt that the United Nations had not given him a mandate, and there would be incalculable risks involved in occupying Iraq. Near the end of his term, President Bush, in conjunction with efforts of the United Nations, involved the United States in the Somali civil war. But efforts to bring about an end to the war failed. It was during the Bush administration that negotiations began on the North American Free Trade Agreement (NAFTA) which would supposedly facilitate trade among Canada, the United States, and Mexico. There was some controversy regarding the agreement, but it was finally passed during the Clinton administration.

For almost twenty years Jack had been training diligently in Shotokan karate. He had begun his training in Saint Cloud and continued in Minneapolis after he and his family moved there. The training had made him stronger physically and mentally. It required a coordination of mind and body and included three pillars which are interdependent and form the karate way: kihon, kumite, and kata. The first, kihon refered to basics including such aspects as structure, movement, stances, breathing, blocks, kicks, and strikes. Kumite entailed different styles of sparring: one step, three step, or free sparring refraining from striking your partner. A great deal of emphasis was placed on proper restraint or control. The kata was a sequence of movements designed to repel the attacks of adversaries. It involved the basics or fundamentals of karate and needed to be done with an awareness of the meaning of various techniques. Every kata began with a block followed with a counter attack of punches and kicks. The essence of karate was "kime": a quick explosion of maximum power expressed in punches, kicks, and blocks. or combination thereof. Back in Minnesota, Jack had tested several times and had progressed from the rank of white belt to purple belt. With further progress he could attain the brown belt, three steps away from a black belt. Jack's sensei or teacher, Robert Fusaro had earned his black belt in Japan shortly after the end of World war Two. He was about Jack's age and a very stimulating and knowledgeable mentor emphasizing proper breathing and a scream "Ei!" which emanated, not from the throat, but from the center of the body. Jack learned that if you did not breathe or breathe properly in kata classes, it could be dangerous. You might even pass out on the floor while training. Sensei Fusaro pointed out that there were two reasons for the "Ei!": It contributed to more effective breathing especially in a series of explosive movements, and it could scare the hell out of adversaries disposing them to turn and run. During the Korean War. nearly a million Chinese communist troops had entered the conflict and were mounting an offensive. Among the defenders were Turkish troops who with fixed bayonets charged screaming. It was reported that many of the Chinese fled frightened and demoralized. Of course, it always better to avoid the use of karate in threatening situations. If possible, the best action is restraint or withdrawal. It should be used only for self-defense and in the event of life or death circumstances.

Karate blows can result in serious internal injuries and even death, and fortunately Jack was never forced to use his karate skills. But sometimes just a karate stance may deter what might have been an unpleasant or even threatening encounter. It was an early evening when Jack had just parked his car along Hennepin Avenue in Minneapolis. It was a depressed neighborhood; and as he headed to his dojo for a training session, a young man slovenly dressed started to approach him. As the man drew nearer, Jack stopped, slowly dropped his arms, clenched his fists, and stood very erect in a ready stance. He looked directly in the eyes of the stranger who had also stopped.

"Mister!" the stranger began, sensing Jack's apprehension. "I don't mean any harm! I only want to ask you for a cigarette."

Jack took a deep breath and relaxed.

"I'm sorry," he replied. "I don't smoke."

The incident ended, and the stranger continued on his way. Simply by moving into a ready stance, Jack had telegraphed a message cautioning the stranger not to draw any closer.

In 1987 the first Palestinian intifada or uprising began in protest to the Israeli occupation of Palestinian territories which followed after the Six Day War in 1967. There was growing dissatisfaction and resistance among the Palestinians in the Gaza Strip and the West Bank. Much of this was expressed in Palestinian strikes, boycotts, refusals to pay taxes, and acts of violence. The violence entailed a widespread throwing of stones and Molotov cocktails at Israeli police and military forces. Other factors contributing to the increased frustration and hostility was the limited availability of land for new buildings and agricultural use. In addition, there was growing population crowding and unemployment as well as Palestinian fears that they might be transferred or displaced from their current territories. Mass demonstrations and escalating violence resulted in repressive measures taken by Israeli defense forces. There were reported beatings of handcuffed Palestinian youths and shootings of school children. Many of the protesters were teenagers and even younger. The high birth rates of the Palestinians had contributed to their disproportionately young population. At the beginning of the first Palestinian uprising, Hamas emerged originating in the Muslim Brotherhood. It was an organization calling for the destruction of the State of Israel and the creation of an Islamic Palestinian state. In later years it split with the PLO and challenged Fatah's leadership role; and in 1990 Hamas began terrorist attacks against Israel comprising indiscriminate suicide bombings and the firing of rockets into civilian settlements. The first Palestinian uprising ended about 1993 with the Oslo Accords which failed to bring about any permanent agreement and peace. Also, Iran had entered the nuclear age and was perceived as a growing threat not only to Israel but to other Arab nations and Western civilization as well.

It was the early 1990's, and in Saint Cloud Jack informed John Kearney that he was ready to retire and wanted to forego any retirement ceremony. However, John insisted on a farewell dinner.

"But Jack, it's tradition. We've always done this for retiring faculty. Everyone in the department will be there, and you can invite faculty from other departments."

Reluctantly Jack consented. He even invited Mike Lusky from the Economics Department, Bob Prow, chairman of the Criminal Justice Department, and Hashim, his luncheon companion from the History Department. The retirement dinner occurred at one of city's restaurants, and Jack delivered a farewell speech which was generally conciliatory.

However, at one point he became blunt and critical.

"Some of you sociologists may not like what I have to say, but I'm going to say it anyway."

"Oh, oh", Bob Prow murmured. "Here it comes."

"I've taught in this department for about twenty years; and there's been very little, if any, growth. Changes have been largely cosmetic. I think we've failed to make meaningful advances in our curriculum or promote research which I have always believed is essential to quality teaching. We couldn't even get a bona fide graduate program off the drawing board."

When the evening was drawing to a close, Mike Lusky said to Jack: "You really got your licks in."

It took almost a year for Jack and Hilda to sell their house in Minnetonka. Originally they had planned to build a new home in Prescott, Arizona, and they had already purchased land in an attractive housing development. But costs of construction had increased substantially, so they decided to move temporarily to Las Vegas. A few months before they departed, Marie gave birth to another baby girl. Now they had two granddaughters: Elizabeth and Maria, the first born. William's responsibilities were indeed growing. Just before their departure, Jack and Hilda had a farewell dinner for the family.

"We'll be back to visit you," Jack reassured his son. And early one spring morning, Jack and Hilda loaded their sport utility vehicle (SUV) with basic necessities and drove south on 35W. Within a few hours they were heading west toward the Great Divide.

CHAPTER NINE:
THE LAS VEGAS EXPERIENCE

During an earlier trip to Las Vegas Jack and Hilda had rented an apartment, and their furniture together with other possessions would be sent there on their arrival. Hilda insisted in doing the driving while Jack perused a series of detailed maps providing directions. It would be a long drive almost 2,000 miles, but they would take their time. They passed many farms and fields of corn as they drove through the countryside of Iowa. Later they crossed into Nebraska at Council Bluffs on the east bank of the Missouri River just across from Omaha. Driving through the flat terrain of Nebraska and along the North Platte River, they viewed herds of cattle grazing in green fields of grass mixed with alfalfa, and periodically repulsive odors emanating from piles of dung pervaded the air. The sun was just beginning to set when they reached Kearney, about halfway across Nebraska, where they stopped at a motel, ate a leisurely dinner, and spent the night. They arose early the next morning; and after a quick breakfast, they were on the road again. By midday they entered Colorado leaving Interstate 80 and continuing on Interstate 76. For a few hours they passed a lot of farmland, and the terrain continued to be level. But as they neared Denver, the massiveness and peaks of the Rocky Mountains loomed ahead. It was already late afternoon, and the sun was beginning to sink behind the mountains, and Jack suggested that they stop at a motel in the foothills waiting until morning before crossing the Continental Divide. Early the following day they started into the mountains, and soon they reached the Eisenhower Tunnel which stretched nearly two miles under the Continental

Divide. The elevation was slightly over 11, 000 feet which was the maximum along Interstate 70. By midday they stopped to relax and eat some packed sandwiches at a picnic area. They were still up several thousand feet, and the view was spectacular. Towering mountain ranges covered with Ponderosa pines, white oak, and dense shrubs were clearly visible. A bald eagle could be seen soaring above a deep canyon. And far below, the waters of the Colorado River glowed in the sunlight flowing incessantly and winding through the mountains like some great serpent. The river's currents were swift and strong as well as lethal. Jack thought of their friends and former neighbors in Minnesota who had retired to Prescott, Arizona and whose son had drowned in the river's rapids. He was their only child, making it an especially sorrowful event. Finishing their lunch and leaving leftover crumbs for some hungry squirrels, they resumed their journey. At twilight they began their descent and stopped for the night at Grand Junction, Colorado close to the border of Utah. The next day they expected to reach Las Vegas.

Again they rose early in the morning and resumed their journey crossing the green rolling hills of Utah. Far to the north were mountain ranges and to the south a desert and more mountains. By early afternoon, they had turned south on Interstate 15, and late in the afternoon they passed through St. George and entered the Mojave Desert. The surrounding landscape changed drastically. The terrain flattened, the air became very hot and dry. Cactuses, Joshua Trees, and other desert flora abounded. Far in the distance were mountains that engulfed Las Vegas. Suddenly Hilda slowed the SUV.

"What is it? Why are you slowing down?" asked Jack.

"Don't you see it?" replied Hilda.

A coyote was sitting in the middle of the highway. The animal seemed unconcerned with their approach. But as they we drew closer, it quickly sprang from the road and disappeared.

By the time they had driven through the mountains, dusk had fallen; and far ahead was Las Vegas. Lights from hotels, casinos, and expanding residential areas were shining brightly. The city was like some great jewel glowing in the desert. Jack reflected that he and Hilda had first visited Las Vegas on one of their wedding anniversaries, and on that first flight there he was bewildered by the strange landscape of the Mojave Desert: so barren and level, except for the sprawling city. Following that, they made many visits to Vegas and enjoyed the entertainment, the buffets, and even the gambling which they did with some restraint. It was rather extraordinary to walk through the airport and casinos hearing the sound of coins falling into the trays of slot machines and the gasps or cries of players at the blackjack tables. Jack enjoyed playing blackjack, and sometimes Hilda joined him. Often when they took their trips to Vegas, they stayed at the Mirage Hotel along the Strip. Occasionally, Jack would rise and begin to play blackjack about five in the morning. By that time the night crowd had dissipated and the casino was relatively quiet. One early morning he sat at a blackjack table permitting a minimum of five dollar bets. Just as he placed a five dollar chip on a betting spot, a woman dressed in a white evening dress falling from her shoulders slipped into a seat next to him. In one hand she held a glass of wine and in the other a rumpled paper bag. She drew five one hundred dollar bills from the bag and placed them all on a betting spot. Then she turned to Jack saying:

"Put your money with mine."

Jack smiled and shook his head incredulously. "No thanks," He replied.

The dealer dealt the hand, and the lady received a seven and a four. Unhesitatingly, she drew another five one hundred dollar bills from her bag.

"I'll double down," she uttered firmly, and placed the additional bills on her betting spot.

The few players at the table gasped, as the dealer dealt cards face up. Instead of a hoped for ten or face card, the woman received only a three. She could win if the dealer busted. But the dealer turned over his hole card. He made a hand totaling seventeen, and quickly scooped up the woman's bet. Subsequently she showed the dealer some identification and asked to draw on her line of credit. The dealer made a quick call, nodded, and then gave the woman a pile of hundred dollar chips. Jack had won his hand. He picked up his two five dollar chips, left the table; and returning to his hotel room, he related the incident to Hilda. Later that morning, he saw the same woman still sipping a glass of wine and playing at a blackjack table. Other curious sights were observed among the slot machine players. One guy covered his eyes as he pulled the lever of a machine. Another pulled the lever and ran back and forth. And a few others were playing two or more machines almost simultaneously. Perhaps they believed their movements would cast magical and beneficial spells. Then there were those players who made claims on particular slot machines. At times when Jack was about to insert some coins in a particular slot machine, he was brazenly interrupted by another player shouting:

"Stop! I've been playing there! That's my machine!"

"Jack, wake up!" Hilda exclaimed. "We're here in Las Vegas. There's a hotel ahead. Shall we stay there for the night?"

"I must have dozed off," he answered, shaking his head. "I think that hotel will be okay."

Hilda drove into valet parking. They registered inside and spent the night at the hotel. Their furniture and other possessions were scheduled for delivery the following day. Their new living quarters were rather cramped compared with their former home back in Minnesota which had been spacious: a large two story house with a finished walk out basement. However, there was adequate space in the two bedroom apartment, and many things were left unpacked and stored away in one of the bedrooms. The apartment was in a neighborhood on the west side of Las Vegas just a few blocks away from Summerlin, an area undergoing rapid residential and commercial development. Also, it was close to some shopping malls with food stores, restaurants, gas stations, pharmacies as well as many other conveniences and only a block away from West Sahara Avenue which ran several miles down to the renown Las Vegas Strip.

For several months Jack and Hilda spent considerable time patronizing the hotels, casinos, shows, and restaurants of the city. They gambled but budgeted themselves very carefully. Whenever Jack played a session of blackjack, it was always with a fixed amount of cash. He would play with either one hundred or two hundred dollars per session depending upon whether his basic bet was five or ten dollars per hand. He put aside a bankroll of one thousand or two thousand dollars from which he drew for each blackjack session. Such discipline was indeed needed for people's lives could be so easily destroyed if they became addicted to gambling. Frequently Jack witnessed players who failed to leave the tables when losing, who simply hung on thinking that if I play long enough their situations would change to winning streaks. Their thinking perhaps was related to the so-called "law of averages" or "law of large numbers". But such players would fail to realize that it could take many dealt hands or trials before the "law of large numbers" kicked in and by that time, they may have had their "clocks cleaned". In contrast, the casino or the "house" possessed virtually inexhaustible resources. Players beware! The glitter and glamour of Las Vegas was built on "losers" not on "winners".

Their favorite place for gambling and buffets was the Golden Nugget Hotel and Casino in the downtown area on the Freemont Street Experience. The hotel was very accessible. It was a short drive on the nearby expressway to the downtown exit and to the hotel only a few blocks away. Parking was no problem as free parking was provided for hotel guests. It was one of the oldest casinos in the city built in 1946 and exuded the ambience of the old Las Vegas. Jack would play at the blackjack tables making conservative bets of five or ten dollars except when it was appropriate to double down or split pairs in which cases the stakes could increase considerably. There were times when he felt like a yoyo alternately winning and losing. But he found it challenging and enjoyed the game especially the interaction with dealers and other players. Some people preferred playing the machines feeling intimidated by the presence of a dealer and other players, but not Jack. Generally he disliked the machines. He might play one now and then if he had a few spare coins. Once in a while, he would even play alone against the dealers which afforded him more of a chance to develop relationships with individual dealers and "pit bosses" or dealer supervisors. Interestingly there were dealers who would even try to help him. One morning Jack stopped to play at an empty table. He was well acquainted with the dealer; they had conversed many times.

"How are we doing today, Harry?" Jack asked as he sat down and dropped some chips on a betting spot.

"Jack," he replied, "Don't play here. Everyone is losing at my table this morning. Try the one behind me. It's hot, lots of winners."

"Thanks for the tip," Jack quickly scooped up his chips and moved to the other table.

He played for a while. Harry was right. It was a hot table. Jack was winning almost a hundred dollars and then left. The tide was turning and the dealer began to take a few consecutive hands. But before leaving the casino, he stopped again at Harry's table and handed him a few five dollar chips.

"Thanks again, Harry. Have a good day. See you another time."

Jack was wary of a casino of empty blackjack tables, except in the very late evening or early morning hours when most players had retired. It could be a "red flag" indicating there had been a preponderance of losers driven from the tables. He learned, too that it was a good idea to scan or scout the blackjack tables before deciding where and when to play. What was the mood of the players? Did they look happy or depressed? Were they winning more often than losing? Did they play with many chips or were they clutching a remaining few? There were many such circumstances to consider. For a time he was ahead a few thousand dollars, but in the end he gave it all back. Certainly this was no way to earn a living or get rich quickly.It was just a kind of entertainment. He played his best to win but was always prepared to lose; and eventually his interest and involvement in the game expired.

Soon after they became settled in their apartment, Jack began searching the martial arts section of the yellow pages of the local phone directory. He needed to resume his karate training. Although there were many listings, he found only one for Shotokan karate. The dojo or "place of training" was located along West Sahara only several miles from Jack's apartment. In the training area was a smooth wooden floor and mirrors on one of the walls. A large photograph of Master Gichin Funakoshi, considered the founding father of Shotokan karate, was mounted on the front wall. Next to his picture was a smaller photograph of his disciple, Shihan Osamu Ozawa who established the Las Vegas Shotokan Dojo. Hanging below both pictures was a plaque inscribed with "Dojo kun" - the five precepts of Gichin Funakoshi. At the end of every training session, they were recited by the highest ranking student and repeated by the rest of the class:

We shall endeavor to build our character.

We shall be faithful in our study.

We shall cultivate courage and tenacity.

We shall attach great importance to etiquette.

We shall be wary of foolishness.

This was only a part of the ritual. At the beginning of each class the students would line up in the order of their ranks:black belts at the head of the line, white belts at the end. Making sure their line was straight; they faced the front wall and their instructor or sensei. They all kneeled, including their sensei, and bowed saying, "shomen ni rei", a salutation to the front. Then their sensei turned and faced the students who then bowed again saying, "sensei ni rei," a salutation to their master or teacher. After that, they would all rise and the training would begin with stretching exercises. The three pillars of Shotokan were kihon, kumite, and kata and each was treated during the training session. Kihon refered to the basics such as stances, blocks, punches. "Kiai" was a fighting yell where "ki" was "spirit" and "ai" was "together", meaning spirit and harmony. It was a yell intended to demoralize an adversary and was essential for proper breathing. The basics or kihon were analogous to the foundation of a house without which the house would fall. Kumite or sparring involved an attacker and a defender. The attacker employed combinations of punches and kicks while the defender responded with appropriate blocks and counter attacks. Form, speed, power, timing, focus, and distance all played an important role in the kumite. A karateka or practitioner of karate was expected to exercise constraint or control when sparring. Bodily contact could be dangerous; and, if possible,should be avoided, as it could result in serious internal injuries. This especially applied in competitive tournaments where a body strike could result in a penalty or even a forfeit of the match. A gross misrepresentation of authentic and traditional karate are the tournament scenes in the movie, "The Karate Kid" where opponents are deliberately and mercilessly inflicting bodily strikes on one another. The kumite training consisted of one step, three step, and free sparring. Although Jack was cautious particularly in free sparring sessions, one time he was careless while blocking a kick with his hand and forearm. His thumb was inappropriately protruding, and his partner's foot struck his extended thumb. Obviously he should've blocked with a clenched fist, or even better moved quickly away from the path of the kick. A blocking arm and hand are usually no match for a powerful front or round house kick. Jack's thumb felt sprained, but he hoped in time it would heal. However, the pain persisted, and finally he visited an orthopedist. A ligament was torn requiring surgery. For about six months Jack's hand and forearm were wrapped in a cast, and the prognosis was not encouraging. The orthopedist believed that he would recover only half of the original flexibility in his injured thumb. But surprisingly, after the cast was removed, he recovered complete flexibility. Equally important was the kata, the third pillar of Shotokan incorporating aspects of kihon and kumite. Although all three pillars were independent, they were inextricably woven together. Each kata began and ended in a bow. After the bow, the karateka executed a block immediately followed by a counter attack. A kata was made up of a sequence of defensive and offensive movements against supposed adversaries or attackers. There was variation in the speed of movements which gave each kata an almost rhythmic and distinctive aura. At this point, Jack had learned the five basic katas or heian katas where the word "heian" derived from "peace and stability"; and such katas highlighted basic techniques.

The ambience of the Las Vegas Shotokan dojo differed somewhat from that of the dojo in Minnesota. To begin with, the Shotokan karate in Minnesota: or the Midwest Karate Association was affiliated with the Japan Karate Association or JKA whereas the Shotokan karate dojo in Las Vegas was associated with the International Traditional Karate Association. The latter placed more emphasis on Japanese customs and language. For example, sometimes students in Las Vegas were asked to recite Dojo Kuhn not only in English but in Japanese as well. Also, bowing was a common greeting as was the expression "Ooss!" Such rituals had not been practiced and class etiquette had been more informal back in Minnesota. In the Vegas dojo testing for higher belts was encouraged more; and except for the black belt, tests were given monthly. Before he left Minnesota, Jack had tested for the purple belt which was the highest rank of the so called color belts but had received only a semi pass. After about a year, he tested again in Vegas and earned a full purple belt rank.

The origins of Japanese karate are unclear; no one is quite sure how it all began. Many styles, including Shotokan, developed on the island of Okinawa dating back some hundreds of years. It is believed that it was first introduced by Buddhist monks journeying from India to monasteries in China where it was adopted and practiced by other monks as a form of exercise to stimulate themselves physically and mentally. Perhaps later it underwent some transformations being influenced by Chinese kick boxing. Eventually it found its way to Okinawa, and at a time when the island's habitants were prohibited by ruling authorities to possess weapons. Since people had no means of protection against bandits or marauders, they began to train in karate or "empty hands". Their feet, legs, arms, and hands became lethal weapons. As mentioned earlier, it was Gichin Funakoshi who was the father of modern Karate do or the "The Karate Way". When Jack Rubin journeyed to Las Vegas and joined the Shotokan dojo, he had the great honor to train under Shihan Osamu Ozawa: a descendent of the Samurai and a renown disciple of Master Funakoshi. His story is extraordinary and played an influential role in Jack Rubin's Las Vegas experience. Much of the following is based upon Osamu Ozawa's autobiography.

Osamu began studying karate at the age of 12. When he was only 17 years old, he entered Hosei University and began training with Master Gichin Funakoshi. During a period of two years, he learned various styles of sparring as well fifteen katas basic to Shotokan. Master Funakoshi was a patient and very watchful teacher who carefully observed his students, pointing out their mistakes, and explaining the meaning of Shotokan techniques. By 1944 Osamu earned his first degree black belt or 1st Dan. But Japan was at war, and Osamu was drafted into the military. At this point in time it was clear that Japan was losing the war, but the general population was unaware of this because of the suppression of information by a military that controlled the government. Often there was much misinformation circulated particularly about Americans who were depicted as savage animals. After his induction into the military, Osamu began training in an aircraft kamikaze unit. This was an elite force comprised of not only aircraft but also tanks, submarines, and speed boats. It was considered an honor to be selected and serve in such a force and eventually die for the Emperor and the nation. Osamu was assigned to plunge his plane into specified enemy targets on the island of Okinawa which had been the home of Gichin Funakoshi, the founder of Shotokan Karate, as well as the home of many other styles of Japanese karate. Was it a stroke of fate or destiny? As Ozawa's plane headed down the runway and took off, it overturned and crashed. His life was spared, but he suffered injuries and was hospitalized. When he recovered, the war had ended; and for a period of time, he felt deep shame and dishonor, He even sought the counsel of a priest at a Zen temple who encouraged him to work for a new Japan.

In the years that followed, Osamu continued his karate training and instructed others in karate. Also, he was active in the Japan Karate Association which was seeking to unify karate throughout Japan. For a time, he became involved in the television industry and became one of Japan's leading television directors. In the early 1960's he immigrated to America where he lived in California for a while and became acquainted with a number of prominent Hollywood actors among then was Chuck Norris who invited Osamu to teach at his dojo in Redondo Beach. He remained in the Los Angeles area for several years before moving to Las Vegas in 1974. He worked there as a blackjack dealer and at poker tables in hotel casinos and was responsible for organizing karate tournaments at major Las Vegas hotels. Over the years the tournament participants grew in number and teams of competitors came from all over the world. During the 1980's, Master Ozawa attained the rank of 8th degree black belt and spent a great deal of his time teaching at his dojo along West Sahara Avenue.

Although Master Ozawa was a short and thin man, he was very muscular and able to generate a great deal of energy when executing karate techniques. One time in demonstrating a rising block, he instructed Jack to punch him. As Osamu blocked, just brushing against the sleeve of Jack's gi, Jack experienced an odd sensation. It felt like an electric shock was passing through his body. When Jack appeared on the dojo floor, bowing before Master Ozawa and other instructors, preparing to test for a full purple belt rank, Ozawa asked:

"How old are you?"

"Sixty seven," he replied. Jack was the oldest student in the dojo.

Ozawa smiled. "Ohhh!" he exclaimed. "It's so good that you train!"

Only three years separated the two men. Ozawa was seventy years old.

About two years later, Jack tested for his brown belt and passed. He was now considered a higher belt only two more ranks away from the black belt.

A lot of changes were occurring in Las Vegas especially along the Vegas Strip. Old hotels and casinos were being displaced by new ones such as Bellagio, Monte Carlo, Venetian Resort, and Paris. Others such as Holiday Inn, Aladdin, the Barbary Coast, and the Flamingo were undergoing expansions or renovations. Both automobile and pedestrian traffic was growing substantially, and overpasses were being constructed to accommodate the increased tourist congestion. The metropolitan area was experiencing an explosive growth in population along with a proliferation of private residences, apartments, neighborhood hotels and casinos, public parks as well as countless malls with businesses providing needed goods and services. Jack and Hilda generally avoided the Strip mainly because of the hectic flow of traffic and increased air pollution. But occasionally they did visit the area to dine or take in a show. After spending several months in the apartment, Hilda suggested that maybe they should think about buying a house in Las Vegas. They had already put their lot in Prescott up for sale since building prices there were still too high. Her suggestion appealed to Jack, so with the help of a real estate agent they began to explore the housing market. They confined their searches to Summerlin and adjacent areas. It wasn't long before they discovered a fairly new housing development next to Angel Park, a very attractive city park covered with trees, bushes, and equipped with an automatic watering system. In addition, there were picnic tables with overhangs and benches as well as a walking path that completely circled the park. Directly buffeting the park was the bright green of the Angel Park golf course. A great deal of vacant land sprawled west of the housing development comprising a few hundred homes and identified as Angel Park Ranch. Some of the empty land was already developed for commercial use consisting of a variety of stores, shops, and a few restaurants. Jack and Hilda found an available house only a block away from the park. Unlike their house in Minnesota, it was a single story structure and a lot smaller. But it was certainly adequate, and the location was excellent. Its construction was nearly finished, and when it was completed they purchased it and moved into their new home.

Jack had grown more involved in his karate training and had become quite friendly with other karate students; and occasionally the dojo scheduled social gatherings especially around the holiday season, Thanksgiving and Christmas. Heidi had joined a Swedish American organization and made new friends among the group. However, Jack had become somewhat restive. He had pretty much abandoned his blackjack playing and had some wish to teach again but only on a part time basis. He phoned the Chairman of the Sociology Department at the University of Nevada Las Vegas (UNLV),and an interview was arranged. During his tenure at Saint Cloud State University, he had recurrently taught a course in World Population Problems; and at his meeting with the chairman he inquired if he could offer the course at UNLV. His instructional materials and lectures would be based on current reports published by the Population Reference Bureau dealing with relationships between population growth and the social, economic, and political ramifications in different parts of the world with emphasis on comparisons between developed and developing nations. The chairman seemed very receptive and impressed. Quickly he agreed to schedule Jack's course for the coming fall semester, and a sufficient number of the reports for prospective students were ordered from the Population Reference Bureau.

UNLV was several blocks east of the Las Vegas Strip. It was obvious that the university was well endowed. Many fairly new buildings academic and administrative occupied a massive campus. Student dormitories and other facilities were abundant. Before fall classes began, Jack explored the university library and computer center. The resources of both were quite extensive and impressive. On the first day of the semester about twenty students filed into Jack's classroom. All were well groomed and seemed attentive. Most had already purchased copies of the United Nations population reports ordered from the Population Reference Bureau. Jack's first lecture was essentially introductory. He handed out a detailed description of material to be covered in the course, the requirements which included midterm and final examinations, and a written research project which could contribute to a student's final course grade. In advance of his lectures, he indicated what he expected students to be reading and that they should be prepared to engage in some discussion of the assigned materials.

But it was an odd situation. As the course progressed, the students were almost completely silent. And it seemed that most were not even bothering to read the population reports or write notes during his lectures. This occurred despite the fact that he had told them their examinations would be based largely on his lectures. Maybe they can't read or write, Jack mused. They're almost like a bunch of zombies.

Prior to the midterm examination, he attempted to prepare the students with an intensive review. But, it was to no avail; generally their performance on the exam was abysmally poor. When the tests were graded and returned, some of the students became boisterous and even insolent. As Jack was taking time to go over the test questions, one student continuously interrupted him with contemptuous statements, claiming to speak for the entire class.

"We didn't like your test and the way you grade!" he shouted.

"You speak for yourself not for the rest of the class!" Jack shot back at him. "You're not listening. You're disrupting the class, and if you don't stop I'll call security and have you removed!"

A few other students were whining, rose from their seats and without a word simply walked out of the room. One student even remarked: "I took this course because I thought it would be easy." Subsequently, many students were absent from the class until a few days before the week of final examinations. On a day when nearly all students were present, a young woman appeared at the door of the classroom clasping a bunch of papers. She entered the room telling Jack he must wait outside while she distributed and subsequently collected teacher evaluation forms from his students.

Jack felt this was absurd. Most of these students hadn't even attended class for several weeks. But he has no choice except to cooperate with the university rules. Consequently he waited about fifteen or twenty minutes before reentering the room and beginning his lecture. Student performance on the final examinations was generally dismal. However, there was one exception: a graduate student from the Economics Department drew an *A* grade for the course. She was indeed a very exceptional student. A few months later Jack happened to encounter her and she complimented him on the course, commenting:

"I don't know what was the matter with the other students. You had a lot of patience and gave them a great deal of help. But it seemed like it was never enough. They were rude and infantile and wanted to be spoon fed."

About a week after Jack had submitted final grades for his World Population Problems class, he received a phone call from one of the students.

"Professor Rubin this is a student, Stanley Rodham from your course on World Population Problems. I'm unhappy about my final grade. It was only a C, and I need a B for admittance to law school. I want to meet with you and go over my final examination."

Jack remembered the student. He was the one, following the midterm exam, who had said that he was taking the course because he thought it would be easy. He was also among the many students who failed to attend class after the midterm reappearing just prior to the final examination. Jack did not grade students on their attendance, but he was careful to keep an attendance record.

"Stanley, there is really no point of our meeting for this," Jack replied. "I am not going to alter my grading procedure as described in the course syllabus, and I'm no longer in residence at UNLV. What I can do is review your final examination and let you know the result."

"No," the student insisted. "You have to meet with me, or I'll call the chairman."

"You can do that."

Within several minutes Jack received a phone call from the chairman.

"Jack, I just received this call from one of your students. He's upset about his grade. Says he needs a *B* to be accepted to law school. Claims he attended class regularly."

"Listen, Brian. The student is lying about his attendance. I keep an attendance record which shows he missed about half of his classes. But that's really irrelevant. I don't grade at all on class attendance only on student performance."

"Will you at least review his final examination, and then drop by my office. Let me know what you decide to do."

"Certainly", Jack responded. "I offered that option to the student, but he refused."

For a few moments, there was silence. Then hesitatingly Brian said,

"You know, Jack. I can't change the grade."

"I know that," Jack answered. The chairman was trying to be subtle, but what he wanted was obvious.

A few days later Jack appeared in the chairman's office, and brought the student's final exam with him. Their conversation was very brief.

"I reviewed the student's final exam, Brian. I can't change the grade. In order to do that, I would have to alter my system of grading indicated in the syllabus given out to the class at the beginning of the semester."

"What about his research paper that he did for extra credit? Wouldn't that help?" the chairman asked.

"No it wouldn't", Jack replied

"Well, that's it then," Brian said with a disapproving tone.

Jack shook his head in disgust, turned, and left the room. He was not a team player and refused to abandon his integrity. Of course, he would not be asked to teach again at UNLV; and as far as he was concerned, it was good riddance. Except for two students, the class was the very worst that he had ever had. Sometime later, he described his UNLV teaching experience to Mike Lusky who occasionally escaped the frigid Minnesota winters and visited relatives in Las Vegas.

"I'm not at all surprised. Jack," Mike commented. "I taught a course in the UNLV Economics Department for one semester. It was very disappointing. The students performed very poorly. I had office hours to meet with students, but nobody ever came. They never had any questions. By comparison, my students at Saint Cloud were stars." He paused for a few moments and then continued. "Another thing, I visited their computer center. It was certainly well equipped with the latest technology, but the staff were a bunch of incompetent nincompoops. They were no help whenever I asked for assistance or had questions."

Mike Lusky's account helped to validate Jack's experience at UNLV. He was very good at assessing situations. Moreover he was an accomplished scholar both in his teaching and research activities. Jack had met him early in his career at Saint Cloud State and had come to know him quite well.

Beginning in 1993, Bill Clinton had become President of the United States. He was the first Democratic president to serve two terms since the Franklin Roosevelt administration. At the very beginning of his administration, he advocated raising taxes on the wealthiest Americans, on the use of energy, and on some Social Security payments. These recommendations, along with cuts in government spending, were in a budget submitted to Congress with aim of reducing deficit spending. There was intense opposition especially from Republican members of Congress. But eventually President Clinton won out. He was a very effective negotiator and had a talent for "reaching across the aisle" and compromising with Republicans. On one occasion, conflicts over the budget even led to a temporary government shutdown. But the president and his opponents were able to work out their differences. There were other domestic achievements of the Clinton administration. Economic growth nearly doubled, the unemployment rate fell below five percent. Especially striking were the drops in the unemployment rates of minorities in particular for African Americans or blacks and Hispanics. Their unemployment rates were cut in half. Similarly, the inflation rate was reduced by nearly one half. Home ownership increased by the end of the Clinton administration, and the poverty rate declined markedly. In addition he was a strong advocate of the North American Fair Trade Agreement (NAFTA) which had been initiated in an earlier administrations.

In foreign policy Clinton encountered many dilemmas and difficulties. From the very beginning of his presidency he was confronted with a number of international conflicts. Civil war raged in Somalia on the Horn of Africa. The prior administration of George H. W. Bush had tried to alleviate the suffering and dying by dispatching American troops to the area. But American intervention failed in 1994, and Clinton was forced to withdraw American troops. There was widespread genocide in Rwanda, an African country; but the Clinton administration and the United Nation did essentially nothing while thousands were slaughtered. The Balkans, sometimes referred to as "the sick man of Europe" was plagued with problems. Yugoslavia had already broken up into separate states: War raged within Bosnia, Herzegovina, and later Kosovo especially between Serbs and Muslims. There had been much instability in Yugoslavia since the breakup of the Ottoman Empire following First World War, and during the Second World War there was continued conflict between the Serbs and Croats. By 1998 the United States and NATO became involved in air strikes against Yugoslavia. Much of the conflict related to the continued dispute over the sovereignty of Kosovo. The fighting was intense between the Muslims and Albanians on the one hand and the Serbs or Yugoslavs on the other. The intervention was not approved by the United Nations and was opposed by Russia and China. But by 1999 NATO the attacks ceased after Yugoslavia withdrew its forces from Kososvo. Clinton was successful in mediating peace agreements between Prime Minister Rabin of Israel and Chairman Arafat of the Palestinian Liberation Organization (PLO). He also helped Israel and Jordan end their state of war and normalize relations. But the peace agreements between Israel and the PLO did not endure. Close to the end of his term in office, Clinton had a phone conversation with Arafat. According to Clinton, Arafat remarked: "You are a great man", and Clinton responded: "The hell I am. I'm a colossal failure, and you made me one." Continued tensions and conflicts persisted in other parts of the Middle East as well. Early in his presidency, Clinton also had to deal with a terrorist attack on the World Trade Center in New York City, the growing threat of Osama bin Laden, and a rising tide of terrorism abroad.

Jack's experience teaching at UNLV had been a fiasco. He concentrated more on his karate training, sometimes attending two consecutive classes. Within a few years, he succeeded in advancing to first

Kyu, a top ranking brown belt. Now he was only one step away from the black belt which would be a very big step. In the meantime he had grown restless and yearned to teach again or engage in research. After all, he had been trained well especially in the latter. He applied to a number of universities, private research organizations, and even the U.S. Bureau of the Census. But they all turned him down. For one thing, he was too old: *You're over the hill, bub.* The chairman of the sociology department at one university, Old Dominion was remarkably candid responding that Jack was too old to be considered for employment. Another hurdle, that had persisted for many years, was the fact that he was not a member of one of the preferred minorities. Had he been the other gender, African American, or other "person of color", he surely would've been in high demand.

Jack had become active in his neighborhood volunteering to serve as a neighborhood watch block captain which helped him establish rapport with his new neighbors. Criminal activity, especially involving delinquent gangs, was an ongoing problem in Las Vegas. At times the walls of the Angel Park Ranch development were defaced with graffiti, and occasionally parked cars along the streets or in driveways and homes were burglarized. Periodically, Jack scheduled meetings of his neighbors to discuss community issues and recommend concerted actions. These meetings, as well as informal contact with neighbors, helped promote a greater degree of social integration and personal security. One neighbor, a young man teaching part time at the Community College of Southern Nevada (CCSN), suggested that Jack might try teaching at the college.

"I believe you'll find it more stimulating than you did at UNLV," he noted. "I think the students there are more motivated".

For a while Jack thought about the suggestion and finally decided to apply to CCSN sending the college his résumé with a letter expressing his interest in teaching. A few weeks had passed when one evening the phone rang, and he picked up the receiver:

"Hello, this is Jack Rubin."

"Hello, Jack. This is Devin McKay at the Department of Human Behavior of the Community College of Southern Nevada. You have an impressive academic record. Listen I'm in charge of hiring the adjunct faculty or part timers. Could you teach two classes in Introductory Sociology here this coming semester?"

"Well, sure," Jack replied.

"Good. Any preference regarding which campus? We have a number of them."

"The Charleston campus would be the best for me." It was the one located closest to Jack's home.

"Very good!" Devin said. "My office happens to be at the Charleston campus. Why don't you drop in here in a week or two, so we can take care of all the details. Our secretary, will set you up with an appointment."

"Thanks Devin. I'll do that."

"Good bye, Jack. Looking forward to meeting you."

It was a brief conversation, but the caller's tone sounded very friendly. About a week later, Jack drove to the Charleston campus. It was only ten minutes away from Angel Park Ranch. Most striking were the colors of the college buildings: a mixture of blue, yellow, and red. It was indeed a colorful campus! He entered the department office where one of the two secretaries greeted him and handed him some forms to fill out. Devin was waiting for him in a nearby cubicle.

"Hello, Jack. Come on in." He reached out and grasped Jack's hand. He had a strong grip.

That's a good sign, Jack reflected. Some people greet you with a very limp handshake. It's like holding a dead fish in your hand.

Devin was a tall, slender man with rumpled brown hair and large blue eyes. He had thin lips, a small upturned nose, and wore a broad smile. He motioned Jack to sit down, and speaking in a soft voice he began telling Jack about salary, his teaching schedule, and other related matters.

"The salaries for adjuncts are quite low, Jack," he said in an almost embarrassed tone.

"That's okay. I'm not doing this for the money."

"Oh, there's one other thing. I tried to schedule both your classes on the Charleston campus; but we didn't get enough students for one of them. Would you mind teaching the class at Nellis Air Force Base? It would just be for one semester."

"No, that'll be alright," Jack replied.

"Good. It will be an evening class of a few hours, and you'll meet with students only once a week. Here's the name and phone number of the education director. Get in touch with him." Devin handed Jack a piece of paper with the information. "By the way, you'll have to make a trip out to Nellis before classes begin. It's just for clearance and getting an identification card. I think we've covered everything. Any questions?"

"No thanks, Devin." The two men shook hands again, and Jack departed.

Jack had a couple of months before he would start teaching again allowing him time to review the introductory sociology text book and to revise his lecture notes. His notes were an important supplement to assigned readings and contained elaborations and criticisms of the latter. He was constrained to use a particular text book for the Introduction to Sociology course. But that didn't really matter. Anyway, no one text book adequately explained basic sociological concepts, and he felt it was especially important to relate sociological content to one's life experiences.

Students in both of his classes appeared very attentive. At Nellis there were about fifteen students all dressed impeccably in U.S. Air Force uniforms. During a lecture dealing with the problem of poverty, one student made some rather revealing comments. He was originally from the island Haiti where he had grown up on a small farm and lived in poverty throughout his childhood. He claimed that most of the island's inhabitants were wretchedly impoverished and abused by a wealthy and powerful minority. Jack encouraged the airman to elaborate further asking: "But hasn't there been a lot of aid flowing into Haiti from the United States?"

"Oh, yes," the student replied. " People from AID, the U.S. Agency for International Development, would fly into Haiti with all kinds of financial assistance. The wealthy and powerful would welcome them at the airport. From there they would be escorted to a plush hotel where they were wined, dined, and entertained. The money from Washington disappeared failing to reach the grass roots level. My family and I never saw any of it."

The student's assessment was a kind of validation. Millions of dollars had already poured into Haiti from American taxpayers and private organizations during the Clinton administration and then later during the presidency of George W. Bush. Where did it all go? There was simply little, if any, accountability.

Jack's class at the Charleston campus met in the mornings twice a week and was somewhat larger with about thirty students. One of his students was really outstanding. She was careful to take detailed notes throughout Jack's lectures and excelled on written examinations. On essay questions she expressed herself superbly. Many of the students in both of Jack's classes had writing problems which reflected the inadequacies of education back in high school and lower grades. Nevertheless they were motivated; and Jack assisted them as much as possible giving them a lengthy review in preparation for each examination. He encouraged them, saying:

"Just because you're here at a community college, don't think small! Think big! Listen, this is where I started as a student many years ago!"

He found CCSN to be a pretty congenial place. Generally students were respectful and tried to meet course requirements. No one interfered with his grading. But there a few of incidents where students engaged in distractive behavior during class. On one occasion he was compelled to eject a student from class when the student persisted in talking to another student during a lecture. It was quite distracting; and when he refused to desist, Jack ordered him out of the classroom. Then there was a young woman sitting in the front row in another class who chatted continually with another student during Jack's lecturing. Several times Jack politely told her to do her chatting only after class. However, she would not shut up! Becoming exasperated, he slammed his fist on the flat surface of her chair. She was stunned, almost flying out of her seat and then became very quiet. After class she approached Jack:

"I'm sorry Doctor Rubin," she uttered apologetically. "But you didn't have to strike my chair so hard. It really shook me up."

Jack smiled and replied, "But it worked. Didn't it?"

A most shameful aspect of the college was its library. It was deplorably inadequate consisting of only a couple of rooms. The smaller room contained some rows of book cases with very limited reading materials. If an instructor wished to disseminate reading lists, generally books would have to be obtained from the UNLV library; and hopefully they would be available for the length of the semester. In contrast, the college had an impressive computer center which occupied nearly the entire first level space of a classroom building. It contained an abundance of personal computers, printers, and other related equipment and was well staffed with assistance personnel. This reflected a growing trend in colleges and universities of an increased reliance on computer technology. Many leading politicians and educators were convinced that more usage of computers would enhance the quality of American education. But as far as Jack was concerned, this trend was both a blessing and a curse. He knew very well, from his own experiences, that computers were wonderful "work horses" saving a great deal of time in computations and contributing greater accuracy in extensive and complex statistical calculations. But there could be certain problems, one being: "Garbage in garbage out". For the scope of intelligence of computers was quite limited. Computer systems could respond to certain programming and other input errors, but not to "dirty data" or many other programming inaccuracies resulting in erroneous or nonsensical output.

When teaching back in Saint Cloud, Jack encountered situations where students became too dependent on the use of computers and even calculators. During a statistics examination one student cried out in desperation as his pocket calculator failed.

"What shall I do? I think the battery has died on me!"

"Finish with a paper and pencil," Jack replied.

"But I don't know how to take a square root."

"There's a long division method for doing it manually. Didn't you learn it back in high school or earlier?" asked Jack. The student replied negatively shaking his head.

Then there was the time when a student came to his office with an armful of printed output generated by a multiple regression program. "Doctor Rubin, can't you help me? I just don't understand all these statistics."

"Have you had any statistics courses?" Jack inquired.

"No," the student replied. "But I've had to do this research project. I don't know anything about multiple regression."

"Hasn't your instructor helped you?"

"Not really. I don't think he knows anything about it either."

I'm sorry," Jack replied. "I can't help you. You need to take at least one and probably two courses in statistics. Multiple regression is very complicated. Your instructor should've never given you such an assignment."

During one semester he had some interesting encounters with another adjunct faculty member. Jack was teaching two classes with an hour break in between. His second class met very close to the school cafeteria, so he would spend the hour poring through lecture notes or simply sipping a cold drink. Usually he sat at an empty table; and on one occasion, a thin, dark skinned man approached him. His long black hair was tied in a ponytail, and he was carrying some books and papers under his arm.

"May I join you?" he asked

"Certainly," Jack quickly replied. He welcomed some company. The other fellow dropped his books and papers on the table and slid into a chair. He extended his arm, and the two men shook hands.

"The name is Henry, an adjunct faculty teaching chemistry."

"I'm Jack Rubin, another adjunct faculty. Sociology is my thing."

The two men chatted with one another for almost an hour. Henry was waiting to hear from UNLV where he had applied for a teaching position. He had been at CCSN for only a year. Before that he had taught and done research back east at Rutgers University.

"I'm doing my community service, teaching here." Henry remarked smiling. "And I hope to move on by the end of this semester."

During the semester Jack and Henry met recurrently in the college cafeteria. Jack was somewhat curious about Henry's background. Was he an American Indian or perhaps from India? But Henry didn't divulge a clue to his ethnic or racial origin, and Jack never inquired. Anyway, Henry appeared to be a rather interesting fellow. He had a number of fascinating stories to tell, and there was one in particular that struck Jack as extraordinary.

"I was invited to an interview at Yale University. All went well, and they offered me a tenure track position in their chemistry department. But there was one thing wrong. It made me walk away from the offer."

"What was it?" Jack asked.

Henry shook his head. An expression of disapproval and disgust flashed across his face. "They stipulated that I could not give any student a grade lower than a *B*."

"Wow!" Jack chuckled, "Yale, the pride of the Ivy League! Good for you for turning them down." Jack reflected for a moment thinking about his experience teaching a course at UNLV which he had already shared with Henry. Expressing a caveat, he added: "Henry you may run into a similar problem accepting a position at UNLV."

"I hadn't thought of that," Henry replied.

The two men continued spending about an hour together at the same place and same time. When the semester ended, they no longer met. Occasionally Jack would visit the cafeteria, but he never encountered Henry again.

Jack had been teaching a few years at the college and was becoming restive. He enjoyed teaching Introductory Sociology but also yearned to teach some advanced courses such as Social Statistics and Social Research Methods. These were courses which he had taught for so many years back in Minnesota. He raised the question with Devin who responded:

"I don't know about you teaching those courses Jack? Richard usually teaches them. You'll have to talk to him about it."

When Jack asked Richard, the chairman of the department, he seemed to equivocate. "We'll see Jack", he answered. "I'll think about it and let you know." But Richard never responded, and Jack was reluctant to press the issue.

Then there other issues that cropped up. On one occasion Jack was called to consult with both Devin and Richard. When he entered the chairman's office, the chairman and Devin were already seated waiting for him. Jack smiled at them and chuckled.

"Both of you are here!" He exclaimed. "What's going on? Are you ganging up on me?" He said jokingly.

"It's nothing like that," Richard replied in a genial tone. "We only want to clarify a few matters. Take a seat, Jack."

"Well, okay. Shoot away." Jack answered, slipping into a nearby chair.

"Look," Richard continued. "I want you to know that your students have a great deal of respect for you. They're really impressed with your knowledge of sociology and feel you are a very outstanding teacher."

"That's nice to hear", Jack responded.

"But there are a few things that we need to talk about. They have to do about your examinations. I understand you test the students on multiple choice and essay questions."

"Yes, that's right," Jack acknowledged.

" Well, Jack a few students have complained about your test requirements; and Devin and I were wondering if you could ease up on the essay questions. You do require them to write on ten questions. Maybe you could have them write on say any five or six out of ten specified questions? Would that be workable?"

Jack became uneasy and began to squirm in his chair. "It would be workable but____"

Richard interrupted him. "I know what you're thinking, Jack. You would be compromising academic standards, and you have a point. But you know, we have open admissions here at the college."

"No, I didn't know that, Richard. A college can self-destruct with a policy like that. It almost happened to CCNY, City College of New York some years back when they also introduced remedial education classes."

"We don't like the policy, but we have to live with it."

"I understand," Jack nodded.

"One other suggestion," Richard added.

"What is it?"

"Some students are having difficulty integrating your lecture material with text book readings. Could you limit the multiple choice questions to text book readings and base the essay questions on your lectures indicating this on the examinations?"

"I can try, but it might be rather difficult because of considerable overlapping. Students are cautioned at the beginning of the course that I would not merely recite what they read, but I would critically elaborate on their readings. Text books alone do not adequately treat most sociological concepts."

"Well, do what you can," Richard responded.

The meeting ended, and Devin turned to Jack thanking him as they left the chairman's office. Although it had been a friendly discourse, a number of things troubled him. To begin with, he felt the open admissions policy of the college was deplorable and especially unfair to students who were ill prepared for higher education. In a number of classes, Jack had to fail students whose reading and writing skills were atrociously poor. Perhaps other teachers passed them through,while others would fail them and increase the numbers of college dropouts. In any event, they were victims of a failing education system not only at the college level but at lower levels of education as well. The erosion of academic standards was further reflected in capitulations to student complaints and preferences. And, of course, there were other contributing factors. It was a complex situation, a malady festering and growing for many years throughout American education institutions: in elementary schools, high schools, colleges and universities. Would it ever end and turn around? Jack asked himself. Certainly not in his lifetime. Perhaps someday in generations to come. But, in the meantime, the driving force of America: its brainpower would probably continue to decline.

CHAPTER TEN:
LEAVING LAS VEGAS

It was early in the morning of September 11, 2001. Yawning and rubbing his eyes, Jack struggled out of bed to answer the telephone. It had been ringing persistently. He picked up the receiver murmuring, "Hello. Who is it?"

The caller shouted excitedly, "Dad! We're under attack!"

"William, what is this all about?"

William was almost breathless as he began to relate the catastrophic events. "Hijackers seized control of two of our planes, American Airlines and United Airlines departing from Logan Airport in Boston and flew the planes into World Trade Center in New York City! Two other planes were hijacked: one out of Washington crashed into the Pentagon; and the fourth left Newark and crashed in Pennsylvania, as the passengers tried to overcome the hijackers."

"This is awful!" Jack replied.

"There were no survivors from plane crashes, and so many people were killed at the World Trade Center!"

They talked only a few minutes longer as Jack was anxious to turn on the television to get a fuller and continuing account of the disaster. "Listen William, I'm saying good bye now. I want to catch up on the news. Take care. Love to you and the family."

By this time Hilda had risen. "I heard you talking to William. It's terrible what happened!" she exclaimed. "I'll make the coffee while you put on the news!"

It was a shocking sight! The two towers of the World Trade Center were enveloped in flames! People were screaming, and many were leaping to their death. Nearly 3,000 died including nineteen hijackers. Besides the 110 floor Twin Towers other buildings were either damaged or destroyed. Throughout the crisis the New York City Fire Department and Police Department responded valiantly.

Later Jack talked with his nephew, Allen who was working in Brooklyn at the time of the attack and was an eyewitness to the horrific event. Allen described the calamity vividly.

"A great deal of excitement was sweeping my office. People were saying something terrible was happening: that the city was being bombed. I dashed up a few flights of stairs to the roof of our building. It was a very clear day; and as I looked across the East River, I saw it! It was a terrifying sight! The World Trade Center was only about a mile away! A large plane was approaching from the south, from Staten Island, and it struck one of the towers about three fourths of the way from the bottom. Then another plane came and crashed into the second tower higher up! I saw flames bursting from the buildings and pillars of smoke curling up into the air.! People were hurling themselves out of the windows trying to escape the flames and smoke! It was awful!"

This massive terrorist attack was carried out by an organization known as al-Qaeda which originated in 1979 when the Soviet Union invaded Afghanistan. Their leader, Osama bin Laden traveled to Afghanistan and helped organize resistance against Soviet forces.

During this time the United States provided considerable aid to Bin Laden and the Arab mujahideen (Islamic fundamentalists and guerrilla fighters), and eventually they were successful in driving out the Russian invaders. But in the years that followed, al-Qaeda and Bin Laden declared a holy war against the West particularly the U.S. and Israel. They called for the indiscriminate killing of Americans, and their terrorist attacks were driven by a multiplicity of motives. Some included: (1) resentment of the stationing of American troops in Saudi Arabia, (2) American support for the state of Israel, (3) sanctions imposed on Iraq. Historically the Middle East had been a focal point of conflict for thousands of years. The earliest civilization of Mesopotamia (Iraq) clashed with the forces of ancient Egypt. Later the Persian Empire dominated the region followed by the ascent of the Greeks and the Macedonian Empire led by Alexander the Great. Then the Roman Empire engulfed much of the Middle East; but with the Empire's decline, a struggle ensued between Christian Crusaders and Saracens for control of the Holy City Jerusalem. In the early 13th century Mongol armies swept through parts of the Middle East. Most enduring was the Ottoman Empire which ruled the area as well as parts of Eastern Europe for several hundred years into the 20th century. But in the aftermath of World War One, the Ottoman Empire collapsed, and much of the Middle East including North Africa fell under the control of the Western powers notably England and France. Egypt was granted independence but was occupied by the British during World War Two. After World War Two, a number of new states arose or regained their independence. British mandates ended in Jordan and Palestine, United Kingdom forces withdrew from Iraq and British and Soviet forces withdrew from Iran, French mandates were terminated in Syria and Lebanon, and the United Kingdom withdrew most of its military from Egypt.

In 1947 the United Nations voted to partition Palestine, and the state of Israel was born. Arab leaders rejected the partition and war between the Arabs and the Jews ensued. In 1948 the armies of five Arab nations together with additional forces from Saudi Arabia and Yemen attempted to destroy the new state of Israel but were defeated amid cries of: "Never again!"

Intervention over so many years by European powers and later by America had helped to fuel fires of animosity and resentment among the masses of the Middle East. The Western nations thirst for vast oil reserves of the region coupled with their support of abusive dictatorships was probably another factor contributing to the growing hostility against the West and the spread of modernism. Adding further to the instability of the region were unabated internal clashes among a medley of ethnic and religious groups. The borders of newly created nations seemed to have been drawn arbitrarily by the former colonial powers. An example was the creation of the Kingdom of Jordan by the British partitioning of Palestine. All this undoubtedly provided fertile ground for the rise of Islamic extremism expressed in acts of terrorism, wrought by the Islamic Jihad and a yearning to resurrect the age of the Caliphs. None of this, however, would ever justify the inhuman acts of violence terror committed by the terrorists. The attacks on September 11, 2001 dwarfed earlier terrorist attacks on American embassies and military, and the country's response was swift and resolute. In 2001 President George W. Bush ordered the invasion of Afghanistan to destroy the Taliban regime which was supporting Bin Ladin and al Qaeda. Later came the invasion of Iraq and the overthrow of its dictator, Saddam Hussein suspected of producing weapons of mass destruction and who had already massacred many thousands of his own people with chemical weapons. A beast was rising in the East, and the War on Terrorism was in full swing.

Any peaceful settlement between Israelis and Palestinians had become less likely. In his last year as U.S. president Clinton attempted to hammer out a failed peace accord with the Palestinian Chairman Yasser Arafat at Camp David, and by fall of 2000 the second Intifada or Palestinian uprising had begun. Although the Israelis had withdrawn their forces from Lebanon and Gaza, the terrorist organizations of Hezbollah and Hamas were insistent upon the destruction of the Jewish national state attacking Israel with persistent suicide bombings and rocket attacks. Both organizations grew in power: Hamas in Gaza and Hezbollah in Lebanon, and both had been aided by other Arab States notably Iran and Syria. Further antagonizing Palestinians was the Israeli military occupation and the continuing construction of Israeli settlements in the West Bank. Concurrently fires of violence, fueled by al Qaeda and allied terrorist groups, became rampant throughout Iraq and Afghanistan. For eight long years during the George W. Bush administration much American blood and treasure was spent in conflict and attempts at nation building or rebuilding of Iraq and Afghanistan.

For sometime Jack and Hilda had thought about eventually moving to Prescott, Arizona where their friends and former neighbors in Minnesota had retired. They still retained their lot in the same Prescott development where their friends had settled and whom they visited occasionally. Although they had speculated about building a home there, they delayed making any definite plans because of the high construction costs. However, in the early years of the 21st century a nationwide real estate boom transpired, and the value of their Las Vegas home virtually doubled. Although Jack failed to make a fortune at the blackjack tables, he and Hilda had done well having purchased a home years ago in Vegas. Hilda deserved much of the credit because it was her suggestion that prompted the purchase. As the real estate boom continued, Jack and Hilda began to seriously contemplate putting their Las Vegas home up for sale and building a new house in Prescott.

The Traditional Karate Tournament International had been initiated by Master Ozawa back in 1981, and throughout the 1980's the tournaments were held at the Maxim Hotel and Casino and the Aladdin Hotel. Later they took place at Bally's Hotel and the Flamingo Hotel and Casino. After Jack had joined the Las Vegas Shotokan Dojo he had the opportunity to help out in this annual event. It was expected that members of the dojo assist since the Shotokan Dojo was the event's chief sponsor, and a great deal of preparation was required. Much time was spent providing instructions on the registration of participants, the recording of scores of kata and kumite competitors, and for other related chores. It was at these times that Jack might interact more directly with Master Ozawa even if it were just an exchange of customary bows. A tournament would last about four days, and Jack would always find time to wander about observing competitors perhaps ranging in age from six to sixty. They came from all over the world: Europe, Japan, Australia, Canada, South America, Africa. There was even a team from the new little country of Kosovo. The opening ceremony was inspiring, a magnificent spectacle! Background music played as hundreds of participants entered a great room in single file: all ages, white belts, colored belts, and black belts. With an arm outstretched each karateka grasped the shoulder of another. On and on they came in separate groups each headed by a karateka proudly carrying his or her national flag. Much of the great room was cordoned off creating separate courts where kata and kumite competitions would take place. A large podium was nearby where Master Ozawa, Sensei James, and other functionaries were seated. There were welcoming speeches and referees and judges rose to be introduced. Many had come from dojos in California and some as far as Japan. After a few more speeches, the tournament officially opened with competitors directed to their respective courts. Other activities included seminars on the Shotokan Katas and Kumite.

Jack and Shihan Ozawa belonged to the same generation, born only a few years apart: Shihan in November of 1925 and Jack in November of 1928. Although they had grown up in very distant places and different cultures, Jack felt that they shared certain common values especially those linked to karate. Jack became more aware of this when he read a copy of Ozawa's autobiography which was a remarkable story, and he learned even more about Master Ozawa during social gatherings at the dojo. Each year a potluck was held about week before Thanksgiving; and there was another get together around Christmas. At these times, shihan would relate some fascinating accounts of his life in Japan. He was a soft spoken man with a pronounced accent and sometimes difficult to understand. But there was one story he told that impressed Jack.

"When I was a young man, living in Tokyo," Ozawa began, "two men were following me along a dark and deserted street. I turned on to other streets, but they were still behind me. There was a park ahead and clumps of bushes; and as I drew nearer to the park, I looked back at my stalkers, screamed, and leaped over the bushes. My scream was the kiai, a fighting yell that seemed to petrify the two men who turned and dashed off. It is important to remember the kiai. It combines physical and spiritual energy and may be enough to scare off attackers."

It was a hot summer morning when Jack arrived at the dojo to attend a karate class. As he passed through the doorway, Sensei James called out to him.

"Jack!"

He stopped at the open doorway to James' office. Sensei was sitting at his desk appearing disconsolate. He drew a deep breath and added, "You're no longer the Kid, Jack."

Jack looked back surprised and puzzled. "What do you mean, sensei?"

"It's shihan. He passed away last night. You know, whenever you came up to test shihan used to say: Here comes the Kid."

"I didn't know that. It's too bad about shihan. I'm very sorry to hear that. I knew him for such a short time."

A wake was held at shihan's home with his wife, other family, and members of the dojo present. Jack and a friend, another karate student, stood before the open casket. Jack's friend gazed down at shihan and crossed himself. Then he turned to Jack saying, "You don't have to do that."

"I know," Jack replied. It was a somber moment, as he bowed and took his last look at Master Osamu Ozawa.

In the days that followed, Jack carried on his karate training. Sometimes he attended two consecutive classes which involved working out for about two hours. One time he felt that his heart was fibrillating when he left the dojo and headed home. "I don't feel right," he said to Hilda. "My heart seems to be beating too fast. Maybe I should see my primary physician."

"Please Jack go see the doctor right away!" Hilda urged. "I can drive you there."

"No,no, I can drive. I don't think it's anything serious."

Shortly he arrived at Doctor Mathew's office. There were no other patients in the waiting room, and a nurse immediately ushered Jack in to see the doctor and he was given an electrocardiogram. The doctor was alarmed by the results of the test for Jack was experiencing a dangerously high heartbeat, and he turned to his nurse exclaiming:

"Call 911 for an ambulance! This patient needs to go to the emergency room at Summerlin Hospital!"

He was treated with medication while on the way to the hospital, but his heart failed to respond. It continued beating very rapidly, and oddly he was experiencing no chest pains or other discomfort. Hilda was notified of Jack's predicament and arrived quickly at the emergency room of the hospital. Jack was treated with more medication and was lying quietly in the emergency room when suddenly he lost consciousness. Hilda screamed loudly causing a physician to rush back into the room reviving Jack with a defibrillator.

Jack spent several days recovering in the hospital. It was a close brush with death. His heart had been considerably weakened by the arrhythmia and his cardiologist and primary physician strongly recommended that he have an implanted pacemaker and defibrillator to strengthen his heart and cope with the possibility of another arrhythmia attack. He was repulsed by the idea of having such alien objects inserted into his chest. He was on prescribed medication, which he hoped would suffice, but it was not adequately effective;

and his primary physician, Doctor Mathew spent a good deal of time trying to convince him of the necessity of having the implants.

"This is a life or death situation," he stressed. "The medications are not enough. Another arrhythmia attack could cost you your life." His doctor finally persuaded him to go ahead and have the implants

After a brief period of further recuperation, Jack resumed his karate training. During the following months, Sensei James Tawatao became the head of the Las Vegas Shotokan Dojo and President of the International Karate Tournament which was renamed the Ozawa Cup in honor of Master Ozawa. Sensei James was an outstanding and inspiring teacher possessing a great understanding of Shotokan karate which he conveyed to his students. Much of his instruction was devoted to basics such as structure or form as well as blocks, punches and kicks all of which were the foundations of kata and kumite. One day something happened in one of Sensei James' classes that was rather unusual and striking. About halfway through teaching a class, Sensei James abruptly stopped, his eyes fixed on a small insect crawling about on the wooden floor. Slowly he reached down, carefully picked up the insect, and quickly walked outside, placing it carefully on the nearby grass. He then returned and continued teaching.

By now, Jack had advanced to first kyu, the top rank of a brown belt. The testing had been rigorous, but he was undaunted. He was only one step away from shodan or first degree black belt. This would be an especially difficult step especially for a man who had passed the age of seventy. Again he was a "Johnny Come Lately" having started his karate training at about the age of forty five little knowing that he would come this far. Was it too late for him to earn the coveted black belt? The test was given every six months. At first he failed, but was determined to try again. Requirements for the black belt were pretty demanding. First, one had to successfully perform the basics which included a variety of blocks, punches, and kicks. Single basics were required, then double basics, triple basics, and finally quadruple basics. Double, triple, and quadruple basics were combinations of blocks, punches, and kicks used for defense and offense. Candidates were scored on their stances: front stance, back stance, fighting stance, and ready stances. These were extremely important, as they were the foundation of all other movements. Also included were free fighting combinations such as: (1) jab, front kick, and lunge punch and (2) jab, reverse punch, round house kick, and lunge punch. After all this, the karateka was expected to perform five katas selected from a total of fifteen katas. If one made any mistakes, it was very important to keep moving, do not hesitate or stop! The final requirement involved semi free and free sparring. With respect to the latter, the karateka was judged on the effectiveness of each of the following criteria: attacking, defending, speed, power, focus, timing, distance, and spirit. It was certainly an arduous test, and correct breathing was essential; otherwise a karateka could pass out on the floor.

It was the fall of 2002, and Jack and Hilda were again planning to spend Thanksgiving with family in Minnesota. But this visit would be special. Before moving to Las Vegas some years ago, Jack and Hilda had parted with their dog: a blue eyed Siberian husky of thirteen years It had been a painful experience, and both were tearful and sobbing when they left Nikki to be cremated. But there was really no other alternative since the animal had become incontinent, and any medication or treatment would only have postponed the inevitable. It happened that Jack and his son were both dog lovers. William had been married several years during which time he had a few Doberman Pinschers. They were beautiful, lovable, and very protective animals although their average longevity was limited to only eight or nine years. Jack especially felt it was time for Hilda and him to adopt another dog, preferably a Doberman Pinscher. He searched the Las Vegas area for a breeder but could find none. William, however, was successful in finding one in Minnesota and procured a puppy which was the last of a litter. And the dog was even house broken by the time Jack and Hilda arrived in Minneapolis for Thanksgiving. William picked up his parents at the airport and when they reached home, Marie and their three granddaughters greeted them with hugs. Their dog was waiting for them as they stepped into the kitchen.

"Here is your puppy," William said. "I hope you don't mind. I already named her, Sophie."

Sophie was sitting upright and barking incessantly. Her tail had already been cropped, and her once droopy ears stood erect wrapped in gauze.

"No, no!" Jack replied excitedly. "She's a beauty!" Sophie's coat was black, and her broad breast was brown. Her eyes were brown, and there were streaks of brown on her legs as well some brown around her jaws. Like all Dobermans she was especially muscular. Jack immediately obtained a book describing the breed. They were described as very astute animals requiring a good deal of attention, care, and training. If left in isolation or neglected frequently and for long periods of time they could become unmanageable and even mean. Jack quickly began to bond with Sophie. Each day he took her on walks along a trail behind his son's home. One time while walking he slipped and fell. Somehow the leash was not secure, and Sophie was loose with Jack on the ground and unhurt. The dog was ahead of him, and he thought she might simply run off. But surprisingly Sophie drew to Jack's side whimpering as if to say, "Master, are you okay?" Jack thought her behavior extraordinary.

It was early evening when William drove Jack, Hilda, and Sophie to the airport for their flight home to Las Vegas. Sophie was in a portable kennel in the rear of the car, and as they drove up to the check in for departures a terrible odor was emanating from the back of the car. Sophie had defecated and vomited. It was a big mess, and it was extremely cold outside with the temperature having fallen to nine or ten degrees Fahrenheit. Jack hurried inside the airport to check in while the others were cleaning up Sophie's mess. The woman at the check in counter argued with Jack about traveling with the dog since animals were not allowed on flights if outside temperatures had fallen to ten degrees or less. Frustrated he returned to the car. They all stood outside shivering, and Marie shouted, "That dog is going to Las Vegas tonight if I have to drive here there!"

"Dad, I'm going back inside with you," William insisted, and they both hurried inside where William sternly confronted the attendant.

"Lady, our dog has to fly tonight! Let me talk with your supervisor." The attendant called her supervisor over, and William was very persuasive.

"All right," she said. "Bring the dog in here. I just want to be sure she can stand on her feet."

Sophie was brought inside, placed in a kennel, and wheeled away to a boarding area. The family all hugged one another saying their farwells. Subsequently Jack and Hilda boarded their flight and when their plane was aloft, the airline stewardess stopped by to reassure them.

"I want you to know that the captain says your dog is doing fine. She's in a warm area and even has a blanket."

"Thank you very much," Jack replied.

Shortly after returning home to Las Vegas, Jack enrolled Sophie in a dog training class. She was very responsive and learned quickly. In about a month she earned her diploma. Nearly every day Jack took her for long walks and spent much time practicing basic commands. It was very important not to leave any objects, especially clothing, on the floors of the house. Once while sitting at his computer, he suddenly heard a choking sound from behind He turned and saw a sock hanging from Sophie's mouth, and he quickly pulled it free. The dog was also inclined to snatch food from the kitchen or dining room table, but that was eventually discouraged. Jack had obtained an electronic training collar and a remote. If she misbehaved, he would give her a mild shock. The shock or simply a command such as, "No!" or "Leave it!" sufficed to deter her. Then something unusual happened one day. Sophie was barking persistently in the backyard. A cement wall completely enclosed the yard except for a gate around a corner in the back of the house. Jack turned to Hilda who was busy in the kitchen.

"I wonder what's going on ? Sophie is really barking, making a racket,"

"Better have a look," Hilda replied.

He stepped out into the patio. Sophie was out of sight. She must be near the gate, he thought, as he walked around the back corner of the house. There she was standing in the yard barking at an open gate. Perhaps Jack had inadvertently left the gate ajar, and the wind had blown it completely open. When he shut the gate she ceased barking.

"What a smart dog we have," he said to Hilda. "Another dog would've taken off. I think she was trying to let us know that something wasn't right."

The day finally came when Jack and Hilda decided to sell their home in Las Vegas and build another house on their lot in Prescott, Arizona. It was still a "seller's market", and they were certain they would get a good price for their Vegas home, enough enabling them to build in Prescott. It would take awhile to sell their home, so Jack continued teaching at the Community College of Southern Nevada. Oddly, the word, "Community" was dropped and the school's name was changed to the "College of Southern Nevada". Jack felt it was a sham, simply a cosmetic change. The college was still only a two year institution not offering baccalaureate degrees and later he learned that the change had been made at the insistence of the students. Perhaps they felt the label, "Community" was a stigma.

During this time Jack was engaged in his karate training. He still had hopes of earning his black belt, but time was running out. He and Hilda finally had a satisfactory offer for their home, and it would only be a matter of weeks before they would depart Las Vegas. Jack had already tested twice for the black belt and had failed. Nevertheless, he spoke to Sensei James about another test.

"Sensei, give me one more shot at it", Jack pleaded.

James hesitated and then consented. The test was given during a karate class. Both Sensei James and Sensei Rey evaluated his performance. After his test Jack wanted to say a few words of fare-well. This was his last time training at the Las Vegas Shotokan Dojo. As he spoke, his voice choked a little with emotion.

"I will have some regrets leaving Las Vegas and will most of all miss my training here at the dojo. So many years ago I became involved in karate, and over the years I think I have learned much, especially in this dojo. I am leaving, but I believe I am taking a great deal of knowledge with me and plan to continue my training either at home or elsewhere. "

There were many "goodbyes" and much handshaking. The following day Jack learned that he had passed the test. At last he had earned his black belt.

The process of building a home at The Ranch, a housing development in Prescott, would be lengthy and tedious. Architectural plans had to be drawn up and approved by an architectural committee that imposed rather stringent rules. Also, Jack and Hilda had made several trips to Prescott to visit their friends and consult with their builder. It was estimated that it might take about a year to complete construction of their new home. In the meantime, all of their furniture and many other possessions were put in storage. William had suggested that they stay at his home in Minneapolis at least until December or January when they could join Hilda's sister living in Florida and escape the Minnesota winter.. Hopefully, they would be able to move into their Prescott home by the following spring. Leaving Las Vegas they drove both of their vehicles to Prescott and visited Tim and Marilyn Grant, their old friends and former neighbors in Minnesota. Sophie, now about three years old, traveled in their Nissan Pathfinder (SUV). The dog was an excellent traveler and had accompanied Jack and Hilda on earlier long drives from Las

Vegas to Minneapolis. They spent a few days with Tim and his wife, and Tim suggested that they leave their smaller car with him which would enable them to travel together in their SUV. It was a hot day in August when they thanked Tim and Marilyn for their hospitality and departed from Prescott. They were on the road about three and a half days before arriving at William's home in Maple Grove, a northwestern suburb of Minneapolis. They stayed with their son, daughter-in-law and three granddaughters for nearly four months. It was very enjoyable being with family during that time. But by January it had turned very cold. Day and night temperatures had plunged to single digits and even well below zero. The Arctic air mass had edged across the upper Midwest. Blankets of snow were accumulating, nearby lakes were frozen over, and driving or walking had become hazardous because of icy conditions. There was a time when Jack could adapt to the frigid Minnesota winters but no longer. He had become accustomed to the more temperate weather of the Far West. Hilda was frequently in touch with her sister who was living in Tampa, Florida, and urged both Jack and Hilda to join her for the remainder of the winter.

On a cold sunny morning they bade farewell to William and his family and headed along route 694 to Interstate 94 East and the turned south on 35W. After driving most of the day, they stopped at a motel outside of Rockford, Illinois. They were on the road again early the following morning continuing south through Illinois, Kentucky, and Tennessee and stopped around Chattanooga.

The next day they drove through Georgia following Interstate 75 all the way to Tampa, Florida. When they arrived at Maya's housing development by early evening, she was outside her home and excitedly greeted Jack, Hilda, and Sophie. It was a very pleasant visit with Hilda's sister and a relief to be away from the ice, snow, and cold of Minnesota. The days and weeks passed quickly, and Jack was on his cell phone nearly every day talking with Tim who was giving him a progress report on the construction of his Prescott home. In all likelihood, Jack and Hilda would not have built this new home without Tim's assistance. He was an experienced engineer with a great deal of knowledge about home construction, and was very helpful in monitoring the construction process. There were a few snags, but essentially everything progressed smoothly. In addition to staying in touch with Tim Grant on an almost daily basis, Jack was in touch with the Director of Northern Arizona University Extension in Prescott. The main campus of the University was located in nearby Flagstaff. After reaching Tampa, he had faxed his vita to the director so as to explore the possibility of teaching at the University Prescott Extension. He received a positive response and was scheduled to teach a course in Criminology beginning in September. He spent much time and effort reviewing a textbook for the course and preparing lecture notes. By March Tim informed Jack that the house was nearing completion, and perhaps he should be thinking about departing for Prescott. It was already becoming warmer and rather humid in Tampa. Near the end of March, Jack, Hilda, and Sophie bade goodbye to Maya and headed west. It was a long drive. Following Interstate 75 they connected with Interstate 10 which would take them all the way across the Gulf coast through Texas, New Mexico, and finally to Prescott, Arizona. It was about a five day trip, and again Sophie was very adaptable. For many hours she would lie quietly in the back of the SUV peering curiously at the passing landscape. Jack and Hilda felt especially secure with her, as she was very alert and protective. In the motels late at night, the dog would growl at any outside sounds. On the fifth day they finally arrived in Prescott. Their house was still not ready to be occupied, and Tim suggested that they stay with him and Marilyn until they could move into their new home. It took about another two weeks before the house was ready to be occupied. There was, of course, much to do in getting resettled. Within a few days their furniture and other belongings arrived from Las Vegas. Appliances, shades for the windows, and many other things were needed. Sophie seemed to be ecstatic in her new home running about the front and back yards. She had been in Prescott before when Jack and Hilda visited their friends; and whenever they were ready to return home to Las Vegas, she was always reluctant to leave. There was a considerable amount and variety of wildlife inhabiting the area: mule deer, peccaries (pig like mammals), coyotes, wildcats, rattlesnakes, and even mountain lions. Residents in the development were not allowed to fence in their properties, but Jack did have an "invisible fence" installed which was an electrically charged wire which bordered his backyard. Wearing a special collar the dog would receive a warning impulse and an electric shock if she attempted to cross the wire. It was very effective in keeping Sophie within the backyard but did not deter wildlife from straying into the yard. Occasionally, Sophie would bark loudly and chase numbers of peccaries, coyotes, and deer from the yard.

The elevation of Prescott varied between five and six thousand feet quite a bit higher than Las Vegas, and the city was situated in North Central Arizona, sometimes referred to as the "high country". Prescott was once the capital of the State when it was still a territory, and in 1867 the territorial capital was transferred to Tucson with Phoenix becoming the capital in 1889. Prominent landmarks of Prescott were Thumb Butte, Granite Mountain, and the National Wildlife Forest. Rolling hills, densely covered with verdant shrubs and trees, valleys, and distant mountains all provided spectacular sights. Also, from certain vantage points the snowcapped San Francisco Peaks near Flagstaff were visible almost a hundred miles away. The Prescott downtown possessed the flavor of the bygone era of the American cowboy. Supposedly Billy the Kid and Doc Holiday, traveling to Tombstone, were once here; and across from the city courthouse was Whiskey Row: a colorful stretch of saloons and shops reminiscent of the Old West.

Shortly after arriving in Prescott, Jack met with the Director of the Northern Arizona University program. She was a short, portly woman with an MA degree in Business Administration; and unsurprisingly she had little if any understanding of sociology. But she was helpful in providing Jack with information related to his teaching schedule. An enrollment of at least six students was required in order for him to teach his course in Criminology. Unfortunately, only three people registered for the course; hence it was canceled. This was disappointing, as Jack had spent a considerable amount of time and effort in preparing to teach the course. He even tried to negotiate with the director suggesting that he was even willing to take a reduction in salary if the course would still be offered, but the director refused despite the fact that such an adjustment was consistent with the rules of the university.

Another disappointing experience followed when Jack began to train at the local Shotokan dojo. Perhaps he should have made one or more visits to the dojo before deciding to move to Prescott. He did attend some classes, but mistakes were being made in the instruction. Also, there was a lack of proper etiquette; and he felt that his new sensei, who was not affiliated with either the Japan Karate Association or the International Traditional Karate Association, was arrogant and offensive. Eventually they clashed, and Jack was forced to leave the dojo. However, he did continue his training in his new home which had a wooden floor and wall mirrors. He remembered that Master Funakoshi had stated in his autobiography: that wherever a karateka performed the basic movements of Shotokan, it was a dojo or training place even if the space were very limited. And there was something else in his autobiography which appeared ostensibly contradictory. Funakoshi referred to a Buddhist saying: "Movement is nonmovement and nonmovement is movement" and wrote that this saying had a special meaning for the karateka.At first this puzzled Jack. Was the expression really contradictory, and how would it apply to karate techniques? After some reflection, he believed he was able to understand its meaning. If a karateka is threatened with an attack or actually attacked, he or she must strategize the situation: Try to extricate yourself from any physical encounter; but if this is not practicable then step aside,. block, and immediately counter with a strike. Also, there are many other aspects to consider: among them are distance, direction, and type of block and strike. But once a karateka is committed and in motion, then it becomes more difficult and even impossible to strategize In this sense *movement becomes non-movement and nonmovement becomes movement.*

Jack was experiencing a growing sense of social isolation. The inhabitants of Prescott seemed rather provincial and aloof very different from people he had known in more cosmopolitan cities like Las Vegas, Minneapolis, and Chicago. For him the people of Prescott were like passing shadows having form but lacking real substance. He would try to talk with neighbors and others, but the conversations tended to be abrupt and shallow confined to trivial or neutral subjects such as the weather or trips taken to far off places. Discussions of personal or controversial issues were generally avoided. Especially distressing was the end of Jack's relationship with Tim. They were currently neighbors in Prescott and had been close friends for over twenty years back in Minnesota. Tim had kept a watchful eye on the construction of Jack's new home in Prescott. He was a trained engineer and possessed quite a bit of knowledge about home construction. If things were not being done right, he complained to the builder and needed corrections were made. Jack was indebted to him for his assistance, and he and Hilda would never have built a home in Prescott without his help. But perhaps the end of their friendship was inevitable. Their temperaments diverged considerably. Unlike Jack, Tim had a very low tolerance level for dissenting views on sundry matters or issues. He was extremely self-righteous and polarized. As the saying goes: *It was his way or the highway.* Usually when Jack disagreed with Tim he would fly into a rage, shouting: "You're not listening to me! Shut up! Shut up!" It seemed like Tim could not agree to disagree and often claimed he knew everything about everything. His behavior became so bizarre, vulgar, and insulting, that it ultimately led to a termination of their friendship.

The two men had very different backgrounds and life experiences which may have contributed to the end of their relationship. Tim was a few years older than Jack and had grown up in Bulgaria in stressful times prior to and during World War Two. He was not reluctant to talk about his native country particularly its history which Jack thought fascinating. He talked in length about Bulgaria when it was part of the Ottoman Empire and about the German occupation as well as the resistance of King Boris III and the people of Bulgaria to the deportation of Bulgarian Jews to Nazi death camps in Poland. In addition, he pointed out that Bulgaria, unlike other East European nations, refused to send troops to fight on the Eastern Front against Russia.

"Generally, Bulgarians including the Jews were treated quite well by the Germans," Tim claimed. "The Bulgarian King defied Hitler in protecting the Bulgarian Jews from extermination. Of course, I was only a teenager at the time perhaps too young to know all that was going on."

Jack did not raise questions or challenge his friend but did suspect that that there were some discrepancies in Tim's assertions. Indeed, his suspicions were verified when he scanned the internet for information on the fate of the Bulgarian Jews shortly before and during the German occupation. According to these other sources, it was true that none of Bulgaria's Jews were sent to die in Nazi extermination camps. In 1940 Bulgarian Jews numbered about 48,000 and comprised only 0.8 percent of Bulgaria's total population. During 1941 Bulgaria joined the Axis Pact consisting of Germany, Italy, Spain, and Japan. In the same year, German troops entered Bulgaria and occupied Greece and Yugoslavia with the assistance of the Bulgarian military.

In the past Jews had experienced a great deal of freedom and tolerance in Bulgaria. There was little evidence of any anti-Semitism. But that was beginning to quickly change. In 1940 the anti-Semitic Prime Minister, controlled by King Boris, promoted a Law for the Protection of the Nation which was introduced into the Bulgarian legislature and specifically targeted Jews. The law, similar to the Nuremburg Laws passed in Germany back in 1935, imposed a number of restrictions on the rights of Bulgarian Jews such as selecting their place of residence, serving in the military, marrying ethnic Bulgarians, entering certain professions, and attending universities. And by 1943 all Jews were ordered to wear the Star of David in public and were subject to insults and physical attacks by fascist gangs. Some lost their jobs or were deprived of their possessions. Also, they were barred from theatres and restaurants as well as prohibited from using main thoroughfares. In the same year the Bulgarian Army and police helped to deport thousands of Jews from territories in Yugoslavia and Macedonia to detention centers in Bulgaria. From these centers they were sent to the extermination camps of Auschwitz and Treblinka. When news of this became known, Orthodox religious leaders and clergy together with members of parliament expressed protests and outrage. There was an even greater wave of protest when Bulgarian Jews were seized, taken from their homes, and sent to internment camps. At this point Dimitar Peshev, vice chairman of the National Assembly, played a leading role in pressuring the cabinet to release the Bulgarian Jews who were waiting to board trains heading for extermination camps. After the war most surviving Jews immigrated to Palestine and the new state of Israel.

In his discussions with Tim, Jack never revealed the additional information that he had gleaned from the internet concerning the fate of the Bulgarian Jews. He knew that any such attempt would've been futile and would only have infuriated Tim. However, Tim had acknowledged that he was perhaps too young to be completely aware of the events transpiring at the time of the German occupation. He did point out that he knew some Jewish families during those years, and that some of them spoke Spanish. They were probably Sephardic Jews whose ancestors had fled from Spain during the years of the Inquisition and had resettled in Bulgaria and other parts of Eastern Europe. What puzzled Jack was the fact that Tim seemed to be unaware of the dire plight of the Bulgarian Jews as well as Jews who were rounded up in Bulgarian occupied territories and sent to extermination camps. How could he not have known about these outrages? He must have been seventeen or eighteen years old at the time. Surely he was not too young to know. This was reminiscent of the times that Jack had served in the U.S. Army occupation forces in Germany. When Jack had asked Germans about the death camps and Nazi atrocities, many simply responded:

"But we didn't know what was happening."

Perhaps this was at least partly true for in totalitarian countries the flow of information is tightly controlled and easily distorted or suppressed. This was certainly the case in Nazi Germany and German occupied Bulgaria. But on the other hand, what did people think in Germany or in Bulgaria when their Jewish neighbors, acquaintances, or friends suddenly disappeared ? To paraphrase in the film *Judgment at Nuremberg*, the wife of a German officer who has been tried for war atrocities, says to the American judge presiding over the war criminal trials:

"It was terrible what happened! But do you think we are monsters? We didn't know what was happening. We just didn't know."

And the American judge replied: "It seems to me that nobody in this country knew what was really happening."

Is it likely, Jack thought, that "pluralistic ignorance" prevailed in such situations where people experienced unusual circumstances but were unaware that these experiences were in fact ubiquitous or shared by many others? Neighbors, acquaintances, or friends unexplainably disappear. Maybe it was believed that they lost their jobs, decided to move, or something else happened. Then such events of circumstances might have been considered as isolated occurrences and dismissed as insignificant. But, on the other hand, perhaps this was problematic with respect to Bulgaria. For when Jews were rounded up in the Bulgarian occupied territories and secretly transported to extermination camps in Poland, it was discovered and there was widespread public outrage and protest. Also, protests mounted particularly from political and religious leaders when similar measures were attempted in the case of Bulgarian Jews.

Tim was still living in Bulgaria when the war in Europe ended and the Russians occupied the country. The Communists seized complete control of social, economic, and political institutions; and unlike the German occupation troops, the Russian military forces were less disciplined and more unruly.

"There was a great deal of suppression", Tim explained. "You had to be very careful criticizing the commies. My brother got picked up one time for making negative comments."

"What happened?" Jack asked.

"Well, Rudolph was on a tram talking with a friend and made some disparaging remarks about the regime. Some plainclothes police overheard him, and whisked him away. He didn't come home that evening, and we had no idea what happened to him. We called the local police station, but they said they didn't know anything about his whereabouts. Our parents then contacted a high official in the local Communist party and found out that the police were indeed holding Rudolph. I went down to the police station, hollered, and threatened to complain to higher authorities. They quickly released Rudolph but cautioned him to be more careful in the future."

Later Tim emigrated from Bulgaria, attended a university in Switzerland where he earned an engineering degree, and immigrated to America where unfortunately his degree was not recognized. He was offered a scholarship to pursue a degree in engineering at a leading American university, but the scholarship did not provide him with adequate funding. Consequently, he abandoned hopes for a career in engineering and earned a Master's degree in Business Administration while working in a major business corporation. Tim's thwarted career in engineering and the accidental death of his only child had possibly left him cynical and embittered.

The breakup of Jack and Tim happened under extraordinary circumstances. Both men and their wives had been invited to a neighbor's home for lunch. After lunch they all sat chatting in the living room. The conversation turned to the question of the need of obtaining immunization from shingles. Jack mentioned that his cardiologist had urged him to get the immunization especially since he had a heart problem. Tim suddenly became very agitated.

"You only need the shingle shots if you've had chicken pox. I know all about it. Your cardiologist doesn't know what he's talking about."

"I'm only telling you what my cardiologist advised," replied Jack.

"Shut up! shut up!" Tim screamed.

"You shut up!" Jack retorted.

Tim gritted his teeth as his face became contorted with anger and hostility. He shouted obscenities and snarled, "The professor!" He looked like he might spring and attack Jack who stared back in disbelief. Years back in Minnesota Jack and Tim had argued concerning a matter, and Tim had rushed at Jack brandishing and shaking his fist. Jack became taut and moved into a ready position. If Tim had attacked, Jack would at least defend himself with a karate block which could send Tim crashing to the floor. Hilda acted very quickly, seizing Jack by the arm.

"Let's get out of here!" she exclaimed.

He and Hilda left quickly. It was a wise move. In all the years of his karate training Jack had never been compelled to use karate to defend himself. It was only to be used only in a life threatening situation, for its use could have lethal consequences. After the incident Jack never spoke to Tim again. He did observe him once when taking Sophie for a walk. As Jack and his dog were passing Tim's house, Tim was in the front yard. For a moment their eyes met, and Tim grimaced quickly disappearing among the trees.

The loss of an old friend reinforced Jack's feeling social isolation and stoked his desire to depart from Prescott. Even before moving there, he and Hilda had agreed that if they became dissatisfied with life in Prescott they would sell their new home and leave within a few years. Hilda was also somewhat unhappy in Prescott. She had joined a Scandinavian American group, but found their members aloof and superficial. She and Jack began to think about returning to the more cosmopolitan ambience of larger metropolitan areas and perhaps even to Minnesota where they would be closer to family and friends

On the other hand, there were advantages living in Prescott. Jack and Hilda were pleased with their new home which had been very well constructed; and certainly Sophie, their very devoted Doberman Pincher, enjoyed the house especially the dining room with large windows granting her a full view of the outside world. She was very vigilant following Jack or Hilda about the house and loudly barking at every passerby, human or animal. The dog romped freely in a large backyard sometimes chasing intruding rabbits, mule deer or peccaries. The air was so fresh free of almost any pollution. Because of the dry climate it could became rather dusty at times especially with increasing winds. But the climate was ideal. All seasons, notably winters and summers, were relatively mild. Nearly every day the skies were clear and the sun shone brightly. Most importantly medical care including both doctors and medical facilities were excellent. And Prescott's hospital had been rated as one of the best in the country.

Considering all the advantages and disadvantages of living in Prescott, Jack and Hilda listed their home for sale. However, it was difficult to sell as the real estate bubble had burst, and prices on homes were plummeting along with competition from a growing number of foreclosures and short sales. In order to sell, it appeared that Jack and Hilda would sacrifice most of their equity which they considered unacceptable. It was decided then they would make the best of a difficult situation and remain in Prescott until the real estate market recovered. Hilda expressed it well, saying: "Wherever I have been planted, I can learn to blossom."

CHAPTER ELEVEN:
A COUNTRY DIVIDED

Even though he had been frustrated from teaching at the Northern Arizona University Extension in Prescott, Jack still hoped he could resume teaching. He sent his résumé and a cover letter expressing interest in teaching to the appropriate departmental chairperson at Arizona State University in Phoenix. In addition, he made an inquiry at the Yavapai Community College in Prescott regarding the possibility of teaching Quickly he received a response from a faculty member at the community college who arranged a meeting with the chairperson of an interdisciplinary department offering courses in psychology and sociology. His initial contact, a faculty member, accompanied him to the chairman's office. Entering the office, Jack introduced himself and shook hands with the Ray Cloud, the chairman. Although Jack grasped the man's hand firmly, the chairman's response was at best tepid. His handshake was limp: like holding a dead fish. He gazed briefly at Jack and motioned him to sit down.

"My name is Ray Cloud and I am a psychologist, "he asserted in a supercilious manner. "You know, we never hired a sociologist. All of our sociology courses have been taught by psychologists."

Jack squirmed slightly in his seat. He didn't particularly like what he was hearing or the chairman's tone. But he simply nodded and continued listening.

"Okay, Jack what textbook would you use in an introductory sociology course? What would you cover in the course?" Cloud asked pointedly.

"There are many suitable textbooks. Back in Minnesota I used one by James Henslin. I would cover different aspects of social structure such as interrelated statuses, roles, social values, norms, social relationships as well as various kinds of social action or social processes, in particular social interaction. The emphasis would be the study of different groups ranging from the micro to the macro level. You could begin with the dyad or two person group and work your way up to social institutions, communities, and larger society."

The chairman looked somewhat flabbergasted and appeared to shake his head in disapproval. He doesn't know what the hell I'm talking about, Jack mused. Then Cloud grasped a book from his desk and waved it in front of Jack.

"This is what I use as a text in my sociology courses, and the students love it!"

"What is it?" Jack asked.

"It's about a relationship between a sociology professor and one of his students. It's titled: *Tuesdays With Morrie.*"

Jack's jaw dropped. His mouth and eyes opened wide in surprise. He was familiar with the story which was surely inappropriate as a textbook for a course in Introductory Sociology. Speechless, he simply stared back at Cloud. The chairman frowned. It was clear that he was not pleased with Jack's response but continued speaking.

"Listen, if you teach part time or just one course you'll be expected to perform the same duties as regular full time faculty.

You'll have to attend faculty meetings, serve on committees, and have several office hours each week for students." Then he asked, "Do you have any questions?"

Jack reflected for a few moments. This was unreal! Never had he heard of part time or adjunct faculty performing such additional duties."What would I be paid for teaching a course?"

"Sixteen hundred dollars," the chairman answered.

Jack didn't need the money. He wanted to teach because he enjoyed it. But he felt that the amount offered and other stipulations were humiliating. Cloud appeared smug and hostile. Eventually Jack would clash with him. All things considered, this was the wrong place for him to teach.

"Any other questions?" the chairman asked again.

"No," Jack answered definitively, rising from his chair and quickly departing.

It had been an unpleasant encounter, and he felt a wave of relief as he drove away from the campus and headed home. A few days later he received an e mail from the chairperson of the Social and Behavioral Sciences Division of at the west campus of Arizona State University (ASU) asking if he were willing to teach a course in Organizational Theory and Behavior for the impending winter semester. It was an upper level course required of junior and senior students and would meet Tuesday and Thursday mornings beginning in January. He replied affirmatively. Later he called the chairperson for additional information such as salary and whether there was already a textbook in use for the course.

"The salary for one course is thirty five hundred dollars," she noted. "The course hasn't been offered for some time, so I have no idea what you can use as a textbook. I'll leave it up to you."

"I'll take care of it. I'm sure I can find something suitable on the internet."

Preparation for the course would take a considerable amount of time, but he had about several months before the winter semester would begin at ASU. First he needed to scan the internet to find an appropriate textbook. Next he would review the book and compile a set of lecture notes. Finally, he would draw up a syllabus or handout describing material to be covered in readings and lectures as well course requirements and grading procedures. Nearly all of this was accomplished by the beginning of January and the winter semester. He only had to complete a few more pages of lecture notes. It was a Monday, the beginning of the first week of classes when Jack received an unexpected phone call.

"Doctor Rubin this is Irene, an administrative assistant at Arizona State University.Where are you? It's past eleven o' clock, and your students have been in my office looking for you."

"Well, I'm home," Jack said surprised. "I was told my classes were on Tuesdays and Thursdays"

"No, your classes meet on Mondays and Wednesdays."

"I received an e mail from your chairperson some time ago stating that my classes would meet on Tuesdays and Thursdays. Has there been a change in the scheduling?"

"There's been no change," Irene answered. "Will you meet with your students on Wednesday?"

"Of course, I'll be there"

Sometimes there's just too much reliance on e mail, Jack thought. It's so easy for the wrong information to be conveyed, ambiguity to arise, or mistakes in spelling or grammar to occur.

It was a long drive of about ninety miles from Prescott to the west campus of ASU. But it was a very picturesque trip from the high country to the Valley of the Sun. It was a steady descent from about 6,000 feet to 2,000 feet elevation along a winding highway that cut through high mountains and deep valleys. Jack exited at Thunderbird Road. From there it was only a few miles to the university campus and faculty parking. Before meeting his class, Jack stopped briefly to speak with the chairperson or head of the Division of Social and Behavioral Sciences. He introduced himself, and they chatted for a short time. He did ask one important question

"Are there any special problems that I can expect to encounter with your students?"

"They do have problems writing," she replied.

Of course, that was not a surprise for Jack. This had been a nearly ubiquitous problem throughout his teaching career.

Some of Jack's students were already waiting for him and gazed with anticipation as he entered the classroom. The room was nearly full with about fifteen students. Jack dropped his attaché case on a table in front of a blackboard and drew out the course textbook, a set of lecture notes, and copies of the course syllabus It was still a little early before the start of class, and a few more students drifted into the room. A bell rang signaling the beginning of classes. Jack cleared his throat and addressed the class.

"I am Doctor or Professor Rubin, and this is Sociology 314: Organizations and Technological Change. Let's be sure we are in the right class. Now, I have a handout for you," then he grasped copies of the syllabus, began distributing them, and spoke further. "The syllabus describes the content of the course as well other things such as course requirements and grading procedures. I want you to look it over, and I will elaborate on it later. First, I would like to know more about you all. What are you majoring in? What sociology courses have you taken? Any special reasons you are taking this course other than it is required? I have a student roster here. Why don't we just begin this with the first row moving from left to right."

One by one the students introduced themselves. Most were students in their senior year majoring in psychology with only two or three having had any sociology courses. Jack discovered quickly that their knowledge of sociology was either completing lacking or very limited. Teaching this course would be a challenging situation. He began by describing the nature of the human group composed of participants occupying different and interrelated or social positions associated with roles specifying expected patterns of behavior. He noted that social relationships arose through the course of social interaction and were guided as well as reinforced by shared values together with social norms specifying approved and disapproved modes of conduct. In some detail he further described the nature of social interaction, expressed by means of social processes such as cooperation, conflict, or competition, manifest in interpersonal or intergroup relationships.

But then Jack stopped lecturing for a few moments thinking he was losing his students for they appeared flummoxed. Maybe all this was too abstract for them to grasp or maybe they were having difficulties understanding a different way of thinking. After all, this was cowboy country, the wild, wild West: the home of rugged individualism.

"Okay," Jack resumed lecturing. "Let's talk about a group with which are all familiar: the family. Members of a family occupy different statuses which are clearly relational. For example, when we refer to husband what does this presume?"

A student raised his hand to volunteer the answer, saying: "Power."

Some other students laughed seemingly amused by the response.

"Wait," Jack said. "That's really not funny. It has some significance, but in a different way. Now, of course, husband presumes wife, father or mother presumes children, and so forth. But what about power? At one time the husbands were the sole providers in families and played a predominant role in decision making processes. That was especially true in so called traditional families, but now much of that has changed. We have moved toward a more companionship and egalitarian type of family structure where the roles or expected patterns of behavior of spouses have become interchangeable. For example, many wives today even with young children are in the work force, and two income families have become more common. Also, husbands are attending more to child care and household chores."

It was not uncommon for Jack to seize upon a student's inappropriate response and discover some meaning and elaborate. Sometimes teaching was like running down a football field, catching a long pass, and then heading for the goal posts. Jack continued talking about the nature of social relationships which emerged in the course of interaction between and among family members, about shared beliefs and rules manifest in episodes of social action, the manifestation of different kinds of interaction or social processes such as cooperation and conflict, and finally the absence of interaction and alienation leading to the termination of social relationships and the eventual breakup of a family. As he elaborated, it became easier to talk about other groups in terms of social structure and social process concepts. Considering larger and more complex groups, Jack described organizations as collectivities with definite boundaries, possessing specific rules and goals as well as hierarchies of statuses or social positions with designated and differentiated functions and where authority flows from upper to lower levels of the hierarchies. Technology was simply defined as the material and nonmaterial means implemented by an organization to deal with endogenous or environmental issues. References were made to the theoretical contributions of Karl Marx, Max Weber, and Emile Durkheim which addressed organizational problems or dilemmas associated with domination and struggle for control, depersonalization and alienation characterizing bureaucracies, and the problem of reconciling the division of labor or role differentiation with overall organizational integration.

In later lectures Jack dealt with problems related to decision making referring to the concept of "bounded rationality" as delineated by Herbert Simon and James March in discussions of administrative theory. The concept specified a number of constraints: (1) a refusal or inability to make decisions, (2) making quick decisions based on inadequate evidence, (3) a dependence on short range solutions, (4) making inappropriate analogies between old and new experiences, (5) oversimplifying, (6) relying upon preconceived beliefs, and (7) *groupthink*. The meaning of these constraints was fairly clear except for groupthink which he felt required some elaboration. In explaining this concept, Jack sought to relate aspects of groupthink to historical and current events. Throughout his teaching career, he had always tried to apply abstract sociological concepts to real life situations which helped to increase student understanding and classroom participation. Consequently, Jack expatiated on the meaning of groupthink.

"Groupthink occurs when members of a group are pressured to conform to a particular course of action which often has dire consequences. Individual creativity and dissent is stifled with members marching in lockstep. A critical evaluation of a group's decision making process is discouraged with an illusion of unanimity. The group tends to isolate itself from outside influences and alternative points of view. Group loyalty predominates, and actions taken are often driven by an ideology or specific beliefs and myths such as: the illusion of invulnerability, actions taken are justifiable and morally right, the conviction that certain out groups are a threat and need to be avoided or eliminated. We can cite many examples, both past and current of this phenomenon. One was our involvement in the Vietnam War which was largely justified on the so called "domino theory": that is the belief that if South Vietnam fell under communist rule the rest of Southeast Asia would follow which was an assumption which later proved fallacious. We were convinced that we could not lose this crusade against what we believed was the spreading threat of communism. After all, America had never lost a war! But we underestimated an enemy that fought back tenaciously. In daylight many were peasants toiling in the fields. But at night they became the Viet Cong: well-armed guerrilla fighters. It was often difficult to distinguish friend from foe. We exaggerated enemy losses insisting that they were on the verge of capitulating.

There were incessant claims that there was a "light at the end of the tunnel", and all the boys would be home by Christmas. But we were not only fighting the Viet Cong but North Vietnam forces as well. And we seemed oblivious to the fact that the North Vietnam army of about 500,000 strong was well armed and made up of seasoned veterans who had fought against Japanese invaders and had defeated the French Foreign Legion signaling the beginning of the end of French colonialism." Jack paused before continuing.

"The Lyndon Johnson administration escalated the conflict, and there was little toleration of dissent regarding the administration's policy with regard to our involvement in Vietnam. However, as the war dragged on for several years, public protest against our involvement and divisiveness grew. Concomitantly, the South Vietnamese regime was corrupt, and its military forces proved inept. The morale of our own troops was steadily sinking and many even became addicted to drugs. The end finally came during the Richard Nixon Administration with the onslaught of the North Vietnamese Army, the fall of Saigon, and the evacuation of our troops."

For a few moments Jack stopped lecturing and scanned the classroom. The students looked alert and attentive.

"Does anyone have any questions or comments?" Jack asked.

One student raised his hand.

"Professor, I have some questions."

"Good!" Jack rejoined. "What are they?"

"Well, what you've been saying about problems of decision making and the nature of groupthink. Wouldn't they also apply to our current situation, especially in the case of our invasion of Iraq?"

"That's a very good point. I certainly think they could apply to our current circumstances. When George W. Bush campaigned to become President of the United States he asserted that he would reduce our participation in nation building and military encounters. But that didn't happen after he was elected. Instead our involvement increased significantly. Also, many of the characteristics of group-think were evident in the George W. Bush administration. Dissent and criticism were stifled, and loyalty to the ongoing policies of the administration was emphasized. The decision to topple the Sadam Hussein regime was supported by the belief that Iraq was linked to both Al Queda and the horrendous terrorist attacks of September 11, 2001 as well as the belief that the regime possessed weapons of mass destruction. But neither belief was confirmed. The September 11 attacks were masterminded by Osama bin Laden and Al Queda. As far as we know, the terrorists had no connections with Iraq. In addition, no weapons of mass destruction were uncovered except for some that were dysfunctional and had been used during the conflict between Iraq and Iran."

Another student raised her hand.

"Didn't we use weapons of mass destruction in World War Two and Vietnam? Atomic bombs were dropped on Hiroshima and Nagasaki, and the chemical weapon Agent Orange was unleashed during the Vietnam conflict."

"That's true," Jack acknowledged. "But I think we had little choice in the case of dropping the atomic bomb. Frequently the Japanese refused to surrender, even committed suicide rather than being taken prisoner. Their leaders had brainwashed them into believing that the enemy would torture or even butcher them. We estimated it would cost us about a million casualties if we attempted

303

to invade Japan proper. As for Agent Orange, it was a defoliant chemical that was extremely harmful even to our own troops. Are there any other questions or comments?"

There was no response, and Jack continued speaking.

"Keep in mind that the problems I've mentioned regarding decision making and aspects of groupthink characterize not only political organizations or governments but other kinds of organizations as well such as education, religious institutions, and business corporations. And another thing, we need to consider in more detail are the unanticipated consequences of courses of action taken by groups and different organizations."

Throughout the semester some students grumbled about the difficulty of the course. On one occasion a student remarked:

"Professor, this course is really hard. I'm a Criminal Justice major, and I sail through other courses easily making A's and B's. I really have to work to make just a C grade in your course."

Maybe Jack had set the bar too high given the continually declining standards in American education. His students had struggled with the readings, lecture materials, and especially the examinations. Their comprehension and writing skills were extremely poor, yet most were in their senior year and preparing to graduate. When the semester ended, students filled out forms evaluating the instruction and content of the course. This had become a common practice at institutions of higher learning and partly availed as a criterion for instructor retention, promotion, and tenure. But by this time it didn't matter any longer to Jack. The nature of higher education had been altered substantially, and he had felt many of the changes were disdainful. He was now a "dinosaur" in academia. His teaching days were over, and he would need to engage in other pursuits.

It was 2008 and time for the election of another U.S. President. George W. Bush had served two terms, and his domestic and foreign policies had proven unpopular. When he left office in 2008 his poll approval ratings had fallen to a low of about 19%. The country had sunk into a recession, and much blood and treasure had been spent fighting two extended wars in Iraq and Afghanistan. In the case of Iraq, Bush had believed we could create a democracy in a country, torn by conflict among Sunnis, Shiites, and Kurds and surrounded by a sea of dictatorships. But now America had become war weary and increasingly divided. There seemed to be a growing desire for new leadership and changes in the directions of domestic and foreign policies. The Democratic candidate, Barack Obama won the presidential election overwhelmingly. Euphoria, an ecstatic reaction swept the country for America had elected its first black president! Over ninety percent of black voters voted for him. But he couldn't have won without the white vote as well, and surely he was as much or perhaps more white as he was black. His mother and grandparents who raised him were white. His father was black and had deserted him as a child. He was well educated having attended Columbia University and later Harvard where he received his law degree and became editor of the Harvard Law Review. He had been a community organizer in Chicago, served as an Illinois state senator, and later as a United States senator. His credentials were impressive enough, and he spoke very eloquently. There was no question that he was a gifted orator with a message of hope and optimism. His message and sweeping promises stirred and elated the voters. Whenever and wherever he spoke he drew enormous crowds that seemed almost mesmerized. He claimed he would promote unity. There are no "red states" or "blue states", he asserted, but only the United States and promised he would promote greater transparency. Other promises were made as well. But the question was: "How many could or would be kept?" And was he sincere or disingenuous? Every U.S. President must endure the restraints of his office: the checks and balances of America's system of government. Perhaps he was reaching too far. Jack had always been a Democrat, but now the party had changed. He felt it was no longer the party of Harry Truman, John Kennedy, and Lyndon Johnson.

In any event, Jack wished the new president well and hoped that he would fulfill his promises of promoting greater national unity and political transparency. But he was perplexed and troubled by the extreme ecstatic reaction of the voters and the media to the election of America's first black President, and the fact that Obama was also white seemed overlooked. Why had "race" become such a prominent factor particularly among white voters? Was the election of a "black man" to the highest office in the land an act of contrition for a dilemma and guilt haunting white America? Years ago, Jack had read a voluminous account of the caste system and institutional racism that prevailed throughout the South. The researcher and author was Gunnar Myrdal, a Swedish sociologist and former member of the Swedish Parliament, who had lived in the Deep South observing and recording the inequities that existed between the white and black races. Perhaps most notable were the statistics he amassed indicating the very unequal resources allocated to segregated black schools.

Myrdal pointed out that separate educational systems for whites and blacks penalized not only black students but whites as well. The dual system was clearly uneconomical and reduced the overall quality of Southern educational institutions. The "separate but equal" doctrine was clearly a fiasco, and the research evidence provided by Myrdal influenced the United States Supreme Court to declare the doctrine unconstitutional years later in the "Brown versus the School Board" decision. Myrdal described the caste system in great detail. Blacks were relegated to a subordinate status in virtually all Southern social and economic institutions and segregated either in or from most public and private places. Racial relationships were controlled by an elaborate etiquette code. Intimate relations between a black man and white woman were prohibited. Blacks were expected to address whites in a deferential manner as "mister, sir, or mam"; whereas whites commonly addressed blacks as "boy or girl". When blacks entered a white home it was usually through the back door or servants' quarters. The nature of the racial caste system could be elaborated further, but more pertinent here is the meaning of the title of Myrdal's work: "An American Dilemma". The oppressive treatment meted out to blacks posed a dilemma for Southern whites especially the better educated who found it difficult to reconcile the conflicting values of equality and justice for all and the discrimination and oppression of blacks? From this perspective, Myrdal concluded that the prevalence of the caste system was largely a white man's problem and engendered feelings of remorse and guilt among middle class and educated Southern whites. Although many abstained in taking an active role in lynching parties and other heinous miscarriages of justice, they failed to take a stand against such acts This dilemma and remorse was also revealed in the writings of some prominent Southern writers, notably William Faulkner.

It appeared that such enthusiasm of voters for a "black" president and his announced policies together with the nearly unanimous support of the media suggested a kind of atonement for the institutional racism and discriminatory acts inflicted on blacks in earlier eras. At the same time, it tended to subordinate and even eclipse transgressions historically suffered by other racial, ethnic and religious minorities in America. Perhaps the worst was the dire plight of the American Indians. Many of their lands, an integral part of their culture, had been taken from them in a forced evacuation of Native Americans from east of the Mississippi referred to as the *Trail of Tears*. In addition, members of the Sioux tribe, unarmed men, women, and children were wantonly massacred by the U.S. Seventh Cavalry at Wounded Knee, South Dakota.

During the early 1830's a Frenchman, Alexis de Tocqueville journeyed throughout America describing the rapidly democratizing of American society. He expressed certain caveats related to the nature of democracy. One was that the nation's obsession with equality could lead to the dominance of mediocrity and to a tyranny of the majority. Ordinary Americans would possess too much power. The more talented and higher educated would be locked out of the halls of power and critical thinking stifled by the rule of the majority. Tocqueville wrote that he knew of no other country with "less independence of mind, and true freedom of discussion than in America." Of course, Tocqueville's observations are only impressions, but they are somewhat prophetic and provocative. For in the 21st century, nearly 200 years later, his speculations have taken hold in education, mass media, politics, and other social institutions and led to a prevalence of mediocrity.

Following the election of Barack Obama, America seemed to become a more divided and polarized country. Political Correctness became more widespread with a "speech police" roaming the campuses of colleges and universities supressing freedom of speech and critical thinking. Discussions of controversial subjects were discouraged or altogether avoided.When they did occur they often deteriorated into shouting matches characterized by hysterical outbursts. People could no longer agree to disagree. At times the opposition was denounced as "racists, misogynists, terrorists, even suicide bombers." In the political realm, battle lines between Democrats and Republicans were hardening. Bipartisanship or compromise failed; it appeared that the tyranny of the majority had triumphed. Then In the late hours of the night and behind closed doors, the president met with members of his party to plot a strategy to pass the Affordable Health Care Act which became popularly known as "Obama Care". The Democrats controlled the House and the Senate, so the bill passed hurriedly and easily; and with the signed approval of the president it became the law of the land. It was over 2000 pages in length which few, if any, legislators bothered to read. The Speaker of the House urged all first to vote for the proposed legislation and then read it. There was virtually no debate or amendments. Legislators claimed the bill was too long to read or the legalese was too incomprehensible. Opinion polls and town meetings indicated growing public opposition to the Affordable Health Care Act, and no thought had been given to the unanticipated consequences of such legislation.

Other issues were fueling discord. Despite the civil rights legislation of the 1960's and the efforts of Martin Luther King, racial epithets were echoed by political and religious leaders as well as the media. Freedom of speech continued to be under attack especially on college campuses once the hallmark of unfettered inquiry and controversy. The national debt had begun to accelerate with unaccountable stimulus spending. Chronic or long term unemployment and underemployment were rising. The latter included: (1) discouraged worker effects where people gave up searching for work and dropped out of the labor force altogether, (2) those who worked part time and were unable to find full time employment, (3) those forced to work at temporary jobs and unable to find more permanent employment, (4) those suffering cuts in wages or fringe benefits, and (5) people employed at jobs substantially below their education or skill levels (e.g. a PhD driving a taxi cab or pumping gas) and (6) there were those unable to work because they lacked required skills Clearly, the unemployment rate was a very inadequate measure of the jobless situation. To begin with, an overall or nationwide rate masked the great variability in unemployment among different subgroups defined by criteria such as age, race, and ethnicity. Also, decreases in the unemployment rate can be rather misleading as they may simply accrue from reductions in labor force participation rates; and such reductions, especially among people in their prime working years (i.e. 25 t0 44 or 54 years of age), may be a harbinger of very serious social and economic problems.

Especially disturbing was the growing hiatus between the federal government and the remainder of the country. Elected leaders and government appointees had become arrogant, self-serving, and disingenuous. Most members of each major political party, Democrats and Republicans, touted a lockstep unity. Few took an independent stand, demonstrated integrity, or were responsive to their constituents. The policies and actions of both parties were too often characterized by aspects of groupthink; and although they could agree on major goals such as universal and quality health care they disagreed on how to attain them. Additionally, the two parties have somewhat different values or ideologies that were frequently difficult to reconcile. Traditionally Democrats had advocated greater social and economic equality as well as an expansion of federal government powers purported to advance equality hence leveling the playing field. In contrast, Republicans favored a more conservative stance with greater emphasis on competitiveness, individual achievement, and more limited government. Both ideologies could complement one another, but unfortunately the major political parties were becoming too influenced by their extreme factions.

Jack wondered: Is America approaching a point where it will cease to be a republic, where our president, elected representatives, and government appointees are no longer public servants, reflecting the will of the people but merely self - serving and ineffectual entities? Perhaps our political leaders should refresh their memories and read the Declaration of Independence, the Preamble to the U.S. Constitution:

We hold these truths to be self-evident, that all men are created equal, that they are endowed by their Creator with certain inalienable Rights, that among these are Life, Liberty, and the pursuit of happiness. That to secure these rights Governments are instituted among Men, deriving their just powers from the consent of the governed. That whenever any form of Government becomes destructive of these ends, it is the Right of the People to alter or abolish it, and to institute New Government, laying the foundation on such principles and organizing its powers in such form, as to them shall seem most likely to affect their Safety and Happiness. Prudence, will indeed dictate that Governments long established should not be changed for light and transient causes; and accordingly all experiences hath shewn, that mankind are more disposed to suffer, while evils are sufferable, than to right themselves by abolishing the forms to which they are accustomed. But when a long train of abuses and usurpations, pursuing invariably the same Object evinces a design to reduce them under Absolute Despotism, it is their right, it is their duty, *to throw off such Government and to provide new Guards for their future security.*

The document, especially the last sentence, is certainly clear. Hopefully American voters will throw the rascals out.

It was time for Jack to move on. He had already abandoned any hopes or desires to teach again and was considering other pursuits. Hilda's sister, Maja proposed an overseas trip. She had friends, living in Michigan who owned a rental house in a small town in Southern France; and learned that the house would be available for occupancy in the coming fall. After some discussion it was decided that Jack, Hilda, Maja, and a friend of Maja would spend about a month at the house beginning in early October. Much preparation was needed: plane reservations, Paris hotel reservations, and train reservations for the journey to Toulouse where they would rent a car to drive to Cuxac a small town in the southeast corner of France. Also, they were cautioned that the inhabitants of Cuxac did not speak English. Hilda and her sister, of course, spoke Swedish but that was not going to help. Jack had a background in French from his high school days, but that was a long time ago. Fortunately there were several months before they would make their trip, so he had time to enroll in a refresher course in conversational French at the local community college.

In late September Jack and Hilda boarded a plane in Phoenix and visited Maja for a few days at her home in Tampa. Subsequently, they flew to Atlanta where they took a lengthy flight to Amsterdam where they connected with another flight to Paris. At Charles de Gaulle Airport they were joined by Maja's friend, Sandra who had arrived earlier. Pulling their baggage through the massive airport, they found their way to the Metro, a subway system extending throughout Paris. The train was crowded, and Jack and the others were forced to sit apart from one another. A young man sat across from Jack, and for a while they simply glanced at each other as the train pulled out of the terminal and gained momentum. Finally, the young man broke the silence speaking impeccable English.

"You look like you've done some traveling," he commented.

"Right," Jack replied. "It's been a long trip, all the way from Arizona and Florida, in America. Say, your English sounds perfect. Where are you from?"

"I'm from Iran, studying engineering at the university here. My government pays my tuition and many other expenses. When I've received my degree, I'll have to return home."

"Sounds like you have a pretty good deal," Jack responded. "But I'm surprised that you speak such good English."

"As a matter of fact my English is better than my French. Back in Iran, our schools require us to learn English."

The two men continued talking until the Iranian slowly rose from his seat and turned to Jack, saying:

"I have to get off at the next stop. It's been very nice talking with you."

Jack also rose. They shook hands, and Jack responded:

"It's been a pleasure. I hope someday our two countries will develop a better understanding of each other."

The young man smiled, nodded, and departed as the train came to a halt.

"Our stop is next!" Sandra shouted. She had made other trips to Paris and claimed that she knew the way to their hotel. As the train made another stop, Jack and the others grasped their luggage, left the train, and stepped on to a "people mover." Suddenly Maja unexpectedly lost her balance and fell backward causing people behind her to topple. Fortunately all recovered. and nobody was injured. Reaching a long stairway exiting to the street, they started to ascend the stairs. Sandra was in the lead, pulling two small suitcases, and moving quickly. Hilda was still near the bottom of the stairway helping her sister. Jack was about halfway up and had nearly fallen on his two large suitcases. He was very tired from the long trip. Then he heard a soft voice and saw an attractive young woman leaning close to him. She was speaking in French, but he was too weary to understand. He simply nodded, uttering:

"Je ne comprends pas."

He was astonished! The woman reached over, grasped his suitcases, pulled them to the top of the stairs, and quickly descended to help Hilda and her sister.

"Merci, mademoiselle! Merci beaucoup!" Jack shouted.

The three of them exited to the street. Sandra was already a block away. The other two women lagged behind Jack; and Hilda was becoming exasperated, crying out:

"Where is our hotel, Hotel Ibis?"

"I think I see it ahead!" Sandra turned crying out at the others but then saying, "Oh, no! That's not it!"

"We're on the wrong street!" Jack exclaimed. "Look at the sign! This isn't Lafayette Street!"

There was a MacDonald's restaurant nearby where they stopped to ask for directions to Rue de Lafayette and Hotel Ibis. When they finally arrived at the hotel, they were exhausted but pleased to find their accomodations quite comfortable. They planned to remain in Paris for only two days before continuing on to Toulouse. Jack spent much of the time either sleeping to recover from the trip or lounging about the hotel conversing in French with hotel employees and guests. The women were more inclined to go sight – seeing and shopping.

This was Jack's second visit to Paris. His first was in the spring of 1953. Of course he was a young man then, serving in the U.S. Army of occupation in Germany and required to be in uniform at all times. The Korean war was still raging and Princess Elizabeth was about to be crowned Queen of England. Jack and a friend, Joe Smith nicknamed "Smitty", were on an eleven day furlough, and had flown directly to Paris where they planned to spend only two or three days. Most of their time was spent sight- seeing places like the Arc de Triumph, Montmartre, the Eiffel Tower, Napoleon's Tomb. They even attended a performance of the Follies Bergaire which was quite a show. Now, so many years later, Jack was more interested in the people especially their language and culture. This was the birth place of August Comte, a mathematician and philosopher who coined the term "sociology" defining it as a science devoted to the study of society. His disciples founded the major school of French sociology which later exerted a significant influence on developments in American sociology. France was the home of great writers and philosophers: Emile Zola, Francois Voltaire, Guy De Maupassant, Alexandre Dumas, Jacque Rousseau and many others. Especially memorable was Emile Zola, a champion of truth and justice who jeopardized his career and risked imprisonment in fighting a gross miscarriage of justice in the infamous Dreyfuss case. Alfred Dreyfuss, a Jewish lieutenant in the French Army in the 1850's, was falsely accused of treason. Stripped of his rank and dishonorably discharged, he was imprisoned on Devil's Island for nearly fifty years. Zola unrelentingly sought the truth exposing members of the General Staff who were directly or indirectly guilty of the acts of treason and who had framed Dreyfuss. In a letter to the President of France, entitled "J'Accuse", he singled out the guilty parties. Subsequently, he was threatened with imprisonment and fled to England to continue his fight for justice. Zola's efforts stirred the conscience of a nation and finally led to the exoneration of Dreyfuss.

The two days in Paris passed quickly. It was early Monday morning when Jack and the women called for a taxi to convey them to the train station. It was more convenient than traveling on the Metro, pulling their luggage, and possibly getting lost again. They were hungry and had sandwiches and coffee after arriving at the station. The trip to Toulouse would take about five to six hours. Boarding the train they found ample seating and storage space for their luggage. Shortly, the train moved slowly out of the station beginning its journey through the French countryside. A number of stops were made at small towns for passengers coming and going. Rumbling along level terrain, the train passed farms, and pasture land where herds of cattle, sheep, and horses were grazing or roaming about. After sitting for a few hours, Jack was feeling a little stiff. He needed to stretch, so he began to rise from his seat. Then an extraordinary thing happened. Seated diagonally across the aisle was a woman and a boy of perhaps nine or ten years old. As he slowly rose, the boy quickly moved toward him extending his arm and an open hand. Jack grasped the boy's hand and responded:

"Merci beaucoup pour votre aider!"

The boy smiled returning to his seat. Jack smiled back at him and thought, I don't believe this would happen in America, not today.

A few hours later the train reached Toulouse where Jack and the women picked up their rental car for the drive to Carcassonne and their final destination, the village of Cuxac. Hilda was their designated driver but relented, and Sandra volunteered to drive. It was late in the day, so they decided to take the expressway in order to reach Cuxac before nightfall. It was still daylight when they drove into the village. Close by was a stream and a few ducks. They drove by a large statue of Virgin Mary holding baby Jesus, a hotel, a small grocery store, and a bakery. Sandra expertly maneuvered through narrow winding cobblestone streets, passing rows of stone houses perhaps centuries old, a community parking area, and what appeared to be a town hall. She then turned up a steep street leading to a house which would be home for about the next three weeks. The owner had given them detailed directions; and the caretaker, an elderly English lady arrived with keys to the house. The house interior was quite compact. One large room was on the first floor, a fireplace, and a few pieces of furniture consisting of a couch, table, and a few chairs. Next to the room was a very small kitchen and a half bathroom. A steep spiral staircase wound up to the second and third floors where there were three bedrooms and a larger bathroom with a shrunken deep tub. A central heating system was lacking but portable electric heaters were on the first and second floors. The house was probably two or three hundred years old.

Cuxac was like a journey back in time. The village had a medieval even Romanesque ambience. In the distance was the Pyrenees, a mountain range stretching along the borders of France and Spain from the Atlantic to the Mediterranean. They had thought of driving up into the mountains and visiting Andorra; but the English lady warned them that the roads might be unsafe, very narrow, windy and even icy at times. The weather was unusually cool for October probably explaining why very few of the village residents were walking about. Nearly every morning Jack headed down to the bakery for a fresh loaf of bread. One morning they found themselves out of butter, so Jack took a longer walk past the bakery to the town grocery store. Inside he searched for butter but was having difficulty finding it, so he approached an elderly lady waiting on customers and inquired:

"Ou est le buerre, si'il vous plais?"

The woman shrugged her shoulder and looked very puzzled. He repeated the question, and she replied: "Je ne sais pas que vous voulez."

There were other customers standing by, and they too appeared puzzled. At this point it was becoming obvious to Jack that he simply wasn't pronouncing the word "buerre" properly. Back in high school his French teacher had often chided him for his incorrect pronunciation of the language. He had an idea! Outstretching the palm of one hand, he brushed the palm with his other hand.

"Oui! Oui! Maintenant je sais que vous voulez!" the woman shouted

Quickly she led Jack to the back of the store and showed him the butter. At the same time, she gave him a lesson in the proper pronunciation of the word, "buerre".

La Cité de Carcassone was only fifteen or twenty miles from the village and had a fascinating history dating back to the time of the Roman Empire. Originally a Roman colony, it was surrounded by outer and inner walls lined with battlements and flanked by towers. Although well fortified, it fell to successive waves of invaders. First came the barbarian hordes followed by the Visgoths, Franks, Arabs, and finally the French. In order to enter the city visitors crossed a bridge elevated above a moat and passed through a high archway. The streets were narrow and winding filled with tourists. Alongside were shops, restaurants, sidewalk cafes, and all kinds of living quarters. Farther in was a chateau and church. After walking some distance, Jack and the women grew tired and hungry and stopped for lunch at one of the sidewalk cafes. Seated nearby was a Frenchman who smiled at them. Jack began to pick up his eating utensils, first a fork and waving it at the Frenchman he asked:

"Comme vous il disez en Francais?"

The Frenchman responded, "fourchette."

He asked the same question holding up a knife and the response was: "couteau" and finally a spoon, and the man answered, "cuillére."

Each time the man responded Jack repeated the French word and exclaimed, "Merci, monsieur! Maintenant, je puis parler Francais!"

Then they both laughed.

"What's so funny?" Hilda asked Jack.

"Oh, I told him that now I'm able to speak French."

Whenever he could Jack would engage the French people in conversations, and they appeared to respond very positively. He would make mistakes in grammar or pronunciation, but it didn't seem to matter. What seemed important to them was that here was an American who was trying to speak their language.

One time they traveled farther east to the city of Narbonne where they encountered throngs of young people demonstrating in a large open area in the center of the city. Barricades blocked some of the streets, and at one point the barricades forced Sandra to stop the car. However, when she rolled down a car window and addressed one of the demonstrators in English, he reacted quickly removing the barricades. It was impossible to park on the streets because of the crowds of demonstrators and spectators as well as gendarmes standing by to assure the peace. They were able to park in a nearby underground garage and walked several blocks to a restaurant for lunch. Seated inside, they asked their waitress what the demonstration was about. She answered rather flippantly and in English:

"Oh, this happens every fall. They really don't know what they're demonstrating about."

But Jack was curious. As they were walking back to the garage, he stopped to speak to one of the demonstrators and even picked up one of the pamphlets being circulated. He thought it was unusual. All these young people were protesting against pending legislation that would increase the age of eligibility for retirement pensions and were so enthusiastically concerned for the welfare of their elders. At the head of the crowd was a podium where several people stood with megaphones delivering speeches to noisy and responsive demonstrators. Jack, Hilda, Maja, and Sandra made additional visits to Carcassone and Narbonne. They even drove farther east and wadded into the calm waters of the Mediterranean Sea. Driving back after dark they became temporarily lost on an expressway because of the inadequate lighting of exit signs and found themselves heading south toward the Spanish border.

The days and weeks passed quickly until it was time to leave France. They departed from Cuxac, returned their rental car in Toulouse where they spent the night at a hotel. The following morning they boarded a train for Paris, and returned to Hotel Ibis on Rue de Layfayatte. They stayed in Paris only a few days, and in a cool early morning a taxi took them to Charles de Gaulle Airport. Along the way, Jack sat next to the driver and carried on a conversation with her in French. At the airport crowds of young people were demonstrating, This had become a common phenomenon. They checked in at departures and moved quickly through security, after which Jack, Hilda, and Maja parted with Sandra who was leaving on a different flight. They headed for their gate and shortly boarded their plane which departed on time. It was an uneventful flight back to America. They landed in Detroit, passed through customs, and flew on to Tampa where Jack and Hilda spent a few days with Maja before returning to Prescott.

The day after they reached home they retrieved Sophie from Runamuck, a kennel run by her veterinarian. She had received excellent care, and seeing Jack and Hilda she jumped with joy almost knocking Jack off his feet. In the months that followed Jack mulled over the disappointments and frustrations of his past which left him somewhat depressed. At the same time, he recalled happy and humorous times. Now he was becoming more disturbed, even agitated by the course of events in America. It was September, 2012. A national election for office of President of the U.S. and members of the House of Representatives and Senate was only months away; and divisions, distortion, suppression, and intolerance were growing throughout the nation. The ideological differences between Democrats and Republicans as well as between so called conservatives and liberals had continued to sharpen. Bipartisanship and a willingness to agree to disagree was dissipating People were more apprehensive about freely expressing their views or dissenting from prevailing opinions. Political adversaries increasingly resorted to character defamation charging one another as "racist", "misogynist" or "sexist", and even "treasonable". There there was the continual use in the media and by politicians of the word, "undocumented" to refer to people who entered the country illegally. But did this make sense? Having broken the law they could easily falsify documents. If so, wasn't the term "undocumented" an oxymoron? Also disconcerting were the distortions or misrepresentations of the meaning of the terms, "liberal" and "conservative", labels often applied in derogatory and scurrilous ways. Jack had always prided himself as a liberal: someone willing to listen and consider different or conflicting points of view, open to compromise, and a strong believer of freedom and justice. At the same time, he was conservative insofar as he respected certain traditions and felt that caution was essential in decision making related to social and political innovations. Too often America's leaders ignored the unanticipated consequences of their actions and even neglected to read proposed legislation which he considered a national disgrace!

Jack talked to Hilda about all this and other issues: his life experiences, the past and current plight of America, and its uncertain future. She was a very patient listener and often suggested:

"Jack, you talk about this a great deal. Why don't you write about it all? It might make you feel better, and other people might be interested in what you have to say."

Perhaps he would do that. It might give him some feeling of relief if he wrote about all this. It would be a way of escaping the boredom of Prescott and sharpen his mental faculties. Finally, it might be a legacy that he could leave his wife, son, and grandchildren. So he began to write, to recreate his life experiences through a fictitious character and against the backdrop of changes in America as well events transpiring in the rest of the world.

Then something horrific occurred! On September 11,2012 our diplomatic facilities in Benghazi, Libya were assaulted by militant Islamists and terrorists. The attacks against the main compound of the consulate began at nightfall and continued for quite a few hours. After a lull in the attack, the compound annex was assaulted in the early morning hours of September 13. The terrorists were armed with sophisticated and heavy weapons including rocket propelled grenades, anti-aircraft machine guns, mortars, and artillery mounted on trucks. The U. S. ambassador and his staff notified Tripoli and Washington that they were under attack and desperately pleaded for help. But no substantial help came. Sean Smith, an information officer, attempted to assist Ambassador Stevens, but both men were killed by the terrorists. Tyrone Woods, a former naval seal, headed a rescue team that rushed from Tripoli in armored Toyota Land Cruisers. Glen Doherty, also a former naval seal, was part of another rescue team that headed from Tripoli. Both Woods and Doherty were killed in attempts to save personnel trapped in the compound annex.

The initial reaction of the Obama administration was that the attack was carried out spontaneously and in response to a provocation: an anti-Islamic video, "Innocence of Muslims". Further investigation, however, determined that such an assumption was false and that the attack was a premeditated, well planned, and organized operation. Extensive inquiries were made and continue to be made by Congress concerning inadequate security of the consulate and the failures of the Obama administration to respond to repeated and desperate calls for help. There had been earlier attacks in Libya indicating a persistence of instability which seemed to be ignored. No one was held responsible or accountable for the Benghazi tragedy. The Secretary of State had said she took responsibility for the lack of adequate security and the failure of our nation to mount a rescue operation; and in answering the question of whether the Benghazi attack was premeditated or spontaneous she simply stated, "What difference does it make!" But no disciplinary actions were taken against anyone The Secretary of Defense claimed that the attacks didn't last long enough for help to arrive on time. But it is estimated by witnesses that the assaults lasted about eight or nine hours. Also, it has been noted by members of the annex security team that their endeavors to save Ambassador Christopher Stevens were delayed by an order to "stand down". Who gave that order? Where were the Secretary of State, Secretary of Defense, and the President of the United States, the Commander in Chief and what were they doing during the hours of the attack? The President has said that he gave orders that sufficient help be given to our people trapped in Benghazi. If that were the case, why weren't his orders carried out? These and related questions continue to go unanswered.

There had been other notorious or scandalous incidents throughout earlier administrations such as Watergate and the Iran

Contra Affair. But especially disconcerting to Jack was the Benghazi debacle. Most disturbing was that there has been no accountability for what happened. Harry Truman expressed it well pointing out that when things go awry," the buck" stops in the Oval Office. But In the case of President Obama and the Benghazi incident it seems that "the buck" never reached the Oval Office. Clearly life is a very precious thing! Jack strongly believed the most significant message here was that you do not abandon comrades in harm's way! Trained by combat veterans during the Korean War, he learned the importance of protecting the backs of fellow soldiers and leaving no one behind. There may, of course, be exceptions when soldiers in combat volunteer or are ordered to remain behind to fight a rear guard action enabling their main force to retreat escaping enemy assaults. And during air combat, pilots may be instructed not to break formation in an attempt to rescue a downed comrade due to the risk of jeopardizing the entire squadron. But such exceptions hardly applied to the Benghazi debacle.

Many years ago during World War Two, a U.S. Marine company was almost wiped out somewhere in the jungles of the South Pacific. There were three survivors, a lieutenant and two enlisted men. They were surrounded by enemy troops, and the lieutenant was badly wounded. The lieutenant ordered the other two marines: "Leave me behind. I'm not going to make it. The enemy is all around us. Save yourselves."

"Sir, we're not leaving you behind! We're bringing you out!" They insisted, refusing to obey the order.

Putting together a bamboo stretcher, the two marines carried their lieutenant out of the jungle. At an aid station, a medic asked the lieutenant, "Sir, how did you make it out of the jungle?"

And the lieutenant replied, "Two of my men brought me out: a Baptist minister and a wandering Jew!"

CHAPTER TWELVE:
REFLECTIONS

Jack began to contemplate his past experiences and many changes that had occurred in America and the larger world. He would try to write about it all weaving it together like some massive tapestry. But there were questions to address. Should the narrative be a medley of fact and fiction? How and where should it begin? How would it end? It could begin in Boston, his place of birth, followed by a description of the experiences of his early years and the tumultuous events leading up to World War Two. Answers to other questions could wait. He had never before he tried to write something like this. In his youth he dabbled in fiction mostly short stories of the supernatural. In later years his writings related to social problems and were more academic in nature. Some were published as articles in academic journals, while other were presented at professional meetings. Sitting in front of his computer, he touched the keyboard, reflecting, and reaching far back into the past. He became detached from his surroundings and felt transported to other times and places. Slowly, he started to press the keys struggling with words, sentences, and paragraphs, which gradually fell into place. Most importantly they all had to have meaning and continuity. Time passed swiftly even when he wrote for hours when he might write only a page or less. Afterwards he would feel somewhat drained. But, at the same time, he sensed a wave of relief and accomplishment.

In certain respects Prescott was an ideal place to write for there were few distractions. It was like living in a cabin in the midst of a remote wilderness. Jack's home was embedded in a breathtaking landscape of mountain ranges, dense forests, and lakes. Throughout his housing development there was little sign of human movement or activity, and any sounds resonated for miles around. Animal life was frequently visible: scurrying rabbits and road runners, mule deer standing motionless then nibbling on trees or bushes, and when disturbed leaping quickly through the brush, and herds of peccaries or javelinas crossing properties and neighborhood roads. Once Jack spied two bears intermittently hugging each other at a distant horizon. What a sight! As the months passed his narrative unfolded, and he decided that it would essentially be an autobiography. There was no need to mix facts with fiction. He believed that the facts alone were adequate to provide the raw material for a unique and meaningful work. Hilda was helpful in editing and making suggestions related to content.

Although not optimistic, considering the nature of the social climate of Prescott, Jack hoped he might connect with other writers in the community. Then one morning, while perusing the local newspaper, he came across a notice of meetings of a group identified as, the "Professional Writers of Prescott". He attended their meetings and was favorably impressed with the agendas and the fact that there were quite a few participants. However, the major reason he joined the group was to interact with others in writing critiques. He found some people who had organized into critique groups but was abruptly told by their members that their groups were "closed". He raised the question of his interest in writer critique groups with the head of Professional Writers of Prescott but received an unsatisfactory response.

"We don't formally organize critique groups. If individual members wish to organize such groups they may do so. Perhaps I'll bring up the issue at one of our meetings."

But the question was not raised at future meetings, and Jack became alienated and left the group. Following that, he received a barrage of e mails from parties in the community offering to edit his writings but always for a price sometimes as high as fifty dollars per hour. There was also a flood of e mails from people claiming to be participants of writer groups who encouraged him to join. One such group met weekly at a downtown coffee house, and he chose to investigate.

It was a Sunday morning when he drove downtown and parked near the coffee house where he hoped to meet other writers and engage in some meaningful discourse People were seated at tables sipping coffee in an outside courtyard. Many inside the coffee house were busy pressing the keys of laptop computers. It was very noisy, almost deafening, as a young woman was singing and strumming on a guitar. Jack approached one of the employees serving coffee and pastries, asking him loudly:

"Can you help me? I'm looking for a group of writers who are meeting here!"

A tall, good looking man was standing nearby. Hearing Jack he waved and pointed at a table.

"We're sitting over there," he said. "Just follow me!"

There was just the two of them seated at the table.

"Where are the others?" Jack inquired.

"They'll be along shortly. Hey, my name is Dan!"

"Very nice to meet you, I'm Jack!"

The two men shook hands. Dan continued speaking in a lower tone as the woman had ceased singing and playing her guitar.

"I see you didn't bring a laptop with you," Dan observed.

"No," Jack replied. "But I did bring a copy of the first chapter of an autobiography that I've been working on over a year."

Like many other patrons in the coffee shop, Dan had an open laptop in front of him. Jack leaned over slightly trying to see the content on the screen. But he could see only a few lines of text as Dan quickly moved his computer away from him.

"I have only some notes, just an outline," Dan said almost defensively.

"What are you writing about?"

"You might say it's science fiction about some creatures from outer space."

For a brief period of time Dan rambled on describing a number of his rather weird creatures. When Jack asked him if he were planning to try to publish his work, Dan replied:

"Yes, but I'll need to raise some money first. Then I'll try to get it on creative space or a web site."

"Say, Dan I brought a copy of the first chapter of my autobiography along. You want to take a look at it? Any comments would be appreciated."

But Dan reacted negatively.

"No! No!" he exclaimed. "We don't do that sort of thing!"

"I don't understand you." Jack was surprised and flummoxed.

"Look," Dan replied. "We used to do that, read and critique each other's writings, but it didn't work out. One member of our group was this retired college professor, and when he reviewed our writings he treated us like we were his students."

"But I don't think that's enough reason to discontinue the practice. Besides, when others read your material they may see deficiencies or problems that you fail to descern."

"I can do all the editing myself," Dan insisted. "I read my stuff forward and backward. I can take care of any problems. What we can do is simply talk about what we have written and raise any questions or invite comments."

This guy is really arrogant, Jack thought. He's really firm about this. It sounds hopeless. There's no use pushing him any further.

"By the way, where is Angela?" Jack asked. "Isn't she the leader of the group?"

"Well, yes, she's been away on a trip to Mexico. We expect her back at our next meeting."

Two others then joined Jack and Dan: a short rather portly woman and a young man. The woman brought a cup of coffee, a dish of pastries, and a laptop to the table. Most of the ensuing conversation was between Dan and the young man. They talked a great deal about their experiences visiting distant places in Asia and Latin America. It was almost a travelogue, but Jack listened politely. At one point, he did mention that he had brought a copy of the first chapter of his autobiography; and the young man asked:

"May I read it?"

"Certainly," Jack responded handing him the manuscript.

He read it and showed some interest but made no comments. When finished he returned the manuscript to Jack and simply said: "Thank you."

There was more conversation, but none of it pertained to writing. Jack had reservations about attending another meeting. It appeared to be a waste of time especially since it appeared unlikely that there would be any exchanges involving writing critiques. However, Hilda encouraged him to participate at least one more time.

A week later he again joined the group at the coffee house. Dan and the short portly woman were the only participants. According to Dan, the leader of the group was still away in Mexico. Jack spent about an hour with them;and during that time, they talked incessantly about creatures in current science fiction films. Finally, Jack grew exasperated and rose from the table.

"You guys have lost me!" He exclaimed. "I'm leaving. Maybe I'll see you another time."

He quickly left and never returned. From that time on, he abandoned any idea of joining any other so called writer groups.

It was November 2012. Barack Obama was reelected President of the United States, and early in his second term the state of the Union and conditions in the larger world were becoming steadily worse. The president and his administration appeared increasingly disingenuous and incompetent. Promises of a transparent or open administration were recurrently violated The Benghazi debacle was just one example of a series of rationalizations, coverups, and an eschewing of responsibility when circumstances went awry. Unlike earlier presidents, Obama has refused to admit mistakes or take responsibility for errors in judgment and policies. He had been disdainful and intolerant of political dissent and, in contrast to past presidents, unwilling or unable to reach across the aisle and compromise with Congressional adversaries. An aura of corruption, incompetence, and negligence enveloped Washington. Illustrative were the Fast and Furious program, begun during the Bush Administration, resulting in government weapons falling into the hands of criminal elements, the targeting and harassment of conservative political groups by the Internal Revenue Service, the failure of the Veterans Administration to adequately serve the country's veterans, the dysfunctional effects of the Affordable Health Care, and illegal migrants increasingly flowing across our open national borders. The president failed to fulfill his promise of promoting national unity, but instead his administration as well as members of Congress stoked divisiveness and conflict among the electorate.

With respect to foreign policy, the threat of global terrorism continued to escalate despite President Obama's assurances that al Queda had been essentially vanquished. Islamic extremism was spreading like a cancer throughout the Middle East, Africa, and Central Asia. The agenda of the Islamic extremists was clear: the destruction of Israel and Western Civilization, the global enforcement of Sharia law or Islamic fundamentalism, and the establishment of an Islamic caliphate. They wore no uniforms nor fought in accordance with international laws and constraints. Their followers were killers, glorifying indiscriminate destruction, death, and the wanton slaughtering of innocent men, women, and children. They were driven by a hatred of democracy and other religions and in battle used their own people as human shields. Unfortunately, America was beginning to abdicate its role as a world leader and was becoming inclined to appeasement. It seemed our nation had lost its way. Our political leaders, particularly President Obama and the Congress, continued to lose credibility at home and abroad in tandem with a growing hiatus between Washington and the electorate. Hopefully this would change, otherwise there was the danger that America might repeat the mistakes and isolationism of the 1930's facilitating World War Two.

About two years had passed since Jack had begun to write his story which was nearing completion. And he still wondered: How should it all end?" He had pondered this question for some time, and then something happened while he was talking with his son. They were conversing on the phone. William, now a high level executive in a large prominent company, had just returned home to Minnesota from a business engagement in California.

"How did the trip go, William?"

"Fine dad, fine. How are you and mom doing?"

"Everything is okay here. How was your presentation at the meeting?"

"Good! It was well received. I covered a lot of separate topics, and then it was *aha*!

"What do you mean by *aha*, William?"

"Well, dad people may be left confused when you talk about so many different things related or unrelated. By *aha*, I mean pulling everything together, so what you've talked about becomes more understandable and meaningful."

"Yes, yes. I think I understand. That makes good sense. Take care, son. Love to you and the family. See you in a few months. We're really looking forward to Maria's graduation. Good bye, son."

That was it! Jack thought. Now he had a clue as to how to conclude his narrative. William had said it with *aha*! This account of Jack's life experiences and events in America and the larger world invoked sundry themes or issues, but there was no need to reiterate them all. Perhaps there was one or more that dwarfed all others, an overriding message connecting the loose ends, drawing them together, and helping to give the reader a better understanding of his story.

He sat in front of his computer, reflecting on what he had written.For a time he was stymied until late one night it began to come to him: There was at least one recurring and salient theme: It had to do with *taking a stand* against such things as bigotry, religious and racial discrimination, and injustice. And this was not just about him but about America too. In boyhood years he fought back with fists against religious epithets. Later at Augusta Military Academy he stood with fellow cadets against what they considered an infringement of their religious freedom. Then as World War Two drew to a close, it was pointed out how many millions of lives might have been spared if only the world had taken an earlier stand against acts of blatant aggression and genocide.

335

During his college years Jack encountered racial and religious discrimination at American University and felt stifled residing on the main uptown campus of the university. But this was no time to take a stand. For he could not really protest or alter these circumstances and simply moved to a rooming house offering him a more congenial environment while taking courses at the downtown campus of the university. About this time, the civil rights movement was beginning to gain momentum; and he joined a protest demonstration against racial injustice in the case of Willie McGee. After he graduated college the Korean War broke out, and he served in the U.S. Army of occupation in Germany. In basic training he was unafraid to speak out against the scurrilous and irresponsible attacks of Senator Joseph McCarthy; and later in Germany he joined his comrades in thwarting the threats and harassments of a noncommissioned officer.

He recalled his years as a graduate student at the University of Chicago in pursuit of a PhD degree in sociology, and the difficulties he encountered in trying to gain faculty support for a dissertation proposal. This was the most arduous part of the PhD program. You took the required courses, passed several hours of written qualifying exams, and then you reached what many students referred to as the "mountain" beginning with an approved proposal for an original and viable research design. Developing the proposal was one thing, but successfully rounding up a faculty committee to approve and guide the research was another. Three times Jack tried to scale that *mountain*. Twice he was forced back. But he was pertinacious and undaunted. He could have given up like some others: "thrown in the towel." But there was too much at stake. And each time he was knocked down, he rose up feeling stronger than before, and grew more determined.

While still a graduate student, he taught a course in Introductory Sociology at the University of Illinois in Chicago where he was pressured to pass an "Arab" student. Actually the student was Iranian. But that didn't matter. He was told that it was deemed unacceptable for a Jewish instructor to fail an "Arab" student, and if he persisted in doing so his teaching contract would not be renewed. He told the administration what they could do with their contract. He persisted, failed the student, and moved on to teach elsewhere. Years later, after earning his PhD, he took a stand again at Roosevelt University and failed almost the entire class of students who had refused to complete a major class requirement. Many of the students lined up outside the office of the Dean of the Business School to register complaints. One full professor even tried to order Jack to change the grades.

"You can't fail all these students!" he shouted. "We need their tuition!" Fortunately, this time the administration defended Jack's action.

There was another incident at Roosevelt University when Jack admonished the acting dean of the business school for inappropriately criticizing Kim, Jack's teaching colleague, for having communication problems because of his different racial and cultural background. Jack lashed back at the administrator:

"This is nonsense. I've attended a number of Kim's classes. He's an excellent teacher. And that's what America is all about: *being different!*"

But perhaps the most ignominious event occurred some years later when Jack was a full tenured professor of sociology at Saint Cloud State University. It was the end of a semester and he had just submitted final grades for courses that he had been teaching. He was sitting at his desk rummaging through some papers when one of his students appeared at the open doorway to his office.

Jack looked up from his paper work to acknowledge the student.

"Come in. What can I do for you?"

"I just received my grade in Urban Sociology, and I'm very angry about it! You gave me only a C and you promised me a B grade!" She was raising her voice and was almost shouting.

Jack shook his head in disbelief firmly replying: "I never made any such promise." Then he continued. "I have your final examination here." He drew the student's examination from the pile of papers on his desk and handed it to her. "If you like, I am willing to review your final examination."

"Don't bother!" the student snapped with growing anger. "I don't like the way you grade!" she added. She then turned and hastily left Jack's office.

Later, with the assistance of some faculty, other students, and the affirmative action officer, the student twisted the facts, conjured up lies, and filed a sexual harassment suit. Jack could have simply appeased the student and granted her the grade she desired. Instead, he chose to take a stand.

As Jack continued to reflect, he thought about something else that loomed in importance:the plight of education in America. The accumulation and sharing of knowledge had been a central part of his life. We live in an age when technology enables us to access vast amounts of information, yet so many wallow in the bowels of ignorance. Throughout his career, Jack had witnessed a steady decline in academic standards which impeded not only the lives of individuals but the welfare of the nation as well. It was one of our Founding Fathers, Thomas Jefferson who is thought to declare: "The price of liberty is eternal vigilance!" But how can we be vigilant if an active and knowledgeable electorate is lacking? If we allow ignorance and apathy to prevail, then surely we jeopardize our freedoms and even the survival of our republic.

Perhaps the deterioration of American education institutions began with the Civil Rights Acts passed by the U.S. Congress so many years ago. Initially, the legislation was indeed needed to alleviate the unjust treatment of segments of our population. But its policies favoring the preferential treatment of select minorities spawned some adverse effects In attempts to correct past wrongs involving discriminatory practices against certain minorities, greater wrongs had sometimes been committed in the preferential hiring, promotion, and retention of teachers based on race, gender, and ethnicity together with the disregard of teacher qualifications.

Of course, many other factors had contributed to the erosion of academic standards such as grade inflation, social passes, indoctrination in lieu of teaching, the growing repression of freedom of speech on college campuses and the deleterious impact of open admission policies of colleges. Pertinent were the consequences of open admission policies is the case of the City College of New York {CCNY} that nearly ceased to be a viable institution of higher learning as a result of open admission policies and remedial education practices. And although people in our society tend to extol the merits of education, it was not uncommon for teachers to be deprecated. Illustrative was a picture which appearing on the front page of the

Daily Courier, Prescott's only local newspaper, dated December 22, 2012 with the caption reading: *What crust! Students throw pies at professors.* Jack felt it was a disgusting and demeaning sight: several faculty smiling and even laughing as they stood covered with dripping pie ingredients.

The foregoing is certainly not exhaustive. The demise of our education institutions has been complex with many ramifications and no easy solutions. Unfortunately our political leaders and even educators have continually proposed oversimplified and failing solutions. Some have suggested that more funds should be allocated for education. But too often additional monies have been spent unwisely or wastefully. Examples are when increased funding has excessively fattened administrative components of higher education or has been used simply for cosmetic purposes. Others have insisted that technology is some kind of panacea and have advocated for more computers in the classrooms. But technology is merely an extension or product of human intelligence and creativity. Most important is that our students and too often our teachers lack basic reading, writing, and mathematical skills as well as the ability to think logically, critically, and analytically.

Suddenly a voice excitingly interrupted Jack's reflections. It was Hilda shaking him from his long sleep.

"Oi, yoi,yoi!" she exclaimed, "Wake up! Wake up, Jack! My goodness! You've slept here all night!"

Jack slowly opened his eyes, shaking his head. Dawn was just breaking over the distant mountains, and turning he said:

"You know, Hilda my story is almost finished. I've wondered for some time how it would end. Now I finally know."

"How will it end?" she asked.

"With our granddaughter's college graduation."

"Sounds like it will be a good ending. But right now, let's have some coffee and breakfast. Later my sister will be arriving to take care of Sophie. In only a few days we'll be on our way to Minnesota and Fargo for Maria's graduation. "

Soon it was time to depart. Jack and Hilda took the shuttle to Sky Harbor Airport in Phoenix where they boarded an Air Bus bound for Minneapolis. When all the passengers were seated and the doors locked, the pilot announced there would be a delay in leaving as a severe thunder storm was raging over the Twin Cities. After about an hour had passed, the pilot again made an announcement. "Ladies and gentlemen I must apologize for this delay. The storm over the Twin Cities has now subsided, and we are ready to leave." Passengers murmured a widespread sigh of relief. The plane taxied slowly down the runway with its engines roaring, and gaining momentum it was aloft beginning its accelerated climb from the Valley of the Sun. Although it was a little bumpy clearing the surrounding mountains, the flight ran smoothly and without interruptions for a few hours. But when the pilot received reports that thunder storms were persisting in Minneapolis, there were further delays with a flight diversion to Omaha and a holding pattern over Sioux City. Finally, the plane began its descent into the Minneapolis-Saint Paul International Airport. Jack gazed out of a window and briefly saw a glimpse of the ground far below. Then suddenly, the plane lurched and shook as it passed through a bank of dark clouds.

"Oh, my god!" Jack exclaimed. "This is really scary!" He gripped Hilda's hand tightly. The woman sitting next to him at the window was coolly playing solitaire on her laptop.

"Doesn't this bother you?" Jack asked her.

"No," she replied. "I've flied a lot and experienced much worse."

Much to Jack's relief the plane touched down, and he commenced to clap. He looked around and cried aloud, "Hey, everyone give the pilot a hand for bringing us in safely!" But no one else clapped.

When he was leaving the plane, Jack shook the pilot's hand. "Thanks, " he said. "Good job."

"Thank you," the pilot responded and smiled.

William met them at the airport and drove them home where they were joined by their daughter-in-law, Marie and Karin, the youngest granddaughter. It was still early evening, and they spent some time talking before retiring. It had been nearly a year since Jack and Hilda had visited family in Minnesota. The first week passed quickly; and on Friday, the day before Marie's graduation, Jack, Hilda, William, Marie, and Karin packed up and headed for Fargo, North Dakota. It was about 300 miles away. They traveled in two cars; and as they passed the Saint Cloud exits and farmland silos, Jack remembered that a prominent American novelist had grown up in a small prairie town a short distance north of Saint Cloud. He pondered, trying to recall the name of the writer. Then he remembered just before they reached Sauk Centre: Sinclair Lewis, yes, that was it. And at the Sauk Centre exit a sign read: *The boyhood home of Sinclair Lewis.* He was the first American writer to win the Nobel

Prize for Literature. Granting of the award was notably influenced by his novel *Babbit*, a satire of American middle class culture.

They passed Alexandria, and as they drew nearer to North Dakota the terrain changed radically. Dense forests and green rolling hills gradually vanished displaced by a vast flattened landscape of ploughed blackened earth, scattered patches of scrawny trees, farm houses, barns, and silos. Not a place where I would want to live, Jack mused. The land is too barren and isolated but I'm sure it's still home to many.

About an hour later they reached the welcome sign to North Dakota and Fargo. Immediately they checked into their hotel where reservations had been made months earlier. A brief family reunion occurred at Maria's apartment across from the university campus. Elizabeth, Jack's third granddaughter, had driven down from Grand Forks where she had completed her second year at the University of North Dakota. Maria took them all on a tour of the university campus which included the business school, student dormitories, class buildings, and the library. The library facilities appeared rather limited, and Maria mentioned that dust had even collected on the rows of books.

"We really don't use the library except to study. Everything we need to read is on the internet."

Later they all dined together before parting for the night.

The following morning they rose early in order to avert the throng of families and friends planning to attend the graduation ceremonies in a large dome shaped building. The doors to the auditorium opened at 9: a.m., an hour before the start of ceremonies; and

Jack's daughter-in-law, Marie hurried over early to secure seats for the rest of the family.

Inside, tiers of seats curved like a giant horseshoe separated only by long columns of steps leading all the way up to the dome roof. Fortunately Jack and his family had to ascend only a few steps. In front was a lit up stage with chairs and a few podiums. By 10: a.m. the dome was almost filled to capacity, and administrators and other staff began filing on to the stage. Faculty members entered and took their seats in front rows. The university band began playing the traditional *Pomp and Circumstance* as the graduate class of 2014, dressed in their caps and gowns, proudly marched in along the aisles of the auditorium. On and on they came grouped by their respective disciplines: Social Sciences, Physical Sciences, Business Administration, and so forth with each group led by a faculty member. When everyone was seated there was a trooping of the colors, and all rose to sing the national anthem. Afterwards, the university president approached a podium and delivered the opening speech which was very brief and somewhat mundane. Then an honor student spoke and reminisced about university student life and challenges of the future. Jack felt her speech was stirring and meaningful. At the end she raised a fist and protruded her forefinger and smallest finger.

"Always remember," she said. "You went to school in Bison country, and be proud of it."

Grouped by their respective disciplines, each student walked across the stage to receive his or her diploma amid scattered cries. Maria's group Business Administration was among the last, and as she strode across the stage her family and friends uttered a cheer.

This is a great day, Jack thought. All these young people are our country's hope and future. Although America is a young nation, it has a rich legacy. We've weathered many storms. We've made many mistakes. But eventually we get things right!

BIBLIOGRAPHY

Bowen, William and T. Aldrich Finegan. 1969. The Economics of Labor Force Participation. Princeton: Princeton University Press.

Coser, Lewis. 1956. The Functions of Social Conflict. New York: The Free Press.

Donne, John. 1623. "Meditation XVII." From Devotions Upon Emergent Occasions. London.

Douglas, Paul. 1934. Theory of Wages. New York: The Macmillan Company.

Durkheim, Emile. 1982. Rules of the Sociological Method. New York: The Free Press.

Funakoshi, Gichin. 1956. Karate-Do My Way of Life. New York: Kodansha International.

Goffman, Erving. 1956. The Presentation of Self in Everyday Life. New York: Doubleday.

Hassell, Randall and Osamu Ozawa. 1957. Samurai Journey. St. Louis, Mo. Focus Publications.

Hemingway, Ernest. 1940. For Whom The Bell Tolls. New York: Scribners and Sons.

Kipling, Rudyard. 1910. A poem "If". In Rewards and Faries. Doubleday, Page, and Company.

Lewis, Sinclair. 1922. Babbitt. New York: Hartcourt, Brace, and Company.

Malkin, Michelle. 1909. Culture of Corruption. Washington, D. C. Regency Publishing, Inc.

March, James and Herbert Simon. 1958. Organizations. New York: John Wiley.

Parsons, Talcott. 1951. The Social System. London: Rutledge.

Simmel, Georg. 1950. The Sociology of Georg Simmel. Il.: The Free Press.

Stouffer, Samuel. 1949. Studies in Social Psychology in World War Two. The American Soldier. Princeton: Princeton University Press.

Tocqueville, Alexis. 1835. Democracy in America. London: Saunders and Otley.

Weber, Max. 2009. The Theory of Economic and Social Organization. New York: The Free Press.

Zuckoff, Mitchell with members of the Annex Security Team. 2014. 13 Hours. New York: Twelve Hachette Book Group.